VOLUME 1 CONTENTS

UNIT 1 Multiplication and Division with 0–5, 9 and 10

UNIT 2 Multiplication and Division with 6, 7, and 8 and Multiply with Multiples of 10

UNIT 3 Measurement, Time, and Graphs

BIG IDEA 1 — Length, Capacity, Weight and Mass

BIG IDEA 2 — Time and Date

VOLUME 1 CONTENTS *(continued)*

Family Letter

Content Overview

Dear Family,

In this unit and the next, your child will be practicing basic multiplications and divisions. *Math Expressions* incorporates studying, practicing, and testing of the basic multiplications and divisions in class. Your child is also expected to practice at home.

Homework Helper Your child will have math homework almost every day. He or she needs a Homework Helper. The helper may be anyone — you, an older brother or sister (or other family member), a neighbor, or a friend. Please decide who the main Homework Helper will be and ask your child to tell the teacher tomorrow. Make a specific time for homework and provide your child with a quiet place to work.

Study Plans Each day your child will fill out a study plan, indicating which basic multiplications and divisions he or she will study that evening. When your child has finished studying (practicing), his or her Homework Helper should sign the study plan.

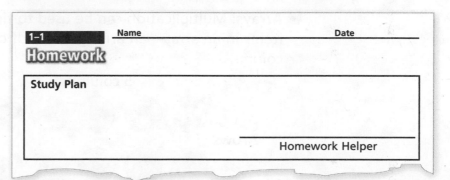

Practice Charts Each time a new number is introduced, students' homework will include a practice chart. To practice, students can cover the products with a pencil or a strip of heavy paper. They will say the multiplications, sliding the pencil or paper down the column to see each product after saying it. Students can also start with the last problem in a column and slide up. It is important that your child studies count-bys and multiplications at least 5 minutes every night. Your child can also use these charts to practice division on the mixed up column by covering the first factor.

In Order	Mixed Up
1 × 5 = 5	9 × 5 = 45
2 × 5 = 10	5 × 5 = 25
3 × 5 = 15	2 × 5 = 10
4 × 5 = 20	7 × 5 = 35
5 × 5 = 25	4 × 5 = 20
6 × 5 = 30	6 × 5 = 30
7 × 5 = 35	10 × 5 = 50
8 × 5 = 40	8 × 5 = 40
9 × 5 = 45	1 × 5 = 5
10 × 5 = 50	3 × 5 = 15

5s

Family Letter

Content Overview

To help students understand the concept of multiplication, the *Math Expressions* program presents three ways to think about multiplication.

- **Repeated groups**: Multiplication can be used to find the total in repeated groups of the same size. In early lessons, students circle the group size in repeated-groups equations to help keep track of which factor is the group size and which is the number of groups.

4 groups of bananas
$4 \times \textcircled{3} = 3 + 3 + 3 + 3 = 12$

- **Arrays**: Multiplication can be used to find the total number of items in an *array*—an arrangement of objects into rows and columns.

5 columns

2 rows

2-by-5 array

2 rows of pennies = $2 \times 5 = 10$

- **Area**: Multiplication can be used to find the area of a rectangle.

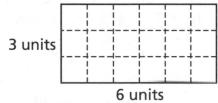

3 units

6 units

Area: 3 units × 6 units = 18 square units

Please call if you have any questions or comments.

Thank you.

Sincerely,
Your child's teacher

© Houghton Mifflin Harcourt Publishing Company

 CA CC

Unit 1 addresses the following standards from the *Common Core State Standards for Mathematics with California Additions*: **3.OA.1, 3.OA.2, 3.OA.3, 3.OA.4, 3.OA.5, 3.OA.6, 3.OA.7, 3.OA.9, 3.MD.5, 3.MD.5a, 3.MD.5b, 3.MD.7, 3.MD.7a, 3.MD.7b, 3.MD.7c, 3.MD.7d,** and all Mathematical Practices.

Estimada familia:

En esta unidad y en la que sigue, su niño practicará multiplicaciones y divisiones básicas. *Math Expressions* incorpora en la clase el estudio, la práctica y la evaluación de las multiplicaciones y divisiones básicas. También se espera que su niño practique en casa.

Ayudante de tareas Su niño tendrá tarea de matemáticas casi a diario y necesitará un ayudante para hacer sus tareas. Ese ayudante puede ser cualquier persona: usted, un hermano o hermana mayor, otro familiar, un vecino o un amigo. Por favor decida quién será esta persona y pida a su niño que se lo diga a su maestro mañana. Designe un tiempo específico para la tarea y un lugar para trabajar sin distracciones.

Planes de estudio Todos los días su niño va a completar un plan de estudio, que indica cuáles multiplicaciones y divisiones debe estudiar esa noche. Cuando su niño haya terminado de estudiar (practicar), la persona que lo ayude debe firmar el plan de estudio.

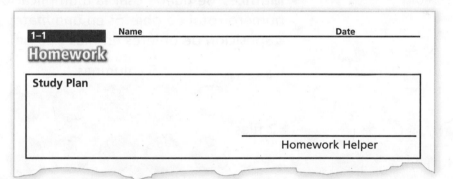

Tablas de práctica Cada vez que se presente un número nuevo, la tarea de los estudiantes incluirá una tabla de práctica. Para practicar, los estudiantes pueden cubrir los productos con un lápiz o una tira de papel grueso. Los niños dicen la multiplicación y deslizan el lápiz o el papel hacia

	En orden	Desordenados
5	1 × 5 = 5	9 × 5 = 45
	2 × 5 = 10	5 × 5 = 25
	3 × 5 = 15	2 × 5 = 10
	4 × 5 = 20	7 × 5 = 35
	5 × 5 = 25	4 × 5 = 20
	6 × 5 = 30	6 × 5 = 30
	7 × 5 = 35	10 × 5 = 50
	8 × 5 = 40	8 × 5 = 40
	9 × 5 = 45	1 × 5 = 5
	10 × 5 = 50	3 × 5 = 15

abajo para revelar el producto después de decirlo. También pueden empezar con el último problema de la columna y deslizar el lápiz o el papel hacia arriba. Es importante que su niño practique el conteo y la multiplicación por lo menos 5 minutos cada noche. Su niño también puede usar estas tablas para practicar la división en la columna de productos desordenados cubriendo el primer factor.

Un vistazo general al contenido

Para ayudar a los estudiantes a comprender el concepto de la multiplicación, el programa *Math Expressions* presenta tres maneras de pensar en la multiplicación. Éstas se describen a continuación.

- **Grupos repetidos**: La multiplicación se puede usar para hallar el total con grupos del mismo tamaño que se repiten. Cuando empiezan a trabajar con ecuaciones de grupos repetidos, los estudiantes rodean con un círculo el tamaño del grupo en las ecuaciones, para recordar cuál factor representa el tamaño del grupo y cuál representa el número de grupos.

4 grupos de bananas

$4 \times ③ = 3 + 3 + 3 + 3 = 12$

- **Matrices**: Se puede usar la multiplicación para hallar el número total de objetos en una *matriz*, es decir, una disposición de objetos en filas y columnas.

5 columnas

2 filas

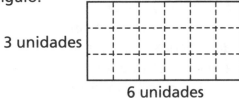
matriz de 2 por 5

2 filas de monedas de un centavo $= 2 \times 5 = 10$

- **Área**: Se puede usar la multiplicación para hallar el área de un rectángulo.

3 unidades

6 unidades

Área: 3 unidades $\times$ 6 unidades $= 18$ unidades cuadradas

Si tiene alguna duda o algún comentario, por favor comuníquese conmigo. Gracias.

Atentamente,

El maestro de su niño

© Houghton Mifflin Harcourt Publishing Company

 CA CC

En la Unidad 1 se aplican los siguientes estándares auxiliares, contenidos en los *Estándares estatales comunes de matemáticas con adiciones para California*: **3.OA.1, 3.OA.2, 3.OA.3, 3.OA.4, 3.OA.5, 3.OA.6, 3.OA.7, 3.OA.9, 3.MD.5, 3.MD.5a, 3.MD.5b, 3.MD.7, 3.MD.7a, 3.MD.7b, 3.MD.7c, 3.MD.7d,** y todos los de prácticas matemáticas.

► **PATH to FLUENCY** **Explore Patterns with 5s**

What patterns do you see below?

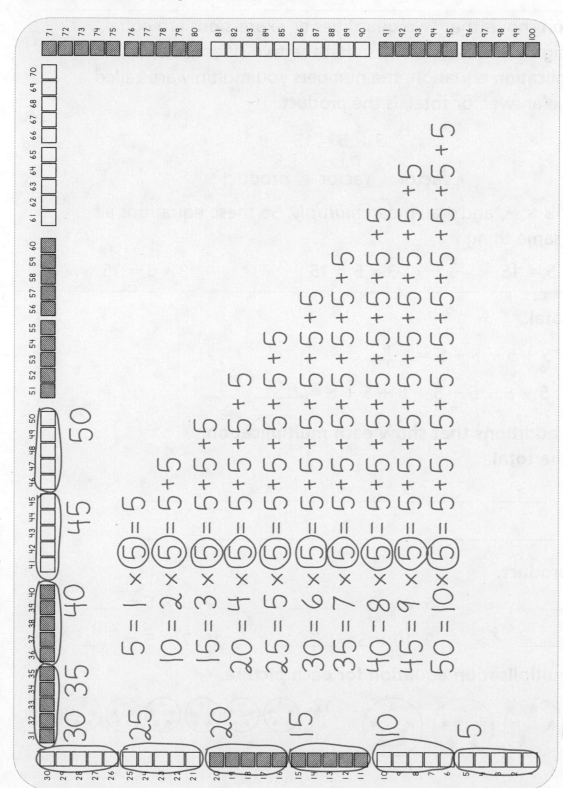

VOCABULARY

equation
multiplication
factor
product

▶ PATH to FLUENCY **Practice Multiplications with 5**

An **equation** shows that two quantities or expressions are equal.
An equal sign (=) is used to show that the two sides are equal.
In a **multiplication** equation, the numbers you multiply are called
factors. The answer, or total, is the **product**.

$$3 \times 5 = 15$$

factor   factor   product

The symbols ×, *, and • all mean *multiply.* So these equations all
mean the same thing.

$$3 \times 5 = 15 \qquad 3 * 5 = 15 \qquad 3 • 5 = 15$$

Write each total.

1. $4 \times ⑤ = 5 + 5 + 5 + 5 =$ _____

2. $7 • ⑤ = 5 + 5 + 5 + 5 + 5 + 5 + 5 =$ _____

Write the 5s additions that show each multiplication.
Then write the total.

3. $6 \times ⑤ =$ _____ = _____

4. $9 * ⑤ =$ _____ = _____

Write each product.

5. $8 \times 5 =$ _____   6. $2 \times 5 =$ _____   7. $5 \times 5 =$ _____

8. $4 \times 5 =$ _____   9. $10 \times 5 =$ _____   10. $7 \times 5 =$ _____

Write a 5s multiplication equation for each picture.

11.

12.

_____   _____

VOCABULARY
equal groups

▶ **PATH to FLUENCY Explore Equal Groups**

You can use multiplication to find the total when you have equal groups.

$2 \times \boxed{5} = 5 + 5 = 10$

▶ **PATH to FLUENCY Write Multiplication Equations**

Write a multiplication equation to find the total number.

1. How many bananas?

_____

2. How many toes?

_____

3. How many wheels?

_____

► **Make a Math Drawing to Solve Problems**

**Make a drawing for each problem. Label your
drawing with a multiplication equation. Then
write the answer to the problem.**

Show your work.

4. Sandra bought 4 bags of lemons. There were
   6 lemons in each bag. How many lemons did
   she buy in all?

   _____

5. Batai baked 2 peach pies. He used 7 peaches
   per pie. How many peaches did he use in all?

   _____

6. The Fuzzy Friends pet store has 3 rabbit cages.
   There are 5 rabbits in each cage. How many
   rabbits does the store have in all?

   _____

7. The Paws Plus pet store has 5 rabbit cages.
   There are 3 rabbits in every cage. How many
   rabbits does the store have in all?

   _____

Multiplication as Equal Groups

► Explore Equal Shares Drawings

Here is a problem with repeated groups. Read the problem, and think about how you would solve it.

Ms. Thomas bought 4 bags of oranges. Each bag contained 5 oranges. How many oranges did she buy in all?

You could also find the answer to this problem by making an **Equal Shares Drawing.**

Think:

⑤ ⑤ ⑤ ⑤
bags of oranges
4 × ⑤ = ☐

Equal Shares Drawing

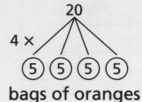

20

4 ×

⑤ ⑤ ⑤ ⑤
bags of oranges
4 × ⑤ = 20

Make an Equal Shares Drawing to solve each problem.

Show your work.

8. Ms. Gonzales bought 6 boxes of pencils. There were 5 pencils in each box. How many pencils did she buy in all?

_____

9. Mr. Franken made lunch for his 9 nieces and nephews. He put 5 carrot sticks on each of their plates. How many carrot sticks did he use in all?

_____

Name _____ Date _____

VOCABULARY
function table

► **PATH to FLUENCY** **Practice with Equal Groups**

Complete each function table.

10.

Number of Tricycles	Number of Wheels
1	
2	
3	
4	
5	

11.

Number of Rabbits	Number of Ears
1	
2	
3	
4	
5	

12.

Number of Cars	Number of Wheels
1	
2	
3	
4	
5	

13.

Number of Spiders	Number of Legs
1	
2	
3	
4	
5	

Multiplication as Equal Groups

Family Letter

Content Overview

Dear Family,

In addition to practice charts for the basic multiplications and divisions for each of the numbers 1 through 10, your child will bring home a variety of other practice materials over the next several weeks.

• **Home Study Sheets:** A Home Study Sheet includes 3 or 4 practice charts on one page. Your child can use the Home Study Sheets to practice all the count-bys, multiplications, and divisions for a number or to practice just the ones he or she doesn't know for that number. The Homework Helper can then use the sheet to test (or retest) your child. The Homework Helper should check with your child to see which basic multiplications or divisions he or she is ready to be tested on. The helper should mark any missed problems lightly with a pencil.

If your child gets all the answers in a column correct, the helper should sign that column on the Home Signature Sheet. When signatures are on all the columns of the Home Signature Sheet, your child should bring the sheet to school.

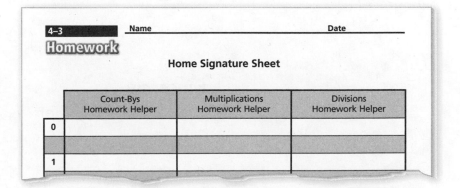

Home Study Sheet A

5s			2s		
Count-bys	Mixed Up ×	Mixed Up ÷	Count-bys	Mixed Up ×	Mixed Up ÷
1 × 5 = 5	2 × 5 = 10	10 ÷ 5 = 2	1 × 2 = 2	7 × 2 = 14	20 ÷ 2 = 10
2 × 5 = 10	9 × 5 = 45	35 ÷ 5 = 7	2 × 2 = 4	1 × 2 = 2	2 ÷ 2 = 1
3 × 5 = 15	1 × 5 = 5	50 ÷ 5 = 10	3 × 2 = 6	3 × 2 = 6	6 ÷ 2 = 3
4 × 5 = 20	5 × 5 = 25	5 ÷ 5 = 1	4 × 2 = 8	5 × 2 = 10	16 ÷ 2 = 8
5 × 5 = 25	7 × 5 = 35	20 ÷ 5 = 4	5 × 2 = 10	6 × 2 = 12	12 ÷ 2 = 6
6 × 5 = 30	3 × 5 = 15	15 ÷ 5 = 3	6 × 2 = 12	8 × 2 = 16	4 ÷ 2 = 2
7 × 5 = 35	10 × 5 = 50	30 ÷ 5 = 6	7 × 2 = 14	2 × 2 = 4	10 ÷ 2 = 5
8 × 5 = 40	6 × 5 = 30	40 ÷ 5 = 8	8 × 2 = 16	10 × 2 = 20	8 ÷ 2 = 4
9 × 5 = 45	4 × 5 = 20	25 ÷ 5 = 5	9 × 2 = 18	4 × 2 = 8	14 ÷ 2 = 7
10 × 5 = 50	8 × 5 = 40	45 ÷ 5 = 9	10 × 2 = 20	9 × 2 = 18	18 ÷ 2 = 9

4–3

Homework

Name _____ Date _____

Home Signature Sheet

	Count-Bys Homework Helper	Multiplications Homework Helper	Divisions Homework Helper
0			
1			

• **Home Check Sheets:** A Home Check Sheet includes columns of 20 multiplications and divisions in mixed order. These sheets can be used to test your student's fluency with basic facts.

• **Strategy Cards:** Students use Strategy Cards in class as flashcards, to play games, and to develop multiplication and division strategies.

Sample Multiplication Card   **Sample Division Card**

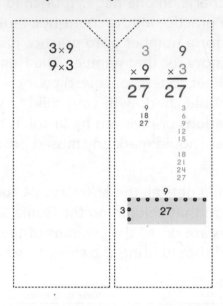   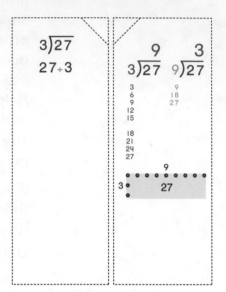

• **Games:** Near the end of this unit, students are introduced to games that provide multiplication and division practice.

Encourage your child to show you these materials and explain how they are used. Make sure your child spends time practicing multiplications and divisions every evening.

Please call if you have any questions or comments.

Thank you.

Sincerely,
Your child's teacher

© Houghton Mifflin Harcourt Publishing Company

 CA CC

Unit 1 addresses the following standards from the *Common Core State Standards for Mathematics with California Additions*: 3.OA.1, 3.OA.2, 3.OA.3, 3.OA.4, 3.OA.5, 3.OA.6, 3.OA.7, 3.OA.9, 3.MD.5, 3.MD.5a, 3.MD.5b, 3.MD.7, 3.MD.7a, 3.MD.7b, 3.MD.7c, 3.MD.7d, and all Mathematical Practices.

Un vistazo general al contenido

Estimada familia:

Además de las tablas de práctica para las multiplicaciones y divisiones básicas para cada número del 1 al 10, su niño llevará a casa una variedad de materiales de práctica en las semanas que vienen.

- **Hojas para estudiar en casa:** Una hoja para estudiar en casa incluye 3 ó 4 tablas de práctica en una página. Su niño puede usar las hojas para practicar todos los conteos, multiplicaciones y divisiones de un número, o para practicar sólo las operaciones para ese número que no domine. La persona que ayude a su niño con la tarea puede usar la hoja para hacerle una prueba (o repetir una prueba). Esa persona debe hablar con su niño para decidir sobre qué multiplicaciones o divisiones básicas el niño puede hacer la prueba. La persona que ayude debe marcar ligeramente con un lápiz cualquier problema que conteste mal. Si su niño contesta bien todas las operaciones de una columna, la persona que ayude debe firmar esa columna de la hoja de firmas. Cuando todas las columnas de la hoja de firmas estén firmadas, su niño debe llevar la hoja a la escuela.

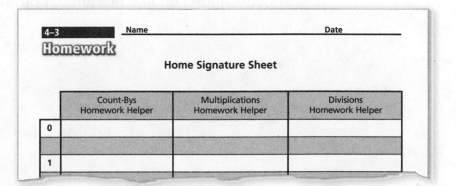

Home Study Sheet A

5s			2s		
Count-bys	**Mixed Up ×**	**Mixed Up ÷**	**Count-bys**	**Mixed Up ×**	**Mixed Up ÷**
1 × 5 = 5	2 × 5 = 10	10 ÷ 5 = 2	1 × 2 = 2	7 × 2 = 14	20 ÷ 2 = 10
2 × 5 = 10	9 × 5 = 45	35 ÷ 5 = 7	2 × 2 = 4	1 × 2 = 2	2 ÷ 2 = 1
3 × 5 = 15	1 × 5 = 5	50 ÷ 5 = 10	3 × 2 = 6	3 × 2 = 6	6 ÷ 2 = 3
4 × 5 = 20	5 × 5 = 25	5 ÷ 5 = 1	4 × 2 = 8	5 × 2 = 10	16 ÷ 2 = 8
5 × 5 = 25	7 × 5 = 35	20 ÷ 5 = 4	5 × 2 = 10	6 × 2 = 12	12 ÷ 2 = 6
6 × 5 = 30	3 × 5 = 15	15 ÷ 5 = 3	6 × 2 = 12	8 × 2 = 16	4 ÷ 2 = 2
7 × 5 = 35	10 × 5 = 50	30 ÷ 5 = 6	7 × 2 = 14	2 × 2 = 4	10 ÷ 2 = 5
8 × 5 = 40	6 × 5 = 30	40 ÷ 5 = 8	8 × 2 = 16	10 × 2 = 20	8 ÷ 2 = 4
9 × 5 = 45	4 × 5 = 20	25 ÷ 5 = 5	9 × 2 = 18	4 × 2 = 8	14 ÷ 2 = 7
10 × 5 = 50	8 × 5 = 40	45 ÷ 5 = 9	10 × 2 = 20	9 × 2 = 18	18 ÷ 2 = 9

4–3
Name _____ Date _____

Homework

Home Signature Sheet

	Count-Bys Homework Helper	Multiplications Homework Helper	Divisions Homework Helper
0			
1			

Carta a la familia

Un vistazo general al contenido

- **Hojas de verificación:** Una hoja de verificación consta de columnas de 20 multiplicaciones y divisiones sin orden fijo. Estas hojas pueden usarse para comprobar el dominio de las operaciones básicas.

- **Tarjetas de estrategias:** Los estudiantes usan las tarjetas de estrategias en la clase como ayuda de memoria, en juegos y para desarrollar estrategias para hacer multiplicaciones y divisiones.

Ejemplo de tarjeta de multiplicación   **Ejemplo de tarjeta de división**

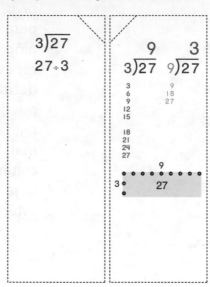

- **Juegos:** Hacia el final de esta unidad se presentan juegos a los estudiantes para practicar la multiplicación y la división.

Anime a su niño a que le muestre estos materiales y a que le explique cómo se usan. Asegúrese de que su niño practique la multiplicación y la división cada noche.

Si tiene alguna duda o pregunta, por favor comuníquese conmigo.

Atentamente,
El maestro de su niño

© Houghton Mifflin Harcourt Publishing Company

CA CC

En la Unidad 1 se aplican los siguientes estándares auxiliares, contenidos en los *Estándares estatales comunes de matemáticas con adiciones para California*: **3.OA.1, 3.OA.2, 3.OA.3, 3.OA.4, 3.OA.5, 3.OA.6, 3.OA.7, 3.OA.9, 3.MD.5, 3.MD.5a, 3.MD.5b, 3.MD.7, 3.MD.7a, 3.MD.7b, 3.MD.7c, 3.MD.7d** y todos los de prácticas matemáticas.

Signature Sheet

	Count-Bys Partner	Multiplications Partner	Divisions Partner	Multiplications Check Sheets	Divisions Check Sheets
5s				1:	1:
2s				1:	1:
10s				2:	2:
9s				2:	2:
				3:	3:
3s				4:	4:
4s				4:	4:
1s				5:	5:
0s				5:	5:
				6:	6:
6s				7:	7:
8s				7:	7:
7s				8:	8:
				9:	9:
				10:	10:

Dash Record Sheet

Dash Number	Accurate	Fast	Really Fast	Dash Number	Accurate	Fast	Really Fast
1				13			
2				14			
3				15			
4				16			
5				17			
6				18			
7				19			
8				19A			
9				19B			
9A				19C			
9B				19D			
9C				20			
10				20A			
10A				20B			
10B				20C			
10C				20D			
11				21			
11A				21A			
11B				21B			
11C				21C			
12				22			
12A				22A			
12B				22B			
12C				22C			

Dash Record Sheet

Study Sheet A

5s

Count-bys	Mixed Up ×	Mixed Up ÷
1 × 5 = 5	2 × 5 = 10	10 ÷ 5 = 2
2 × 5 = 10	9 × 5 = 45	35 ÷ 5 = 7
3 × 5 = 15	1 × 5 = 5	50 ÷ 5 = 10
4 × 5 = 20	5 × 5 = 25	5 ÷ 5 = 1
5 × 5 = 25	7 × 5 = 35	20 ÷ 5 = 4
6 × 5 = 30	3 × 5 = 15	15 ÷ 5 = 3
7 × 5 = 35	10 × 5 = 50	30 ÷ 5 = 6
8 × 5 = 40	6 × 5 = 30	40 ÷ 5 = 8
9 × 5 = 45	4 × 5 = 20	25 ÷ 5 = 5
10 × 5 = 50	8 × 5 = 40	45 ÷ 5 = 9

2s

Count-bys	Mixed Up ×	Mixed Up ÷
1 × 2 = 2	7 × 2 = 14	20 ÷ 2 = 10
2 × 2 = 4	1 × 2 = 2	2 ÷ 2 = 1
3 × 2 = 6	3 × 2 = 6	6 ÷ 2 = 3
4 × 2 = 8	5 × 2 = 10	16 ÷ 2 = 8
5 × 2 = 10	6 × 2 = 12	12 ÷ 2 = 6
6 × 2 = 12	8 × 2 = 16	4 ÷ 2 = 2
7 × 2 = 14	2 × 2 = 4	10 ÷ 2 = 5
8 × 2 = 16	10 × 2 = 20	8 ÷ 2 = 4
9 × 2 = 18	4 × 2 = 8	14 ÷ 2 = 7
10 × 2 = 20	9 × 2 = 18	18 ÷ 2 = 9

10s

Count-bys	Mixed Up ×	Mixed Up ÷
1 × 10 = 10	1 × 10 = 10	80 ÷ 10 = 8
2 × 10 = 20	5 × 10 = 50	10 ÷ 10 = 1
3 × 10 = 30	2 × 10 = 20	50 ÷ 10 = 5
4 × 10 = 40	8 × 10 = 80	90 ÷ 10 = 9
5 × 10 = 50	7 × 10 = 70	40 ÷ 10 = 4
6 × 10 = 60	3 × 10 = 30	100 ÷ 10 = 10
7 × 10 = 70	4 × 10 = 40	30 ÷ 10 = 3
8 × 10 = 80	6 × 10 = 60	20 ÷ 10 = 2
9 × 10 = 90	10 × 10 = 100	70 ÷ 10 = 7
10 × 10 = 100	9 × 10 = 90	60 ÷ 10 = 6

9s

Count-bys	Mixed Up ×	Mixed Up ÷
1 × 9 = 9	2 × 9 = 18	81 ÷ 9 = 9
2 × 9 = 18	4 × 9 = 36	18 ÷ 9 = 2
3 × 9 = 27	7 × 9 = 63	36 ÷ 9 = 4
4 × 9 = 36	8 × 9 = 72	9 ÷ 9 = 1
5 × 9 = 45	3 × 9 = 27	54 ÷ 9 = 6
6 × 9 = 54	10 × 9 = 90	27 ÷ 9 = 3
7 × 9 = 63	1 × 9 = 9	63 ÷ 9 = 7
8 × 9 = 72	6 × 9 = 54	72 ÷ 9 = 8
9 × 9 = 81	5 × 9 = 45	90 ÷ 9 = 10
10 × 9 = 90	9 × 9 = 81	45 ÷ 9 = 5

VOCABULARY
array
row
column

► **Explore Arrays**

An **array** is an arrangement of objects in **rows** and **columns**. You can use multiplication to find the total number of objects in an array.

row

column

2-by-5 array
5 columns

2 rows of 5 = 2 × 5 = 10   2 rows

► **PATH to FLUENCY** **Write Multiplication Equations**

Write a multiplication equation for each array.

1. How many flowers?

_____

2. How many stamps?

_____

3. How many mugs?

_____

4. Math Journal Write a problem that you can solve by using this array. Show how to solve your problem.

► Compare Arrays

Without counting the dots in the array, write >, < or = in the circle.

5.

6.

7.

8.

9.

10.

11.

12.

13. **Create Your Own** Draw two dot arrays and compare them using symbols. Then write an equation for each array to show that your comparison is correct.

▶ Make a Math Drawing to Solve a Problem

Make a drawing for each problem. Label your drawing with a multiplication equation. Then write the answer to the problem.

Show your work.

14. The clarinet section of the band marched in 6 rows, with 2 clarinet players in each row. How many clarinet players were there in all?

   _____

15. Mali put some crackers on a tray. She put the crackers in 3 rows, with 5 crackers per row. How many crackers did she put on the tray?

   _____

16. Ms. Shahin set up some chairs in 7 rows, with 5 chairs in each row. How many chairs did she set up?

   _____

17. Zak has a box of crayons. The crayons are arranged in 4 rows, with 6 crayons in each row. How many crayons are in the box?

   _____

VOCABULARY
Commutative Property of Multiplication

► Explore Commutativity

Multiplication is commutative. The **Commutative Property of Multiplication** states that you can switch the order of the factors without changing the product.

Arrays: 4 × 5 = 5 × 4   **Groups:** 4 × ⑤ = 5 × ④

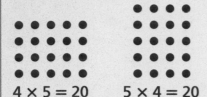

4 × 5 = 20   5 × 4 = 20   4 × ⑤ = 20   5 × ④ = 20

► Solve Problems Using the Commutative Property

Make a math drawing for each problem. Write a multiplication equation and the answer to the problem.

18. Katie bought some stickers. She put the stickers on her folder in 6 rows of 2. How many stickers did she buy?

_____

19. Marco also bought some stickers. He put the stickers on his folder in 2 rows of 6. How many stickers did he buy?

_____

20. On Monday, Juan helped Ms. Chang clean the art cabinet. He packed jars of paint in 3 boxes, with 7 jars per box. How many jars of paint did Juan pack?

_____

21. On Tuesday, Therese helped Ms. Chang. She packed jars of paint in 7 boxes, with 3 jars per box. How many jars of paint did Therese pack?

_____

Name _____   **Date** _____

CA CC Content Standards **3.OA.1, 3.OA.2, 3.OA.3, 3.OA.4, 3.OA.6, 3.OA.7** Mathematical Practices **MP.1, MP.3, MP.4, MP.6, MP.7**

> **VOCABULARY**
> division   divisor
> dividend   quotient

▶ Explore Division

Write an equation and solve the problem.

1. Marc bought some bags of limes. There were 5 limes in each bag. He bought 15 limes altogether. How many bags did he buy?

   _____

2. There were 10 photographs on one wall of an art gallery. The photographs were in rows, with 5 photographs in each row. How many rows were there?

   _____

The problems above can be represented by multiplication equations or by **division** equations.

Problem 1	**Multiplication**				**Division**			
	$\square$	×	⑤	= **15**	**15**	÷	⑤	= $\square$
	number of groups (factor)		group size (factor)	total (product)	total (product)		group size (factor)	number of groups (factor)
Problem 2	**Multiplication**				**Division**			
	$\square$	×	**5**	= **10**	**10**	÷	**5**	= $\square$
	number of rows (factor)		number in each row (factor)	total (product)	total (product)		number in each row (factor)	number of rows (factor)

Here are ways to write a division. The following all mean "15 divided by 5 equals 3."

$15 \div 5 = 3$ $15 / 5 = 3$ $\frac{15}{5} = 3$

$$\overset{3 \leftarrow \text{quotient}}{5\overline{)15}} \leftarrow \text{dividend}$$
$\uparrow$
divisor

The number you divide into is called the **dividend**. The number you divide by is called the **divisor**. The number that is the answer to a division problem is called the **quotient**.

▶ Math Tools: Equal Shares Drawings

You can use Equal Shares Drawings to help solve division problems. Here is how you might solve Problem 1 on Student Activity Book page 23.

Start with the total, 15.

$15 \div ⑤ = \square$

Draw groups of 5, and connect them to the total. Count by 5s as you draw the groups. Stop when you reach 15, the total. Count how many groups you have: 3 groups.

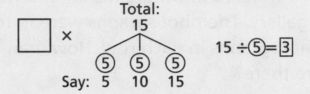

Say: 5   10   15

$15 \div ⑤ = \boxed{3}$

You can use a similar type of drawing to find the number of rows or columns in an array. Here is how you might solve problem 2 on page 23.

Start with the total, 10.

$10 \div ⑤ = \square$

Draw rows of 5, and connect them to the total. Count by 5s as you draw the rows. Stop when you reach 10, the total. Count how many rows you have: 2 rows.

5 ⟨ 5 ⟩
          Total:
10 ⟨ 5 ⟩ 10 $10 \div ⑤ = \boxed{2}$

Write an equation and solve the problem.

3. At a bake sale, Luisa bought a lemon square for 35¢. If she paid using only nickels, how many nickels did she use?

_____

4. Mr. Su bought a sheet of 20 stamps. There were 5 stamps in each row. How many rows of stamps were there?

_____

▶ **What's the Error?**

Dear Math Students,

Today I found the unknown number in this division equation by using a related multiplication. Is my calculation correct?

$40 \div 5 = \boxed{}$ $\boxed{9} \times 5 = 40$

If not, please correct my work and tell me what I did wrong. How do you know my answer is wrong?

Your friend,
Puzzled Penguin

5. Write an answer to the Puzzled Penguin.

_____

_____

_____

_____

▶ (PATH to FLUENCY) **Relate Division and Multiplication Equations with 5**

Find the unknown numbers.

6. $20 \div \boxed{5} = \boxed{}$ $\boxed{} \times \boxed{5} = 20$ $20 \div \boxed{4} = \boxed{}$ $\boxed{} \times \boxed{4} = 20$

7. $10 \div \boxed{5} = \boxed{}$ $\boxed{} \times \boxed{5} = 10$ $10 \div \boxed{2} = \boxed{}$ $\boxed{} \times \boxed{2} = 10$

8. $15 \div \boxed{5} = \boxed{}$ $\boxed{} \times \boxed{5} = 15$ $15 \div \boxed{3} = \boxed{}$ $\boxed{} \times \boxed{3} = 15$

9. $30 \div \boxed{5} = \boxed{}$ $\boxed{} \times \boxed{5} = 30$ $30 \div \boxed{6} = \boxed{}$ $\boxed{} \times \boxed{6} = 30$

10. $5 \div \boxed{5} = \boxed{}$ $\boxed{} \times \boxed{5} = 5$ $5 \div \boxed{1} = \boxed{}$ $\boxed{} \times \boxed{1} = 5$

11. $25 \div \boxed{5} = \boxed{}$ $\boxed{} \times \boxed{5} = 25$ $25 \div \boxed{5} = \boxed{}$ $\boxed{} \times \boxed{5} = 25$

▶ Find the Number in Each Group

Write an equation and solve the problem.   *Show your work.*

12. Aziz put 15 ice cubes in 5 glasses. He put the same number of ice cubes in each glass. How many ice cubes did he put in each glass?

_____

13. Lori's uncle gave her 20 stickers. She put the same number of stickers on each of 5 folders. How many stickers did she put on each folder?

_____

14. Todd cut a board that measured 45 inches in length into 5 pieces. Each piece he cut measures the same number of inches. How many inches does each piece measure?

_____

15. Paige placed 35 books on 5 shelves. She placed the same number of books on each shelf. How many books did she place on each shelf?

_____

16. Ten students gathered into 5 groups to play a math game. The same number of students are in each group. How many students are in each group?

_____

▶ Write a Word Problem

17. Write a word problem for $30 \div 5$ where the 5 is the size of the group.

_____

The Meaning of Division

CA CC Content Standards **3.OA.1, 3.OA.2, 3.OA.3, 3.OA.4, 3.OA.7, 3.OA.9** Mathematical Practices **MP.1, MP.2, MP.7, MP.8**

► PATH to FLUENCY **Explore Patterns with 2s**

What patterns do you see below?

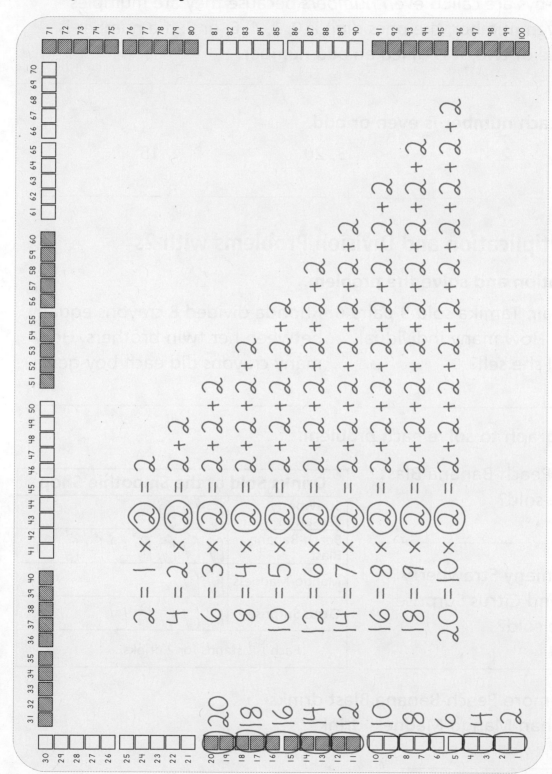

VOCABULARY
even number
odd number

▶ Even and Odd Numbers

The 2s count-bys are called *even numbers* because they are multiples of 2. In an **even number**, the ones digit is 0, 2, 4, 6, or 8. If a number is not a multiple of two, it is called an **odd number**.

Tell whether each number is even or odd.

1. 7

2. 4

3. 20

4. 15

_____ _____ _____ _____

▶ Solve Multiplication and Division Problems with 2s

Write an equation and solve the problem.

5. At the art fair, Tamika sold 9 pairs of earrings. How many individual earrings did she sell?

6. Rhonda divided 8 crayons equally between her twin brothers. How many crayons did each boy get?

_____ _____

Use the pictograph to solve each problem.

7. How many Peach-Banana Blast drinks were sold?

_____

8. In all, how many Strawberry Sensation and Citrus Surprise drinks were sold?

_____

Drinks Sold at the Smoothie Shop	
Strawberry Sensation	🥤 🥤 🥤
Peach-Banana Blast	🥤 🥤 🥤 🥤 🥤 🥤 🥤
Mango-Madness	🥤 🥤
Citrus Surprise	🥤 🥤 🥤 🥤
Each 🥤 stands for 2 drinks.	

9. How many more Peach-Banana Blast drinks were sold than Mango Madness drinks?

_____

© Houghton Mifflin Harcourt Publishing Company

Multiply and Divide with 2

► **PATH to FLUENCY** **Check Sheet 1: 5s and 2s**

5s Multiplications	5s Divisions	2s Multiplications	2s Divisions
$2 \times 5 = 10$	$30 / 5 = 6$	$4 \times 2 = 8$	$8 / 2 = 4$
$5 \cdot 6 = 30$	$5 \div 5 = 1$	$2 \cdot 8 = 16$	$18 \div 2 = 9$
$5 * 9 = 45$	$15 / 5 = 3$	$1 * 2 = 2$	$2 / 2 = 1$
$4 \times 5 = 20$	$50 \div 5 = 10$	$6 \times 2 = 12$	$16 \div 2 = 8$
$5 \cdot 7 = 35$	$20 / 5 = 4$	$2 \cdot 9 = 18$	$4 / 2 = 2$
$10 * 5 = 50$	$10 \div 5 = 2$	$2 * 2 = 4$	$20 \div 2 = 10$
$1 \times 5 = 5$	$35 / 5 = 7$	$3 \times 2 = 6$	$10 / 2 = 5$
$5 \cdot 3 = 15$	$40 \div 5 = 8$	$2 \cdot 5 = 10$	$12 \div 2 = 6$
$8 * 5 = 40$	$25 / 5 = 5$	$10 * 2 = 20$	$6 / 2 = 3$
$5 \times 5 = 25$	$45 / 5 = 9$	$2 \times 7 = 14$	$14 / 2 = 7$
$5 \cdot 8 = 40$	$20 \div 5 = 4$	$2 \cdot 10 = 20$	$4 \div 2 = 2$
$7 * 5 = 35$	$15 / 5 = 3$	$9 * 2 = 18$	$2 / 2 = 1$
$5 \times 4 = 20$	$30 \div 5 = 6$	$2 \times 6 = 12$	$8 \div 2 = 4$
$6 \cdot 5 = 30$	$25 / 5 = 5$	$8 \cdot 2 = 16$	$6 / 2 = 3$
$5 * 1 = 5$	$10 \div 5 = 2$	$2 * 3 = 6$	$20 \div 2 = 10$
$5 \times 10 = 50$	$45 / 5 = 9$	$2 \times 2 = 4$	$14 / 2 = 7$
$9 \cdot 5 = 45$	$35 \div 5 = 7$	$1 \cdot 2 = 2$	$10 \div 2 = 5$
$5 * 2 = 10$	$50 \div 5 = 10$	$2 * 4 = 8$	$16 \div 2 = 8$
$3 \times 5 = 15$	$40 / 5 = 8$	$5 \times 2 = 10$	$12 / 2 = 6$
$5 \cdot 5 = 25$	$5 \div 5 = 1$	$7 \cdot 2 = 14$	$18 \div 2 = 9$

Check Sheet 1: 5s and 2s

1-6

Class Activity

Name

Date

CA CC Content Standards **3.OA.1, 3.OA.2, 3.OA.3, 3.OA.4, 3.OA.6, 3.OA.7** Mathematical Practices **MP.1, MP.2, MP.4, MP.6, MP.7**

▶ PATH to FLUENCY **Use the Target**

×	0	1	2	3	4	5	6	7	8	9
0	0	0	0	0	0	0	0	0	0	0
1	0	1	2	3	4	5	6	7	8	9
2	0	2	4	6	8	10	12	14	16	18
3	0	3	6	9	12	15	18	21	24	27
4	0	4	8	12	16	20	24	28	32	36
5	0	5	10	15	20	25	30	35	40	45
6	0	6	12	18	24	30	36	42	48	54
7	0	7	14	21	28	35	42	49	56	63
8	0	8	16	24	32	40	48	56	64	72
9	0	9	18	27	36	45	54	63	72	81

1. Discuss how you can use the Target to find the product for 8×5.

2. Discuss how you can use the Target to practice division.

3. Practice using the Target.

4. When using the Target, how are multiplication and division alike? How are they different?

_____

_____

_____

▶ Make Sense of Problems

Write an equation and solve the problem.   *Show your work.*

5. Mrs. Cheng bought 8 pairs of mittens. How many individual mittens did she buy?

    _____

6. Brian divided 10 crayons equally between his two sisters. How many crayons did each girl get?

    _____

7. Maria has 5 piles of flash cards. There are 9 cards in each pile. How many flash cards does Maria have?

    _____

8. A parking lot has 5 rows of parking spaces with the same number of spaces in each row. There are 35 parking spaces in the lot. How many spaces are in each row?

    _____

9. Ari arranged his bottle cap collection into 9 rows with 2 bottle caps in each row. How many bottle caps are in his collection?

    _____

▶ Write a Word Problem

10. Write a word problem that can be solved using the equation $45 \div 5 =$ where 5 is the number of groups.

    _____

    _____

Name _____ Date _____

CA CC Content Standards **3.OA.1, 3.OA.2, 3.OA.3, 3.OA.4, 3.OA.6, 3.OA.7, 3.OA.9** Mathematical Practices **MP.1, MP.2, MP.4, MP.6, MP.7, MP.8**

► PATH to FLUENCY **Explore Patterns with 10s**

What patterns do you see below?

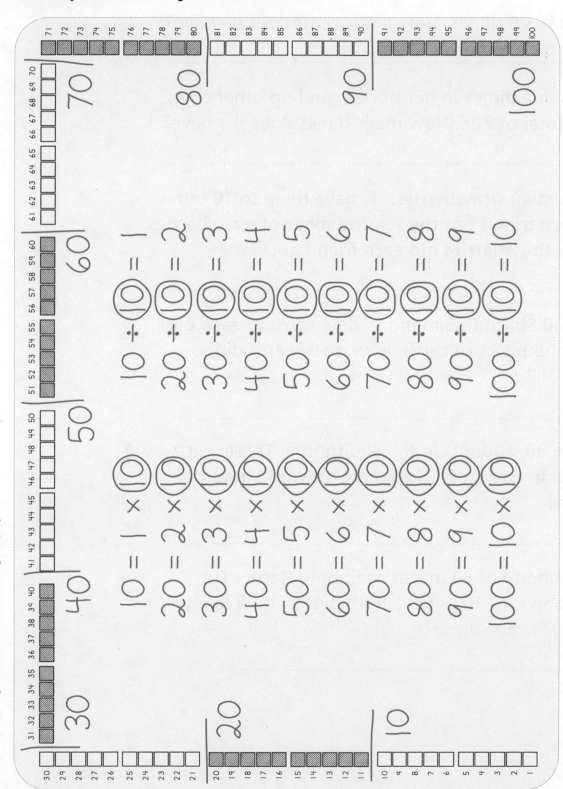

► Solve Problems with 10s

Write an equation and solve the problem.   *Show your work.*

1. Raymundo has 9 dimes. How many cents does he have?

_____

2. Yoko has some dimes in her pocket, and no other coins. She has a total of 70¢. How many dimes does she have?

_____

3. Jonah picked 40 strawberries. He gave them to 10 of his friends. Each friend got the same number of strawberries. How many strawberries did each friend get?

_____

4. There are 10 Space Command trading cards in each pack. Zoe bought 5 packs of cards. How many cards did she buy in all?

_____

5. There were 80 students in the auditorium. There were 10 students in each row. How many rows of students were there?

_____

6. A roll of ribbon has 60 inches of ribbon. Harper cut all the ribbon into 10 equal length pieces. How many inches long is each piece?

_____

Multiply and Divide with 10

VOCABULARY
equation
variable

▶ Use Variables in Equations

When you write **equations** you can use a letter to represent an unknown number. This letter is called a **variable**.

Each of these equations has a variable.

$a \times 10 = 60$	$70 = c \times 7$	$w = 80 \div 10$	$9 = 90 \div c$
$2 \times y = 18$	$p = 9 \times 2$	$f = 18 \div 2$	$18 \div n = 2$

Solve each equation.

7. $14 = 7 \times a$

$a =$ _____

8. $90 \div g = 9$

$g =$ _____

9. $10 \div n = 5$

$n =$ _____

10. $8 \times f = 40$

$f =$ _____

▶ Write and Solve Equations with Variables

Write an equation and solve the problem.

11. A box of straws holds 60 straws. There are 10 straws in each row. How many rows are there?

_____

12. Ethan used 9 dimes to pay for his book. How much did his book cost?

_____

13. There are 10 relay teams with an equal number of people on each team running a race. There are 50 people running the race. How many people are there on each team?

_____

14. Amanda has 20 bracelets. She gave the same number of bracelets to 2 of her friends. How many bracelets did she give to each friend?

_____

▶ What's the Error?

Dear Math Students,

Today my teacher asked me to write a word problem that can be solved using the division 40 ÷ 10. Here is the problem I wrote:

Kim has 40 apples and puts 4 apples in each bag. How many bags did Kim use?

Is my problem correct? If not, please correct my work and tell me what I did wrong.

Your friend,
Puzzled Penguin

15. Write an answer to the Puzzled Penguin.

_____

_____

_____

▶ Write and Solve Problems with 10s

16. Write a word problem that can be solved using the division 60 ÷ 10. Then write a related multiplication word problem.

_____

_____

17. Write a word problem that can be solved using the multiplication 10 × 3. Then write a related division word problem.

_____

_____

► PATH to FLUENCY **Check Sheet 2: 10s and 9s**

10s Multiplications	10s Divisions	9s Multiplications	9s Divisions
$9 \times 10 = 90$	$100 / 10 = 10$	$3 \times 9 = 27$	$27 / 9 = 3$
$10 \cdot 3 = 30$	$50 \div 10 = 5$	$9 \cdot 7 = 63$	$9 \div 9 = 1$
$10 * 6 = 60$	$70 / 10 = 7$	$10 * 9 = 90$	$81 / 9 = 9$
$1 \times 10 = 10$	$40 \div 10 = 4$	$5 \times 9 = 45$	$45 \div 9 = 5$
$10 \cdot 4 = 40$	$80 / 10 = 8$	$9 \cdot 8 = 72$	$90 / 9 = 10$
$10 * 7 = 70$	$60 \div 10 = 6$	$9 * 1 = 9$	$36 \div 9 = 4$
$8 \times 10 = 80$	$10 / 10 = 1$	$2 \times 9 = 18$	$18 / 9 = 2$
$10 \cdot 10 = 100$	$20 \div 10 = 2$	$9 \cdot 9 = 81$	$63 \div 9 = 7$
$5 * 10 = 50$	$90 / 10 = 9$	$6 * 9 = 54$	$54 / 9 = 6$
$10 \times 2 = 20$	$30 / 10 = 3$	$9 \times 4 = 36$	$72 / 9 = 8$
$10 \cdot 5 = 50$	$80 \div 10 = 8$	$9 \cdot 5 = 45$	$27 \div 9 = 3$
$4 * 10 = 40$	$70 / 10 = 7$	$4 * 9 = 36$	$45 / 9 = 5$
$10 \times 1 = 10$	$100 \div 10 = 10$	$9 \times 1 = 9$	$63 \div 9 = 7$
$3 \cdot 10 = 30$	$90 / 10 = 9$	$3 \cdot 9 = 27$	$72 / 9 = 8$
$10 * 8 = 80$	$60 \div 10 = 6$	$9 * 8 = 72$	$54 \div 9 = 6$
$7 \times 10 = 70$	$30 / 10 = 3$	$7 \times 9 = 63$	$18 / 9 = 2$
$6 \cdot 10 = 60$	$10 \div 10 = 1$	$6 \cdot 9 = 54$	$90 \div 9 = 10$
$10 * 9 = 90$	$40 \div 10 = 4$	$9 * 9 = 81$	$9 \div 9 = 1$
$10 \times 10 = 100$	$20 / 10 = 2$	$10 \times 9 = 90$	$36 / 9 = 4$
$2 \cdot 10 = 20$	$50 \div 10 = 5$	$2 \cdot 9 = 18$	$81 \div 9 = 9$

► PATH to FLUENCY **Explore Patterns with 9s**

What patterns do you see below?

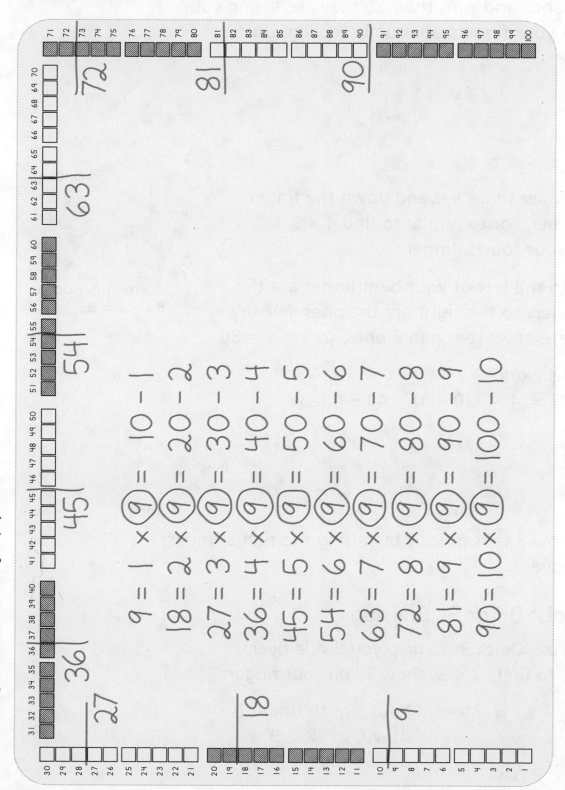

PATH to
FLUENCY

► Math Tools: Quick 9s Multiplication

You can use the Quick 9s method to help you multiply by 9.
Open your hands and turn them so they are facing you.
Imagine that your fingers are numbered like this.

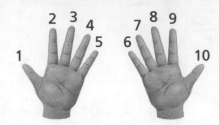

To find a number times 9, bend down the finger
for that number. For example, to find 4 × 9,
bend down your fourth finger.

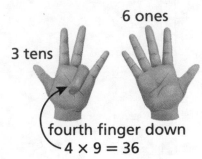

6 ones

3 tens

fourth finger down
4 × 9 = 36

The fingers to the left of your bent finger are the
tens. The fingers to the right are the ones. For this
problem, there are 3 tens and 6 ones, so 4 × 9 = 36.

Why does this work?
Because 4 × 9 = 4 × (10 − 1) = 40 − 4 = 36

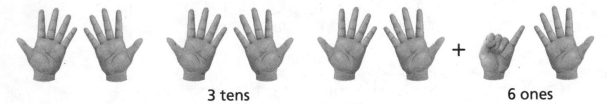

3 tens   6 ones

You could show 3 tens quickly by raising the first 3 fingers
as shown above.

► Math Tools: Quick 9s Division

You can also use Quick 9s to help you divide by 9.
For example, to find 72 ÷ 9, show 72 on your fingers.

7 tens   2 ones

Your eighth finger is
down, so 72 ÷ 9 = 8.
8 × 9 = 80 − 8 = 72

► **PATH to FLUENCY** **Check Sheet 3: 2s, 5s, 9s, and 10s**

2s, 5s, 9s, 10s Multiplications	2s, 5s, 9s, 10s Multiplications	2s, 5s, 9s, 10s Divisions	2s, 5s, 9s, 10s Divisions
$2 \times 10 = 20$	$5 \times 10 = 50$	$18 / 2 = 9$	$36 / 9 = 4$
$10 \cdot 5 = 50$	$10 \cdot 9 = 90$	$50 \div 5 = 10$	$70 \div 10 = 7$
$9 * 6 = 54$	$4 * 10 = 40$	$72 / 9 = 8$	$18 / 2 = 9$
$7 \times 10 = 70$	$2 \times 9 = 18$	$60 \div 10 = 6$	$45 \div 5 = 9$
$2 \cdot 3 = 6$	$5 \cdot 3 = 15$	$12 / 2 = 6$	$45 / 9 = 5$
$5 * 7 = 35$	$6 * 9 = 54$	$30 \div 5 = 6$	$30 \div 10 = 3$
$9 \times 10 = 90$	$10 \times 3 = 30$	$18 / 9 = 2$	$6 / 2 = 3$
$6 \cdot 10 = 60$	$3 \cdot 2 = 6$	$50 \div 10 = 5$	$50 \div 5 = 10$
$8 * 2 = 16$	$5 * 8 = 40$	$14 / 2 = 7$	$27 / 9 = 3$
$5 \times 6 = 30$	$9 \times 9 = 81$	$25 / 5 = 5$	$70 / 10 = 7$
$9 \cdot 5 = 45$	$10 \cdot 4 = 40$	$81 \div 9 = 9$	$20 \div 2 = 10$
$8 * 10 = 80$	$9 * 2 = 18$	$20 / 10 = 2$	$45 / 5 = 9$
$2 \times 1 = 2$	$5 \times 1 = 5$	$8 \div 2 = 4$	$54 \div 9 = 6$
$3 \cdot 5 = 15$	$9 \cdot 6 = 54$	$45 / 5 = 9$	$80 / 10 = 8$
$4 * 9 = 36$	$10 * 1 = 10$	$63 \div 9 = 7$	$16 \div 2 = 8$
$3 \times 10 = 30$	$7 \times 2 = 14$	$30 / 10 = 3$	$15 / 5 = 3$
$2 \cdot 6 = 12$	$6 \cdot 5 = 30$	$10 \div 2 = 5$	$90 \div 9 = 10$
$4 * 5 = 20$	$8 * 9 = 72$	$40 \div 5 = 8$	$100 \div 10 = 10$
$9 \times 7 = 63$	$10 \times 6 = 60$	$9 / 9 = 1$	$12 / 2 = 6$
$1 \cdot 10 = 10$	$2 \cdot 8 = 16$	$50 \div 10 = 5$	$35 \div 5 = 7$

Name _____ **Date** _____

CA CC Content Standards **3.OA.1, 3.OA.2, 3.OA.3, 3.OA.4, 3.OA.6, 3.OA.7** Mathematical Practices **MP.1, MP.4, MP.5**

► Make Sense of Problems with 2s, 5s, 9s, and 10s

**Write an equation to represent each problem.
Then solve the problem.**

Show your work.

1. Ian planted tulip bulbs in an array with 5 rows and 10 columns. How many bulbs did he plant?

   _____

2. Erin gave 30 basketball cards to her 5 cousins. Each cousin got the same number of cards. How many cards did each cousin get?

   _____

3. Martina bought 7 cans of racquetballs. There were 2 balls per can. How many racquetballs did she buy in all?

   _____

4. The 27 students in the orchestra stood in rows for their school picture. There were 9 students in every row. How many rows of students were there?

   _____

5. Lindsey needs 40 note cards. The note cards are packaged 10 to a box. How many boxes of cards should Lindsey buy?

   _____

6. There are 25 student desks in the classroom. The desks are arranged in 5 rows with the same number of desks in each row. How many desks are in each row?

   _____

► Math Tools: Fast Array Drawings

When you solve a word problem involving an array, you can save time by making a Fast Array drawing. This type of drawing shows the number of items in each row and column, but does not show every single item.

Here is how you might use a Fast Array drawing for problem 1 on Student Activity Book page 43.

Show the number of rows and the number of columns. Make a box in the center to show that you don't know the total.

Here are three ways to find the total.

- Find 5×10.

- Use 10s count-bys to find the total in 5 rows of 10: 10, 20, 30, 40, 50.

- Use 5s count-bys to find the total in 10 rows of 5: 5, 10, 15, 20, 25, 30, 35, 40, 45, 50.

Here is how you might use a Fast Array drawing for problem 4 on page 43.

Show the number in each row and the total. Make a box to show that you don't know the number of rows.

Here are two ways to find the number of rows.

- Find $27 \div 9$ or solve $\square \times 9 = 27$.

- Count by 9s until you reach 27: 9, 18, 27.

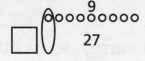

Math Journal **Make a Fast Array drawing to solve each problem.**

7. Beth planted tulip bulbs in an array with 9 rows and 6 columns. How many bulbs did she plant?

8. The 36 students in the chorus stood in 4 rows for their school picture. How many students were in each row?

Name _____ **Date** _____

CA CC Content Standards **3.OA.1, 3.OA.2, 3.OA.3, 3.OA.4, 3.OA.7, 3.OA.9** Mathematical Practices **MP.1, MP.2, MP.4, MP.7, MP.8**

► **PATH to FLUENCY** **Explore Patterns with 3s**

What patterns do you see below?

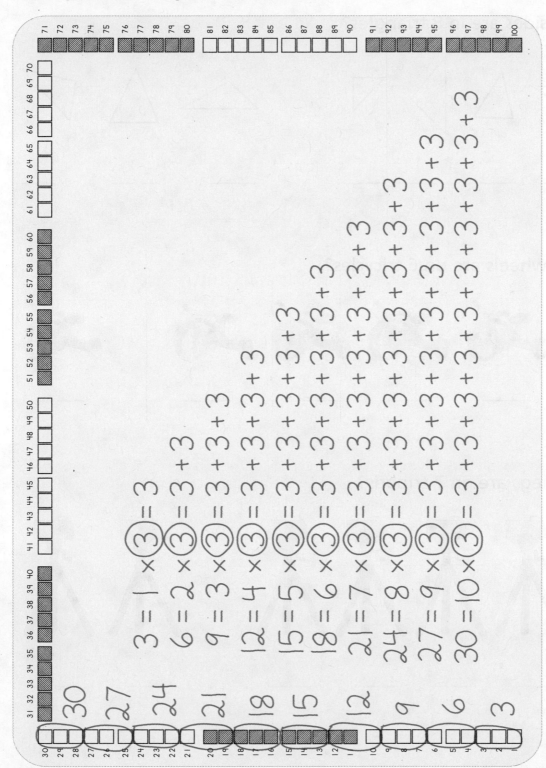

► ◌PATH to FLUENCY◌ **Use the 5s Shortcut for 3s**

Write the 3s count-bys to find the total.

1. How many sides are in 8 triangles?

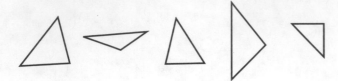

_____ _____ _____ _____

2. How many wheels are on 6 tricycles?

_____ _____ _____ _____ _____ _____

3. How many legs are on 7 tripods?

_____ _____ _____ _____ _____ _____ _____

► (PATH to FLUENCY) **Use the 5s Shortcut for 3s (continued)**

Find the total by starting with the fifth count-by and counting by 3s from there.

4. How many sides are in 7 triangles?

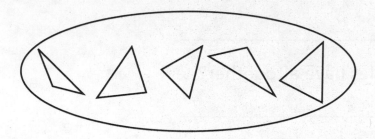

_____   _____ _____

5. How many wheels are on 9 tricycles?

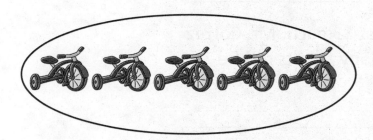

_____   _____ _____ _____ _____

6. How many legs are on 8 tripods?

_____   _____ _____ _____

▶ Make Sense of Problems

Write an equation and solve the problem.

Show your work.

7. Spencer arranged his soccer trophies in 3 equal rows. If he has 12 trophies, how many trophies are in each row?

_____

8. How many sides do 8 triangles have altogether?

_____

9. For Sophie's class picture, the students stood in 3 rows with 5 students in each row. How many students were in the picture?

_____

10. Tickets to the school play cost $3 each. Mr. Cortez spent $27 on tickets. How many tickets did he buy?

_____

11. Jess solved 21 multiplication problems. If the problems were arranged in rows of 3, how many rows of problems did Jess solve?

_____

12. Last year, 6 sets of triplets were born at Watertown Hospital. During this time, how many triples were born at the hospital in all?

_____

Name

Study Sheet B

© Houghton Mifflin Harcourt Publishing Company

4s

Count-bys	Mixed Up ×	Mixed Up ÷
1 × 4 = 4	4 × 4 = 16	12 ÷ 4 = 3
2 × 4 = 8	1 × 4 = 4	36 ÷ 4 = 9
3 × 4 = 12	7 × 4 = 28	24 ÷ 4 = 6
4 × 4 = 16	3 × 4 = 12	4 ÷ 4 = 1
5 × 4 = 20	9 × 4 = 36	20 ÷ 4 = 5
6 × 4 = 24	10 × 4 = 40	28 ÷ 4 = 7
7 × 4 = 28	2 × 4 = 8	8 ÷ 4 = 2
8 × 4 = 32	5 × 4 = 20	40 ÷ 4 = 10
9 × 4 = 36	8 × 4 = 32	32 ÷ 4 = 8
10 × 4 = 40	6 × 4 = 24	16 ÷ 4 = 4

3s

Count-bys	Mixed Up ×	Mixed Up ÷
1 × 3 = 3	5 × 3 = 15	27 ÷ 3 = 9
2 × 3 = 6	1 × 3 = 3	6 ÷ 3 = 2
3 × 3 = 9	8 × 3 = 24	18 ÷ 3 = 6
4 × 3 = 12	10 × 3 = 30	30 ÷ 3 = 10
5 × 3 = 15	3 × 3 = 9	9 ÷ 3 = 3
6 × 3 = 18	7 × 3 = 21	3 ÷ 3 = 1
7 × 3 = 21	9 × 3 = 27	12 ÷ 3 = 4
8 × 3 = 24	2 × 3 = 6	24 ÷ 3 = 8
9 × 3 = 27	4 × 3 = 12	15 ÷ 3 = 5
10 × 3 = 30	6 × 3 = 18	21 ÷ 3 = 7

1s

Count-bys	Mixed Up ×	Mixed Up ÷
1 × 1 = 1	5 × 1 = 5	10 ÷ 1 = 10
2 × 1 = 2	7 × 1 = 7	8 ÷ 1 = 8
3 × 1 = 3	10 × 1 = 10	4 ÷ 1 = 4
4 × 1 = 4	1 × 1 = 1	9 ÷ 1 = 9
5 × 1 = 5	8 × 1 = 8	6 ÷ 1 = 6
6 × 1 = 6	4 × 1 = 4	7 ÷ 1 = 7
7 × 1 = 7	9 × 1 = 9	1 ÷ 1 = 1
8 × 1 = 8	3 × 1 = 3	2 ÷ 1 = 2
9 × 1 = 9	2 × 1 = 2	5 ÷ 1 = 5
10 × 1 = 10	6 × 1 = 6	3 ÷ 1 = 3

0s

Count-bys	Mixed Up ×
1 × 0 = 0	3 × 0 = 0
2 × 0 = 0	10 × 0 = 0
3 × 0 = 0	5 × 0 = 0
4 × 0 = 0	8 × 0 = 0
5 × 0 = 0	7 × 0 = 0
6 × 0 = 0	2 × 0 = 0
7 × 0 = 0	9 × 0 = 0
8 × 0 = 0	6 × 0 = 0
9 × 0 = 0	1 × 0 = 0
10 × 0 = 0	4 × 0 = 0

© Houghton Mifflin Harcourt Publishing Company

Study Sheet B

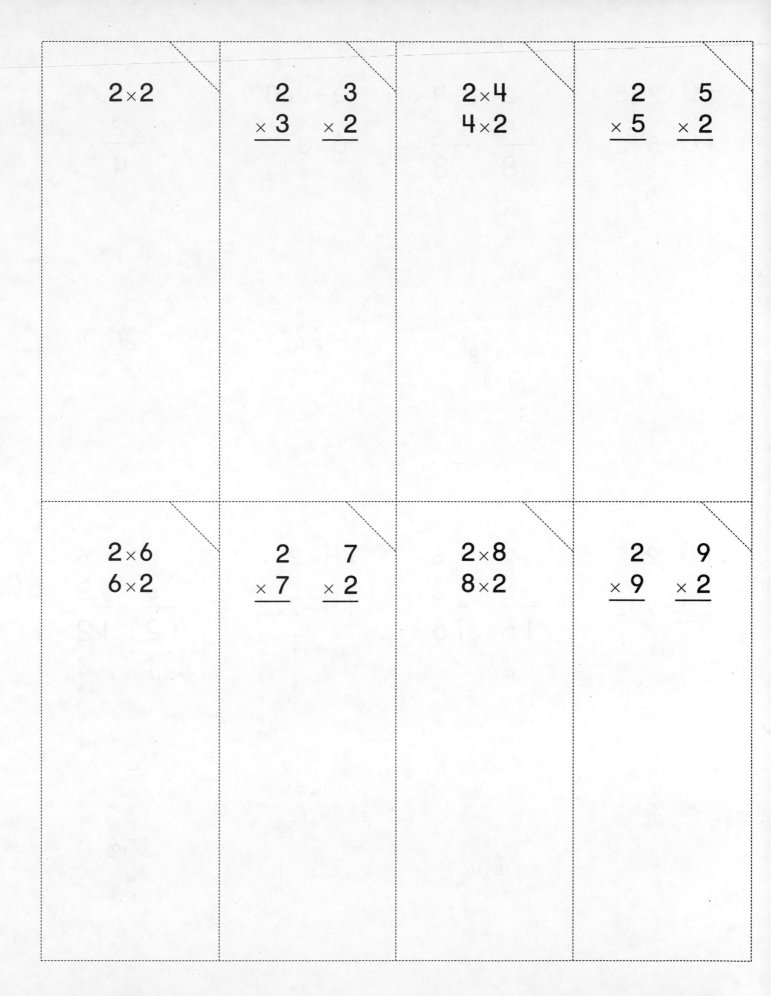

2×2	$\begin{array}{r} 2 \\ \times 3 \end{array}$ $\begin{array}{r} 3 \\ \times 2 \end{array}$	$\begin{array}{c} 2 \times 4 \\ 4 \times 2 \end{array}$ $\begin{array}{r} 2 \\ \times 5 \end{array}$ $\begin{array}{r} 5 \\ \times 2 \end{array}$

2×2

$\begin{array}{r} 2 \\ \times 3 \end{array}$ $\begin{array}{r} 3 \\ \times 2 \end{array}$

2×4
4×2

$\begin{array}{r} 2 \\ \times 5 \end{array}$ $\begin{array}{r} 5 \\ \times 2 \end{array}$

2×6
6×2

$\begin{array}{r} 2 \\ \times 7 \end{array}$ $\begin{array}{r} 7 \\ \times 2 \end{array}$

2×8
8×2

$\begin{array}{r} 2 \\ \times 9 \end{array}$ $\begin{array}{r} 9 \\ \times 2 \end{array}$

$10 = 2 \times 5$

$10 = 5 \times 2$

5 10

2 4 6 8 10

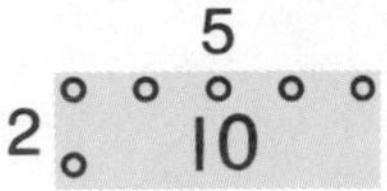

$$\begin{array}{r}2\\ \times 4\\ \hline 8\end{array} \qquad \begin{array}{r}4\\ \times 2\\ \hline 8\end{array}$$

2 4 6 8

4 8

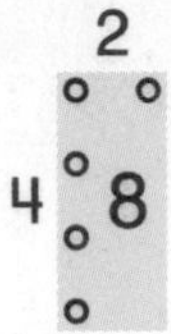

$6 = 2 \times 3$

$6 = 3 \times 2$

3 6

2 4 6

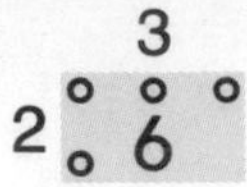

$$\begin{array}{r}2\\ \times 2\\ \hline 4\end{array}$$

2 4

$18 = 2 \times 9$

$18 = 9 \times 2$

9 18

2 4 6 8 10 12 14 16 18

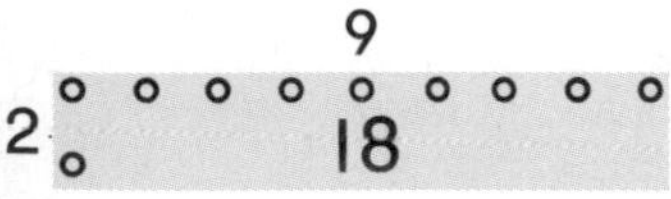

$$\begin{array}{r}2\\ \times 8\\ \hline 16\end{array} \qquad \begin{array}{r}8\\ \times 2\\ \hline 16\end{array}$$

8 16

2 4 6 8 10 12 14 16

$14 = 2 \times 7$

$14 = 7 \times 2$

7 14

2 4 6 8 10 12 14

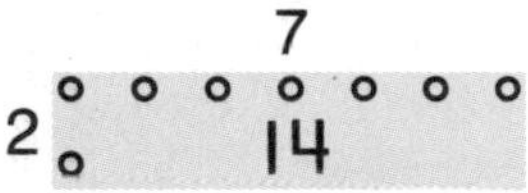

$$\begin{array}{r}2\\ \times 6\\ \hline 12\end{array} \qquad \begin{array}{r}6\\ \times 2\\ \hline 12\end{array}$$

6 12

2 4 6 8 10 12

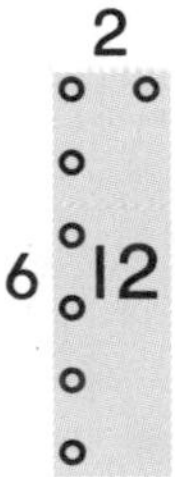

3×3

$3 \quad 4$
$\times 4 \quad \times 3$

3×5
5×3

$3 \quad 6$
$\times 6 \quad \times 3$

3×7
7×3

$3 \quad 8$
$\times 8 \quad \times 3$

3×9
9×3

4
$\times 4$

$18 = 3 \times 6$

$18 = 6 \times 3$

6, 12, 18

3, 6, 9, 12, 15, 18

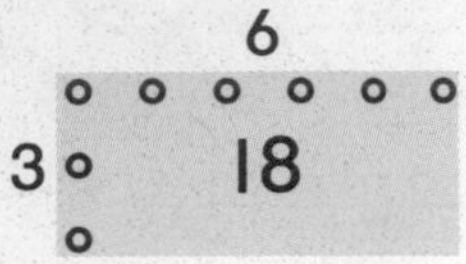

$\begin{array}{r} 3 \\ \times\, 5 \\ \hline 15 \end{array} \qquad \begin{array}{r} 5 \\ \times\, 3 \\ \hline 15 \end{array}$

5, 10, 15

3, 6, 9, 12, 15

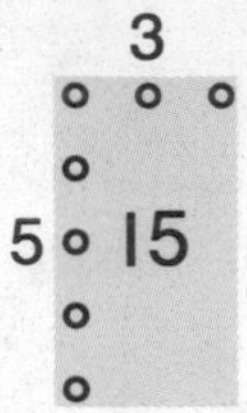

$12 = 3 \times 4$

$12 = 4 \times 3$

4, 8, 12

3, 6, 9, 12

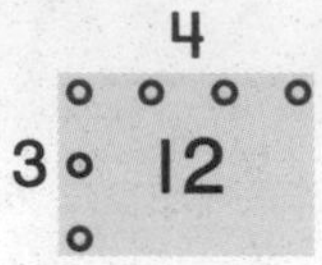

$\begin{array}{r} 3 \\ \times\, 3 \\ \hline 9 \end{array}$

3, 6, 9

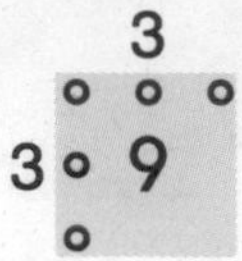

$16 = 4 \times 4$

4, 8, 12, 16

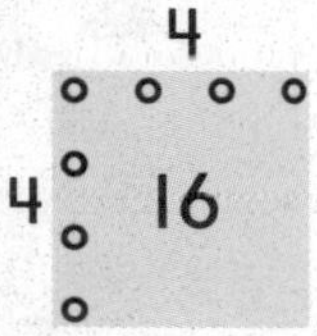

$\begin{array}{r} 3 \\ \times\, 9 \\ \hline 27 \end{array} \qquad \begin{array}{r} 9 \\ \times\, 3 \\ \hline 27 \end{array}$

9, 18, 27

3, 6, 9, 12, 15, 18, 21, 24, 27

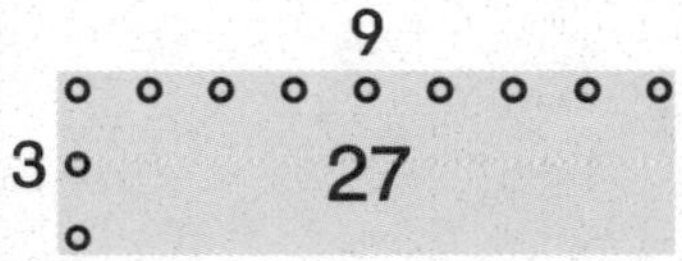

$24 = 3 \times 8$

$24 = 8 \times 3$

8, 16, 24

3, 6, 9, 12, 15, 18, 21, 24

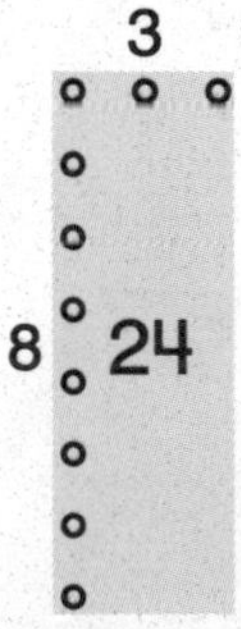

$\begin{array}{r} 3 \\ \times\, 7 \\ \hline 21 \end{array} \qquad \begin{array}{r} 7 \\ \times\, 3 \\ \hline 21 \end{array}$

7, 14, 21

3, 6, 9, 12, 15, 18, 21

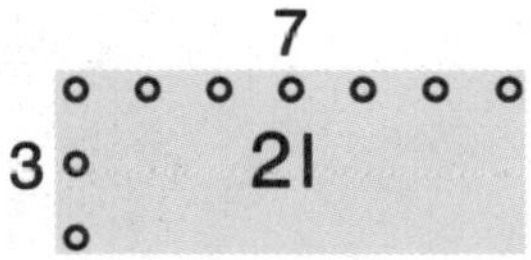

| 4×5 | 4 | 6 | 4×7 | 4 | 8 |
| 5×4 | $\times 6$ | $\times 4$ | 7×4 | $\times 8$ | $\times 4$ |

| 4×9 | 5 | 5×6 | 5 | 7 |
| 9×4 | $\times 5$ | 6×5 | $\times 7$ | $\times 5$ |

Card 1

$32 = 4 \times 8$

$32 = 8 \times 4$

8	4
16	8
24	12
32	16
	20
	24
	28
	32

4

8 — 32

Card 2

$\begin{array}{r} 4 \\ \times 7 \\ \hline 28 \end{array}$ $\begin{array}{r} 7 \\ \times 4 \\ \hline 28 \end{array}$

7	4
14	8
21	12
28	16
	20
	24
	28

7

4 — 28

Card 3

$24 = 4 \times 6$

$24 = 6 \times 4$

6	4
12	8
18	12
24	16
	20
	24

4

6 — 24

Card 4

$\begin{array}{r} 4 \\ \times 5 \\ \hline 20 \end{array}$ $\begin{array}{r} 5 \\ \times 4 \\ \hline 20 \end{array}$

5	4
10	8
15	12
20	16
	20

5

4 — 20

Card 5

$35 = 5 \times 7$

$35 = 7 \times 5$

7	5
14	10
21	15
28	20
35	25
	30
	35

7

5 — 35

Card 6

$\begin{array}{r} 5 \\ \times 6 \\ \hline 30 \end{array}$ $\begin{array}{r} 6 \\ \times 5 \\ \hline 30 \end{array}$

6	5
12	10
18	15
24	20
30	25
	30

5

6 — 30

Card 7

$25 = 5 \times 5$

5
10
15
20
25

5

5 — 25

Card 8

$\begin{array}{r} 4 \\ \times 9 \\ \hline 36 \end{array}$ $\begin{array}{r} 9 \\ \times 4 \\ \hline 36 \end{array}$

9	4
18	8
27	12
36	16
	20
	24
	28
	32
	36

9

4 — 36

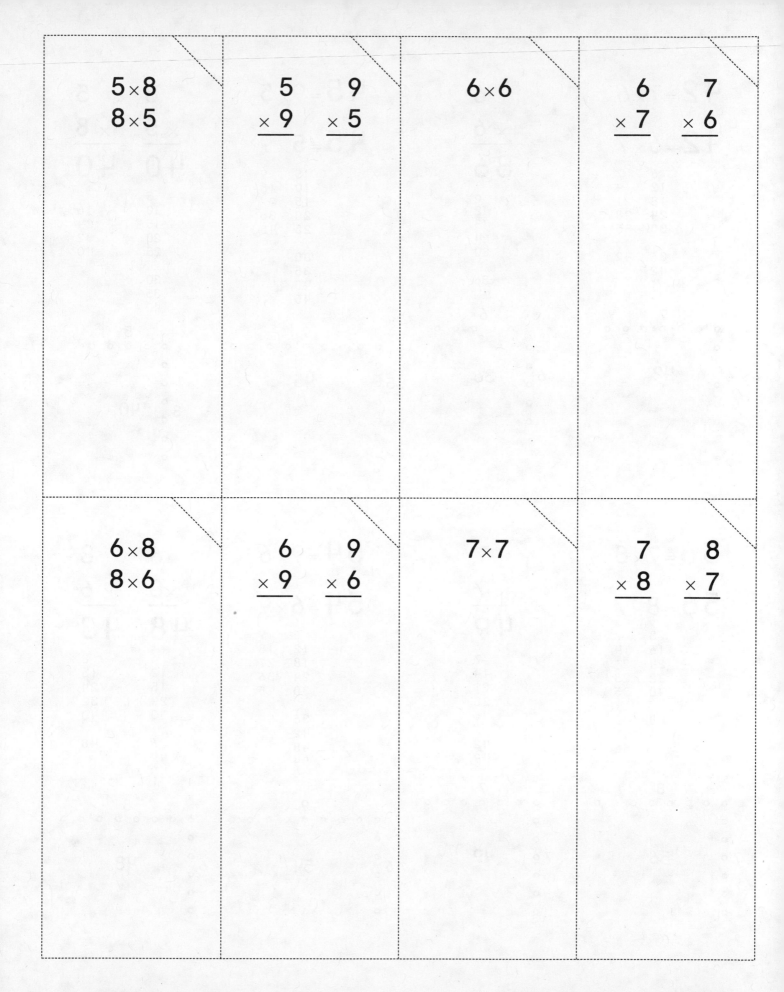

5×8
8×5

$\begin{array}{r} 5 \\ \times 9 \end{array}$ $\begin{array}{r} 9 \\ \times 5 \end{array}$

6×6

$\begin{array}{r} 6 \\ \times 7 \end{array}$ $\begin{array}{r} 7 \\ \times 6 \end{array}$

6×8
8×6

$\begin{array}{r} 6 \\ \times 9 \end{array}$ $\begin{array}{r} 9 \\ \times 6 \end{array}$

7×7

$\begin{array}{r} 7 \\ \times 8 \end{array}$ $\begin{array}{r} 8 \\ \times 7 \end{array}$

Card 1

$42 = 7 \times 6$

$42 = 6 \times 7$

6	7
12	14
18	21
24	28
30	35
36	42
42	

7

6   42

Card 2

$\begin{array}{r} 6 \\ \times\,6 \\ \hline 36 \end{array}$

6
12
18
24
30

36

6

6   36

Card 3

$45 = 9 \times 5$

$45 = 5 \times 9$

5	9
10	18
15	27
20	36
25	45
30	
35	
40	
45	

9

5   45

Card 4

$\begin{array}{r} 8 \\ \times\,5 \\ \hline 40 \end{array}$ $\begin{array}{r} 5 \\ \times\,8 \\ \hline 40 \end{array}$

5	8
10	16
15	24
20	32
25	40
30	
35	
40	

5

8   40

Card 5

$56 = 7 \times 8$

$56 = 8 \times 7$

8	7
16	14
24	21
32	28
40	35
48	42
56	49
	56

8

7   56

Card 6

$\begin{array}{r} 7 \\ \times\,7 \\ \hline 49 \end{array}$

7
14
21
28
35

42
49

7

7   49

Card 7

$54 = 9 \times 6$

$54 = 6 \times 9$

6	9
12	18
18	27
24	36
30	45
36	54
42	
48	
54	

9

6   54

Card 8

$\begin{array}{r} 6 \\ \times\,8 \\ \hline 48 \end{array}$ $\begin{array}{r} 8 \\ \times\,6 \\ \hline 48 \end{array}$

6	8
12	16
18	24
24	32
30	40
36	48
42	
48	

8

6   48

$$7 \times 9$$
$$9 \times 7$$

$$8$$
$$\times\,8$$

$$9 \times 8$$
$$8 \times 9$$

$$9$$
$$\times\,9$$

81 = 9 × 9

9
18
27
36
45

54
63
72
81

9

9 | 81

9   8
×8   ×9
72   72

8   9
16   18
24   27
32   36
40   45

48   54
56   63
64   72
72

9

8 | 72

64 = 8 × 8

8
16
24
32
40

48
56
64

8

8 | 64

7   9
×9   ×7
63   63

9   7
18   14
27   21
36   28
45   35

54   42
63   49
     56
     63

9

7 | 63

Multiplication Strategy Cards

$2\overline{)4}$

$4 \div 2$

$2\overline{)6}$

$6 \div 2$

$2\overline{)8}$

$8 \div 2$

$2\overline{)10}$

$10 \div 2$

$2\overline{)12}$

$12 \div 2$

$2\overline{)14}$

$14 \div 2$

$2\overline{)16}$

$16 \div 2$

$2\overline{)18}$

$18 \div 2$

Card 1

$$5 \quad\quad 2$$
$$2\overline{)10} \quad 5\overline{)10}$$

2	5
4	10
6	
8	
10	

$$\begin{array}{c} 5 \\ 2\,\boxed{\substack{\circ\circ\circ\circ\circ \\ \circ \quad 10}} \end{array}$$

Card 2

$$4 \quad\quad 2$$
$$2\overline{)8} \quad 4\overline{)8}$$

2	4
4	8
6	
8	

$$\begin{array}{c} 4 \\ 2\,\boxed{\substack{\circ\circ\circ\circ \\ \circ \quad 8}} \end{array}$$

Card 3

$$3 \quad\quad 2$$
$$2\overline{)6} \quad 3\overline{)6}$$

2	3
4	6
6	

$$\begin{array}{c} 3 \\ 2\,\boxed{\substack{\circ\circ\circ \\ \circ \quad 6}} \end{array}$$

Card 4

$$2$$
$$2\overline{)4}$$

| 2 |
| 4 |

$$\begin{array}{c} 2 \\ 2\,\boxed{\substack{\circ\circ \\ \circ\,4}} \end{array}$$

Card 5

$$9 \quad\quad 2$$
$$2\overline{)18} \quad 9\overline{)18}$$

2	9
4	18
6	
8	
10	
12	
14	
16	
18	

$$\begin{array}{c} 9 \\ 2\,\boxed{\substack{\circ\circ\circ\circ\circ\circ\circ\circ\circ \\ \circ \quad\quad 18}} \end{array}$$

Card 6

$$8 \quad\quad 2$$
$$2\overline{)16} \quad 8\overline{)16}$$

2	8
4	16
6	
8	
10	
12	
14	
16	

$$\begin{array}{c} 8 \\ 2\,\boxed{\substack{\circ\circ\circ\circ\circ\circ\circ\circ \\ \circ \quad\quad 16}} \end{array}$$

Card 7

$$7 \quad\quad 2$$
$$2\overline{)14} \quad 7\overline{)14}$$

2	7
4	14
6	
8	
10	
12	
14	

$$\begin{array}{c} 7 \\ 2\,\boxed{\substack{\circ\circ\circ\circ\circ\circ\circ \\ \circ \quad\quad 14}} \end{array}$$

Card 8

$$6 \quad\quad 2$$
$$2\overline{)12} \quad 6\overline{)12}$$

2	6
4	12
6	
8	
10	
12	

$$\begin{array}{c} 6 \\ 2\,\boxed{\substack{\circ\circ\circ\circ\circ\circ \\ \circ \quad\quad 12}} \end{array}$$

Division Strategy Cards

$3\overline{)6}$

$6 \div 3$

$4\overline{)8}$

$8 \div 4$

$5\overline{)10}$

$10 \div 5$

$6\overline{)12}$

$12 \div 6$

$7\overline{)14}$

$14 \div 7$

$8\overline{)16}$

$16 \div 8$

$9\overline{)18}$

$18 \div 9$

$3\overline{)9}$

$9 \div 3$

Row 1

$$2 \atop 6\overline{)12}$$
$$6 \atop 12$$

$$6 \atop 2\overline{)12}$$
$$2 \atop 4 \atop 6 \atop 8 \atop 10 \atop 12$$

$$2 \atop 5\overline{)10}$$
$$5 \atop 10$$

$$5 \atop 2\overline{)10}$$
$$2 \atop 4 \atop 6 \atop 8 \atop 10$$

$$2 \atop 4\overline{)8}$$
$$4 \atop 8$$

$$4 \atop 2\overline{)8}$$
$$2 \atop 4 \atop 6 \atop 8$$

$$2 \atop 3\overline{)6}$$
$$3 \atop 6$$

$$3 \atop 2\overline{)6}$$
$$2 \atop 4 \atop 6$$

6 • 12   (with 2 at top)
5 • 10   (with 2 at top)
4 • 8   (with 2 at top)
3 • 6   (with 2 at top)

Row 2

$$3 \atop 3\overline{)9}$$
$$3 \atop 6 \atop 9$$

$$2 \atop 9\overline{)18}$$
$$9 \atop 18$$

$$9 \atop 2\overline{)18}$$
$$2 \atop 4 \atop 6 \atop 8 \atop 10 \atop 12 \atop 14 \atop 16 \atop 18$$

$$2 \atop 8\overline{)16}$$
$$8 \atop 16$$

$$8 \atop 2\overline{)16}$$
$$2 \atop 4 \atop 6 \atop 8 \atop 10 \atop 12 \atop 14 \atop 16$$

$$2 \atop 7\overline{)14}$$
$$7 \atop 14$$

$$7 \atop 2\overline{)14}$$
$$2 \atop 4 \atop 6 \atop 8 \atop 10 \atop 12 \atop 14$$

3 • 9   (with 3 at top)
9 • 18   (with 2 at top)
8 • 16   (with 2 at top)
7 • 14   (with 2 at top)

Division Strategy Cards

$3\overline{)12}$
$12 \div 3$

$3\overline{)15}$
$15 \div 3$

$3\overline{)18}$
$18 \div 3$

$3\overline{)21}$
$21 \div 3$

$3\overline{)24}$
$24 \div 3$

$3\overline{)27}$
$27 \div 3$

$4\overline{)12}$
$12 \div 4$

$5\overline{)15}$
$15 \div 5$

Card 1

$$3\overline{)21}\quad 7\overline{)21}$$

3	7
6	14
9	21
12	
15	
18	
21	

7
3 · 21

Card 2

$$3\overline{)18}\quad 6\overline{)18}$$

3	6
6	12
9	18
12	
15	
18	

6
3 · 18

Card 3

$$3\overline{)15}\quad 5\overline{)15}$$

3	5
6	10
9	15
12	
15	

5
3 · 15

Card 4

$$3\overline{)12}\quad 4\overline{)12}$$

3	4
6	8
9	12
12	

4
3 · 12

Card 5

$$5\overline{)15}\quad 3\overline{)15}$$

5	3
10	6
15	9
	12
	15

3
5 · 15

Card 6

$$4\overline{)12}\quad 3\overline{)12}$$

4	3
8	6
12	9
	12

3
4 · 12

Card 7

$$3\overline{)27}\quad 9\overline{)27}$$

3	9
6	18
9	27
12	
15	
18	
21	
24	
27	

9
3 · 27

Card 8

$$3\overline{)24}\quad 8\overline{)24}$$

3	8
6	16
9	24
12	
15	
18	
21	
24	

8
3 · 24

Division Strategy Cards

$6 \overline{)18}$	$7 \overline{)21}$	$8 \overline{)24}$	$9 \overline{)27}$
$18 \div 6$	$21 \div 7$	$24 \div 8$	$27 \div 9$

$4 \overline{)16}$	$4 \overline{)20}$	$4 \overline{)24}$	$4 \overline{)28}$
$16 \div 4$	$20 \div 4$	$24 \div 4$	$28 \div 4$

Card 1

$$3 \qquad 9$$
$$9\overline{)27} \quad 3\overline{)27}$$

9	3
18	6
27	9
	12
	15
	18
	21
	24
	27

3

9 ○ 27

Card 2

$$3 \qquad 8$$
$$8\overline{)24} \quad 3\overline{)24}$$

8	3
16	6
24	9
	12
	15
	18
	21
	24

3

8 ○ 24

Card 3

$$3 \qquad 7$$
$$7\overline{)21} \quad 3\overline{)21}$$

7	3
14	6
21	9
	12
	15
	18
	21

3

7 ○ 21

Card 4

$$3 \qquad 6$$
$$6\overline{)18} \quad 3\overline{)18}$$

6	3
12	6
18	9
	12
	15
	18

3

6 ○ 18

Card 5

$$7 \qquad 4$$
$$4\overline{)28} \quad 7\overline{)28}$$

4	7
8	14
12	21
16	28
20	
24	
28	

7

4 ○ 28

Card 6

$$6 \qquad 4$$
$$4\overline{)24} \quad 6\overline{)24}$$

4	6
8	12
12	18
16	24
20	
24	

6

4 ○ 24

Card 7

$$5 \qquad 4$$
$$4\overline{)20} \quad 5\overline{)20}$$

4	5
8	10
12	15
16	20
20	

5

4 ○ 20

Card 8

$$4$$
$$4\overline{)16}$$

4
8
12
16

4

4 ○ 16

51R UNIT 1 LESSON 11
© Houghton Mifflin Harcourt Publishing Company

Division Strategy Cards

$4\overline{)32}$	$4\overline{)36}$	$5\overline{)20}$	$6\overline{)24}$
$32 \div 4$	$36 \div 4$	$20 \div 5$	$24 \div 6$

$7\overline{)28}$	$8\overline{)32}$	$9\overline{)36}$	$5\overline{)25}$
$28 \div 7$	$32 \div 8$	$36 \div 9$	$25 \div 5$

4	6
$6\overline{)24}$	$4\overline{)24}$

6
12
18
24

4
8
12
16
20
24

4	5
$5\overline{)20}$	$4\overline{)20}$

5
10
15
20

4
8
12
16
20

9	4
$4\overline{)36}$	$9\overline{)36}$

4
8
12
16
20
24
28
32
36

9
18
27
36

8	4
$4\overline{)32}$	$8\overline{)32}$

4
8
12
16
20
24
28
32

8
16
24
32

5
$5\overline{)25}$

5
10
15
20
25

4	9
$9\overline{)36}$	$4\overline{)36}$

9
18
27
36

4
8
12
16
20
24
28
32
36

4	8
$8\overline{)32}$	$4\overline{)32}$

8
16
24
32

4
8
12
16
20
24
28
32

4	7
$7\overline{)28}$	$4\overline{)28}$

7
14
21
28

4
8
12
16
20
24
28

Division Strategy Cards

$5\overline{)30}$ $30 \div 5$	$5\overline{)35}$ $35 \div 5$	$5\overline{)40}$ $40 \div 5$	$5\overline{)45}$ $45 \div 5$
$6\overline{)30}$ $30 \div 6$	$7\overline{)35}$ $35 \div 7$	$8\overline{)40}$ $40 \div 8$	$9\overline{)45}$ $45 \div 9$

Card 1

$$9 \qquad 5$$
$$5\overline{)45} \quad 9\overline{)45}$$

5	9
10	18
15	27
20	36
25	45
30	
35	
40	
45	

9
5 | 45

Card 2

$$8 \qquad 5$$
$$5\overline{)40} \quad 8\overline{)40}$$

5	8
10	16
15	24
20	32
25	40
30	
35	
40	

8
5 | 40

Card 3

$$7 \qquad 5$$
$$5\overline{)35} \quad 7\overline{)35}$$

5	7
10	14
15	21
20	28
25	35
30	
35	

7
5 | 35

Card 4

$$6 \qquad 5$$
$$5\overline{)30} \quad 6\overline{)30}$$

5	6
10	12
15	18
20	24
25	30
30	

6
5 | 30

Card 5

$$5 \qquad 9$$
$$9\overline{)45} \quad 5\overline{)45}$$

9	5
18	10
27	15
36	20
45	25
	30
	35
	40
	45

5
9 | 45

Card 6

$$5 \qquad 8$$
$$8\overline{)40} \quad 5\overline{)40}$$

8	5
16	10
24	15
32	20
40	25
	30
	35
	40

5
8 | 40

Card 7

$$5 \qquad 7$$
$$7\overline{)35} \quad 5\overline{)35}$$

7	5
14	10
21	15
28	20
35	25
	30
	35

5
7 | 35

Card 8

$$5 \qquad 6$$
$$6\overline{)30} \quad 5\overline{)30}$$

6	5
12	10
18	15
24	20
30	25
	30

5
6 | 30

Division Strategy Cards

$6 \overline{)36}$

$36 \div 6$

$6 \overline{)42}$

$42 \div 6$

$6 \overline{)48}$

$48 \div 6$

$6 \overline{)54}$

$54 \div 6$

$7 \overline{)42}$

$42 \div 7$

$8 \overline{)48}$

$48 \div 8$

$9 \overline{)54}$

$54 \div 9$

$7 \overline{)49}$

$49 \div 7$

9	6
6)54	9)54
6	9
12	18
18	27
24	36
30	45
36	54
42	
48	
54	

9
6 54

8	6
6)48	8)48
6	8
12	16
18	24
24	32
30	40
36	48
42	
48	

8
6 48

7	6
6)42	7)42
6	7
12	14
18	21
24	28
30	35
36	42
42	

7
6 42

6
6)36
6
12
18
24
30
36

6
6 36

7
7)49
7
14
21
28
35
42
49

7
7 49

6	9
9)54	6)54
9	6
18	12
27	18
36	24
45	30
54	36
	42
	48
	54

6
9 54

6	8
8)48	6)48
8	6
16	12
24	18
32	24
40	30
48	36
	42
	48

6
8 48

6	7
7)42	6)42
7	6
14	12
21	18
28	24
35	30
42	36
	42

6
7 42

$7 \overline{)56}$

$56 \div 7$

$7 \overline{)63}$

$63 \div 7$

$8 \overline{)56}$

$56 \div 8$

$9 \overline{)63}$

$63 \div 9$

$8 \overline{)64}$

$64 \div 8$

$8 \overline{)72}$

$72 \div 8$

$9 \overline{)72}$

$72 \div 9$

$9 \overline{)81}$

$81 \div 9$

Card 1
$$7 \overline{)63}^{\,9} \qquad 9 \overline{)63}^{\,7}$$

9	7
18	14
27	21
36	28
45	35
54	42
63	49
	56
	63

7

9 | 63

Card 2
$$8 \overline{)56}^{\,7} \qquad 7 \overline{)56}^{\,8}$$

8	7
16	14
24	21
32	28
40	35
48	42
56	49
	56

7

8 | 56

Card 3
$$7 \overline{)63}^{\,9} \qquad 9 \overline{)63}^{\,7}$$

7	9
14	18
21	27
28	36
35	45
42	54
49	63
56	
63	

9

7 | 63

Card 4
$$7 \overline{)56}^{\,8} \qquad 8 \overline{)56}^{\,7}$$

7	8
14	16
21	24
28	32
35	40
42	48
49	56
56	

8

7 | 56

Card 5
$$9 \overline{)81}^{\,9}$$

9
18
27
36
45
54
63
72
81

9

9 | 81

Card 6
$$9 \overline{)72}^{\,8} \qquad 8 \overline{)72}^{\,9}$$

9	8
18	16
27	24
36	32
45	40
54	48
63	56
72	64
	72

8

9 | 72

Card 7
$$8 \overline{)72}^{\,9} \qquad 9 \overline{)72}^{\,8}$$

8	9
16	18
24	27
32	36
40	45
48	54
56	63
64	72
72	

9

8 | 72

Card 8
$$8 \overline{)64}^{\,8}$$

8
16
24
32
40
48
56
64

8

8 | 64

Division Strategy Cards

Name   **Date**

CA CC Content Standards **3.OA.5, 3.OA.7, 3.MD.5, 3.MD.5a, 3.MD.5b, 3.MD.7, 3.MD.7a, 3.MD.7b, 3.MD.7c, 3.MD.7d** Mathematical Practices **MP.2, MP.7**

► **PATH to FLUENCY** **Find the Area**

The area of a rectangle is the number of square units that fit inside of it.

Write a multiplication equation to represent the area of each rectangle. Then shade a whole number of rows in each rectangle and write a multiplication and addition equation to represent the area of each rectangle.

1.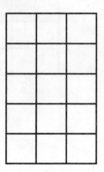

2.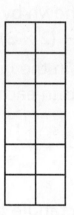

3.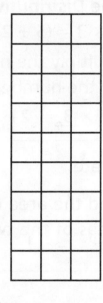

_____   _____   _____

_____   _____   _____

_____   _____   _____

Make a rectangle drawing to represent each problem. Then give the product.

4. $5 \times 3 = $ _____   **5.** $7 * 2 = $ _____   **6.** $2 \cdot 9 = $ _____

► PATH to FLUENCY **Different Ways to Find Area**

The large rectangle has been divided into two small rectangles.
You can find the area of the large rectangle in two ways:

- Add the areas of the two small rectangles:

  $5 \times 3 =$ ____ 15 square units

  $2 \times 3 =$ ____ 6 square units

  _____

  21 square units

  The **Distributive Property** is shown by

  $7 \times 3 = (5 + 2) \times 3 = (5 \times 3) + (2 \times 3)$

- Multiply the number of rows in the large rectangle by the number of square units in each row:

  $7 \times 3 = 21$ square units

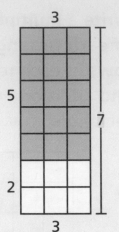

Complete.

7. Find the area of the large rectangle by finding the areas of the two small rectangles and adding them.

   _____

   _____

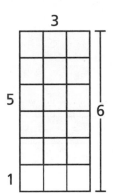

8. Find the area of the large rectangle by multiplying the number of rows by the number of square units in each row.

   _____

   _____

9. Find this product: $5 \times 4 =$ _____

10. Find this product: $2 \times 4 =$ _____

11. Use your answers to Exercises 9 and 10 to find this product: $7 \times 4 =$ _____

Multiplication and Area

Name _____

► (PATH to FLUENCY) **Check Sheet 4: 3s and 4s**

3s Multiplications	3s Divisions	4s Multiplications	4s Divisions
8 × 3 = 24	9 / 3 = 3	1 × 4 = 4	40 / 4 = 10
3 • 2 = 6	21 ÷ 3 = 7	4 • 5 = 20	12 ÷ 4 = 3
3 * 5 = 15	27 / 3 = 9	8 * 4 = 32	24 / 4 = 6
10 × 3 = 30	3 ÷ 3 = 1	3 × 4 = 12	8 ÷ 4 = 2
3 • 3 = 9	18 / 3 = 6	4 • 6 = 24	4 / 4 = 1
3 * 6 = 18	12 ÷ 3 = 4	4 * 9 = 36	28 ÷ 4 = 7
7 × 3 = 21	30 / 3 = 10	10 × 4 = 40	32 / 4 = 8
3 • 9 = 27	6 ÷ 3 = 2	4 • 7 = 28	16 ÷ 4 = 4
4 * 3 = 12	24 / 3 = 8	4 * 4 = 16	36 / 4 = 9
3 × 1 = 3	15 / 3 = 5	2 × 4 = 8	20 / 4 = 5
3 • 4 = 12	21 ÷ 3 = 7	4 • 3 = 12	4 ÷ 4 = 1
3 * 3 = 9	3 / 3 = 1	4 * 2 = 8	32 / 4 = 8
3 × 10 = 30	9 ÷ 3 = 3	9 × 4 = 36	8 ÷ 4 = 2
2 • 3 = 6	27 / 3 = 9	1 • 4 = 4	16 / 4 = 4
3 * 7 = 21	30 ÷ 3 = 10	4 * 6 = 24	36 ÷ 4 = 9
6 × 3 = 18	18 / 3 = 6	5 × 4 = 20	12 / 4 = 3
5 • 3 = 15	6 ÷ 3 = 2	4 • 4 = 16	40 ÷ 4 = 10
3 * 8 = 24	15 ÷ 3 = 5	7 * 4 = 28	20 ÷ 4 = 5
9 × 3 = 27	12 / 3 = 4	8 × 4 = 32	24 / 4 = 6
2 • 3 = 6	24 ÷ 3 = 8	10 • 4 = 40	28 ÷ 4 = 7

© Houghton Mifflin Harcourt Publishing Company

CA CC Content Standards **3.OA.2, 3.OA.3, 3.OA.4, 3.OA.5, 3.OA.7, 3.OA.9, 3.MD.7, 3.MD.7b, 3.MD.7c, 3.MD.7d**
Mathematical Practices **MP.1, MP.2, MP.3, MP.6, MP.7, MP.8,**

► **PATH to FLUENCY** **Explore Patterns with 4s**

What patterns do you see below?

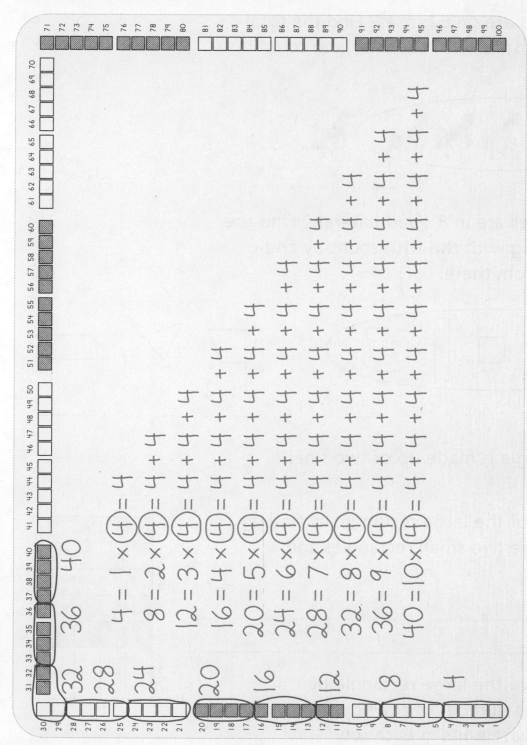

Name _____ Date _____

▶ **PATH to FLUENCY** **Use the 5s Shortcut for 4s**

Solve each problem.

1. How many legs are on 6 horses? Find the total by starting with the fifth count-by and counting up from there.

_____ _____

2. How many sides are in 8 quadrilaterals? Find the total by starting with the fifth count-by and counting up from there.

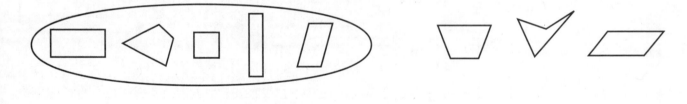

_____ _____ _____ _____

This large rectangle is made up of two small rectangles.

3. Find the area of the large rectangle by finding the areas of the two small rectangles and adding them.

_____

_____

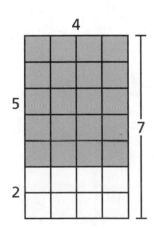

4. Find the area of the large rectangle by multiplying the number of rows by the number of square units in each row.

_____

▶ **PATH to FLUENCY** **Use Multiplications You Know**

You can combine multiplications to find other multiplications.

This Equal Shares Drawing shows that 7 groups of 4 is the same as 5 groups of 4 plus 2 groups of 4.

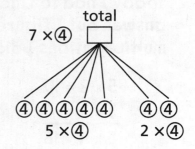

5. Find $5 \times ④$ and $2 \times ④$ and add the answers.

_____

6. Find $7 \times ④$. Did you get the same answer as in exercise 5?

_____

7. Find this product: $5 \times 4 =$ _____

8. Find this product: $4 \times 4 =$ _____

9. Use your answers to exercises 7 and 8 to find this product: $9 \times 4 =$ _____

10. Make a drawing to show that your answers to exercises 7–9 are correct.

▶ What's the Error?

Dear Math Students,

Today I had to find 8 × 4. I didn't know the answer, but I figured it out by combining two multiplications I did know:

$$5 \times 2 = 10$$
$$\underline{3 \times 2 = 6}$$
$$8 \times 4 = 16$$

Is my answer right? If not, please correct my work and tell me why it is wrong.

Your friend,
The Puzzled Penguin

11. **Write an answer to the Puzzled Penguin.**

_____

_____

_____

▶ Make Sense of Problems

Write an equation and solve the problem.

12. Galen has 20 pictures to place in his book. If he puts 4 pictures on each page, how many pages will he fill?

_____

13. Emery arranged the tiles in an array with 4 columns and 7 rows. How many tiles were in the array? _____

CA CC Content Standards **3.OA.1, 3.OA.2, 3.OA.3, 3.OA.4, 3.OA.6, 3.OA.7** Mathematical Practices **MP.1, MP.4, MP.5**

► Make Sense of Problems

Write an equation and solve the problem.

Show your work.

1. The garden shop received a shipment of 12 rose bushes. They arranged the rose bushes in 3 rows with the same number of bushes in each row. How many rose bushes were in each row?

_____

2. Eric saw 4 stop signs on the way to school. Each stop sign had 8 sides. How many sides were on all 4 stop signs?

_____

3. Ed needs 14 batteries. If he buys the batteries in packages of 2, how many packages of batteries will he need to buy?

_____

4. A flag has 5 rows of stars with the same number of stars in each row. There are 35 stars on the flag. How many stars are in each row?

_____

5. Melia learned in science class that insects have 6 legs. What is the total number of legs on 9 insects?

_____

6. Stan has 4 model car kits. Each kit comes with 5 tires. How many tires does Stan have altogether?

_____

► **Make Sense of Problems (continued)**

Write an equation and solve the problem.

Show your work.

7. Maria bought a shoe rack. The shoe rack has 3 rows with places for 6 shoes on each row. How many shoes can be placed on the shoe rack?

_____

8. The park has 4 swing sets with the same number of swings on each set. There is a total of 16 swings at the park. How many swings are on each swing set?

_____

9. Amanda has 27 seashells in her collection. She displayed the seashells in 3 rows with the same number of seashells in each row. How many seashells are in each row?

_____

10. The art room has 4 round tables. There are 6 chairs around each table. Altogether, how many chairs are around the tables?

_____

11. Shanna is making bead necklaces for the craft fair. She can make 3 necklaces a day. She plans to make 21 necklaces. How many days will it take her to make the necklaces?

_____

12. One section on a plane has 9 rows of seats. Five passengers can sit in each row. How many passengers could sit in this section of the plane?

_____

► (PATH to FLUENCY) Play *Solve the Stack*

Read the rules for playing *Solve the Stack*. Then play the game with your group.

Rules for *Solve the Stack*

Number of players: 2–4

What you will need: 1 set of multiplication and division Strategy Cards

1. Shuffle the cards. Place them exercise side up in the center of the table.

2. Players take turns. On each turn, a player finds the answer to the multiplication or division on the top card and then turns the card over to check the answer.

3. If a player's answer is correct, he or she takes the card. If it is incorrect, the card is placed at the bottom of the stack.

4. Play ends when there are no more cards in the stack. The player with the most cards wins.

▶ **PATH to FLUENCY** Play *High Card Wins*

Read the rules for playing *High Card Wins*. Then play the game with your partner.

Rules for *High Card Wins*

Number of players: 2

What you will need: 1 set of multiplication and division Strategy Cards for 2s, 3s, 4s, 5s, 9s

1. Shuffle the cards. Deal all the cards evenly between the two players.

2. Players put their stacks in front of them, exercise side up.

3. Each player takes the top card from his or her stack and puts it exercise side up in the center of the table.

4. Each player says the multiplication or division answer and then turns the card over to check. Then players do one of the following:

   • If one player says the wrong answer, the other player takes both cards and puts them at the bottom of his or her pile.

   • If both players say the wrong answer, both players take back their cards and put them at the bottom of their piles.

   • If both players say the correct answer, the player with the higher product or quotient takes both cards and puts them at the bottom of his or her pile. If the products or quotients are the same, the players set the cards aside and play another round. The winner of the next round takes all the cards.

5. Play continues until one player has all the cards.

Use the Strategy Cards

CA CC Content Standards **3.OA.1, 3.OA.2, 3.OA.3, 3.OA.4, 3.OA.5, 3.OA.6, 3.OA.7, 3.MD.7, 3.MD.7c, 3.MD.7d** Mathematical Practices **MP.1, MP.4, MP.6**

► PATH to FLUENCY **Review Strategies**

Complete.

1. Emily knows that 4 × 10 = 40. How can she use subtraction and multiples of 9 to find 4 × 9?

   _____

2. Joey knows the multiplications 5 × 4 and 4 × 4. How can he use their products to find 9 × 4?

   _____

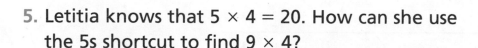

3. Hannah knows that each division has a related multiplication. What related multiplication fact can she use to find 18 ÷ 3?

   _____

4. Kyle knows that 5 × 3 = 15. How can he use the 5s shortcut to find 8 × 3?

   _____

5. Letitia knows that 5 × 4 = 20. How can she use the 5s shortcut to find 9 × 4?

   _____

6. Jorge knows that 6 × 9 = 54. How can he use the Commutative Property or arrays to find 9 × 6?

   _____

   _____

► **Make Sense of Problems**

Write an equation and solve the problem.   *Show your work.*

7. Jordan has 32 peaches. He wants to divide them equally among 4 baskets. How many peaches will he put in each basket?

_____

8. A guitar has 6 strings. If Taylor replaces all the strings on 3 guitars, how many strings does he need?

_____

9. Kassler's photograph album holds 5 pictures on each page. Kassler has 40 pictures. How many pages will he fill?

_____

10. Emily rides her bike 3 miles every day. How many miles does she ride her bike in a week?

_____

11. Ruel has a board 36 inches long. He wants to saw it into equal pieces 9 inches long. How many pieces will he get?

_____

► **Write a Word Problem**

12. Write a word problem that can be solved using the equation $7 \times 10 = 70$.

_____

_____

Name _____   **Date** _____

CA CC Content Standards **3.OA.5, 3.OA.7, 3.OA.9**
Mathematical Practices **MP.7, MP.8**

PATH to FLUENCY

► Explore Patterns with 1s

What patterns do you see below?

1.

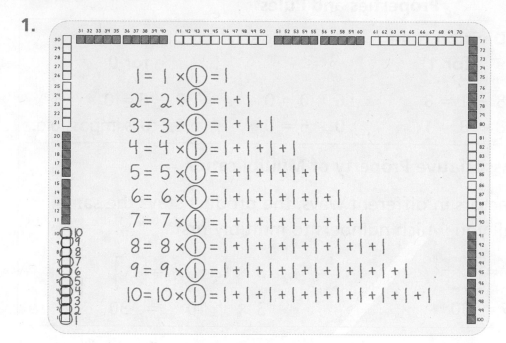

$$1 = 1 \times \boxed{1} = 1$$
$$2 = 2 \times \boxed{1} = 1 + 1$$
$$3 = 3 \times \boxed{1} = 1 + 1 + 1$$
$$4 = 4 \times \boxed{1} = 1 + 1 + 1 + 1$$
$$5 = 5 \times \boxed{1} = 1 + 1 + 1 + 1 + 1$$
$$6 = 6 \times \boxed{1} = 1 + 1 + 1 + 1 + 1 + 1$$
$$7 = 7 \times \boxed{1} = 1 + 1 + 1 + 1 + 1 + 1 + 1$$
$$8 = 8 \times \boxed{1} = 1 + 1 + 1 + 1 + 1 + 1 + 1 + 1$$
$$9 = 9 \times \boxed{1} = 1 + 1 + 1 + 1 + 1 + 1 + 1 + 1 + 1$$
$$10 = 10 \times \boxed{1} = 1 + 1 + 1 + 1 + 1 + 1 + 1 + 1 + 1 + 1$$

► Explore Patterns with 0s

What patterns do you see below?

2.

$$1 \times \boxed{0} = 0$$
$$2 \times \boxed{0} = 0 + 0$$
$$3 \times \boxed{0} = 0 + 0 + 0$$
$$4 \times \boxed{0} = 0 + 0 + 0 + 0$$
$$5 \times \boxed{0} = 0 + 0 + 0 + 0 + 0$$
$$6 \times \boxed{0} = 0 + 0 + 0 + 0 + 0 + 0$$
$$7 \times \boxed{0} = 0 + 0 + 0 + 0 + 0 + 0 + 0$$
$$8 \times \boxed{0} = 0 + 0 + 0 + 0 + 0 + 0 + 0 + 0$$
$$9 \times \boxed{0} = 0 + 0 + 0 + 0 + 0 + 0 + 0 + 0 + 0$$
$$10 \times \boxed{0} = 0 + 0 + 0 + 0 + 0 + 0 + 0 + 0 + 0 + 0$$

► PATH to FLUENCY **Multiplication Properties and Division Rules**

Properties and Rules

Property for 1	Division Rule for 1	Zero Property	Division Rule for 0
$1 \times 6 = 6$ $6 \times 1 = 6$	$8 \div 1 = 8$ $8 \div 8 = 1$	$6 \times 0 = 0$ $0 \times 6 = 0$	$0 \div 6 = 0$ $6 \div 0$ is impossible.

Associative Property of Multiplication

When you group factors in different ways, the product stays the same. The parentheses tell you which numbers to multiply first.

$$(3 \times 2) \times 5 = \boxed{}$$
$$6 \quad \times 5 = 30$$

$$3 \times (2 \times 5) = \boxed{}$$
$$3 \times \quad 10 \quad = 30$$

Find each product.

3. $2 \times (6 \times 1) = \boxed{}$

4. $(4 \times 2) \times 2 = \boxed{}$

5. $7 \times (1 \times 5) = \boxed{}$

6. $(9 \times 8) \times 0 = \boxed{}$

7. $3 \times (2 \times 3) = \boxed{}$

8. $6 \times (0 \times 7) = \boxed{}$

Solve each problem.

Show your work.

9. Shawn gave 1 nickel to each of his sisters. If he gave away 3 nickels, how many sisters does Shawn have? _____

10. Kara has 3 boxes. She put 0 toys in each box. How many toys are in the boxes? _____

11. There are 3 tables in the library. Each table has 2 piles of books on it. If there are 3 books in each pile, how many books are on the tables?

► PATH to FLUENCY **Identify Addition and Multiplication Properties**

Addition Properties	Multiplication Properties
A. Commutative Property of Addition The order in which numbers are added does not change their sum. $3 + 5 = 5 + 3$	**D. Commutative Property of Multiplication** The order in which numbers are multiplied does not change their product. $3 \times 5 = 5 \times 3$
B. Associative Property of Addition The way in which numbers are grouped does not change their sum. $(3 + 2) + 5 = 3 + (2 + 5)$	**E. Associative Property of Multiplication** The way in which numbers are grouped does not change their product. $(3 \times 2) \times 5 = 3 \times (2 \times 5)$
C. Identity Property of Addition If 0 is added to a number, the sum equals that number. $3 + 0 = 3$	**F. Identity Property of Multiplication** The product of 1 and any number is that number. $3 \times 1 = 3$
	G. Zero Property of Multiplication If 0 is multiplied by a number, the product is 0. $3 \times 0 = 0$

Write the letter of the property that is shown.

12. $1 \times 9 = 9$ ____

13. $5 + (6 + 7) = (5 + 6) + 7$ ____

14. $5 \times 0 = 0$ ____

15. $8 + 0 = 8$ ____

16. $3 \times 9 = \boxed{} \times 3$ ____

17. $(2 \times 1) \times 3 = 2 \times (\boxed{} \times 3)$ ____

▶ Use Properties to Solve Equations

Use properties and rules to find the unknown numbers.

18. $5 \times 8 = \boxed{} \times 5$ **19.** $4 + 3 = \boxed{} + 4$ **20.** $0 \div 8 = \boxed{}$

21. $4 \div 4 = \boxed{}$ **22.** $(3 \times 2) \times 4 = 3 \times (\boxed{} \times 4)$ **23.** $6 \times 2 = 2 \times \boxed{}$

24. $5 \times 3 = \boxed{} \times 5$ **25.** $(6 + 2) + 2 = 6 + (\boxed{} + 2)$ **26.** $11 + 0 = \boxed{}$

27. $65 \times 1 = \boxed{}$ **28.** $5 \times (2 \times 6) = (5 \times 2) \times \boxed{}$ **29.** $17 \times 0 = \boxed{}$

▶ Use Equations to Demonstrate Properties

Write your own equation that shows the property.

30. Commutative Property of
Multiplication

_____

31. Associative Property of
Addition

_____

32. Identity Property of
Addition

_____

33. Identity Property of
Multiplication

_____

34. Associative Property of
Multiplication

_____

35. Zero Property of
Multiplication

_____

36. Commutative Property of
Addition

► Identify Types of Problems

Read each problem and decide what type of problem it is. Write the letter from the list below. Then write an equation to solve the problem.

a. Array Multiplication

b. Array Division

c. Equal Groups Multiplication

d. Equal Groups Division with an Unknown Group Size

e. Equal Groups Division with an Unknown Multiplier (number of groups)

f. None of the above

1. Mrs. Ostrega has 3 children. She wants to buy 5 juice boxes for each child. How many juice boxes does she need?

_____

2. Sophie picked 15 peaches from one tree and 3 peaches from another. How many peaches did she pick in all?

_____

3. Zamir brought 21 treats to the dog park. He divided the treats equally among the 7 dogs that were there. How many treats did each dog get?

_____

4. Art said he could make 12 muffins in his muffin pan. The pan has space for 3 muffins in a row. How many rows does the muffin pan have?

_____

5. Bia is helping with the lights for the school play. Each box of light bulbs has 6 rows, with 3 bulbs in each row. How many light bulbs are in each box?

_____

6. Tryouts were held to find triplets to act in a commercial for Triple-Crunch Cereal. If 24 children tried out for the commercial, how many sets of triplets tried out?

_____

▶ Make Sense of Problems

Write an equation and solve the problem.   *Show your work.*

7. The produce market sells oranges in bags of 6.
   Santos bought 1 bag. How many oranges did he buy?

   _____

8. Janine bought a jewelry organizer with 36 pockets.
   The pockets are arranged in 9 rows with the same
   number of pockets in each row. How many pockets
   are in each row?

   _____

9. A parking lot has 9 rows of parking spaces. Each row
   has 7 spaces. How many cars can park in the lot?

   _____

10. Keshawn bought 18 animal stickers for his sisters.
    He gave 6 stickers to each sister and had none left.
    How many sisters does Keshawn have?

    _____

11. The pet store put 3 fish bowls on a shelf. The store
    put 0 goldfish in each bowl. How many goldfish
    are in the bowls?

    _____

▶ Write a Word Problem

12. Write a word problem that can be solved
    using $0 \div 5$, where 5 is the group size.

    _____

    _____

► PATH to FLUENCY **Check Sheet 5: 1s and 0s**

1s Multiplications	1s Divisions	0s Multiplications
1 × 4 = 4	10 / 1 = 10	4 × 0 = 0
5 • 1 = 5	5 ÷ 1 = 5	2 • 0 = 0
7 * 1 = 7	7 / 1 = 7	0 * 8 = 0
1 × 8 = 8	9 ÷ 1 = 9	0 × 5 = 0
1 • 6 = 6	3 / 1 = 3	6 • 0 = 0
10 * 1 = 10	10 ÷ 1 = 10	0 * 7 = 0
1 × 9 = 9	2 / 1 = 2	0 × 2 = 0
3 • 1 = 3	8 ÷ 1 = 8	0 • 9 = 0
1 * 2 = 2	6 / 1 = 6	10 * 0 = 0
1 × 1 = 1	9 / 1 = 9	1 × 0 = 0
8 • 1 = 8	1 ÷ 1 = 1	0 • 6 = 0
1 * 7 = 7	5 / 1 = 5	9 * 0 = 0
1 × 5 = 5	3 ÷ 1 = 3	0 × 4 = 0
6 • 1 = 6	4 / 1 = 4	3 • 0 = 0
1 * 1 = 1	2 ÷ 1 = 2	0 * 3 = 0
1 × 10 = 10	8 / 1 = 8	8 × 0 = 0
9 • 1 = 9	4 ÷ 1 = 4	0 • 10 = 0
4 * 1 = 4	7 ÷ 1 = 7	0 * 1 = 0
2 × 1 = 2	1 / 1 = 1	5 × 0 = 0
1 • 3 = 3	6 ÷ 1 = 6	7 • 0 = 0

Name _____

► **PATH to FLUENCY** **Check Sheet 6: Mixed 3s, 4s, 0s, and 1s**

3s, 4s, 0s, 1s Multiplications	3s, 4s, 0s, 1s Multiplications	3s, 4s, 1s Divisions	3s, 4s, 1s Divisions
5 × 3 = 15	0 × 5 = 0	18 / 3 = 6	4 / 1 = 4
6 • 4 = 24	10 • 1 = 10	20 ÷ 4 = 5	21 ÷ 3 = 7
9 * 0 = 0	6 * 3 = 18	1 / 1 = 1	16 / 4 = 4
7 × 1 = 7	2 × 4 = 8	21 ÷ 3 = 7	9 ÷ 1 = 9
3 • 3 = 9	5 • 0 = 0	12 / 4 = 3	15 / 3 = 5
4 * 7 = 28	1 * 2 = 2	5 ÷ 1 = 5	8 ÷ 4 = 2
0 × 10 = 0	10 × 3 = 30	15 / 3 = 5	5 / 1 = 5
1 • 6 = 6	5 • 4 = 20	24 ÷ 4 = 6	30 ÷ 3 = 10
3 * 4 = 12	0 * 8 = 0	7 / 1 = 7	12 / 4 = 3
5 × 4 = 20	9 × 2 = 18	12 / 3 = 4	8 / 1 = 8
0 • 5 = 0	10 • 3 = 30	36 ÷ 4 = 9	27 ÷ 3 = 9
9 * 1 = 9	9 * 4 = 36	6 / 1 = 6	40 / 4 = 10
2 × 3 = 6	1 × 0 = 0	12 ÷ 3 = 4	4 ÷ 1 = 4
3 • 4 = 12	1 • 6 = 6	16 / 4 = 4	9 / 3 = 3
0 * 9 = 0	3 * 6 = 18	7 ∶ 1 = 7	16 ÷ 4 = 4
1 × 5 = 5	7 × 4 = 28	9 / 3 = 3	10 / 1 = 10
2 • 3 = 6	6 • 0 = 0	8 ÷ 4 = 2	9 ÷ 3 = 3
4 * 4 = 16	8 * 1 = 8	2 ÷ 1 = 2	20 ÷ 4 = 5
9 × 0 = 0	3 × 9 = 27	6 / 3 = 2	6 / 1 = 6
1 • 1 = 1	1 • 4 = 4	32 ÷ 4 = 8	24 ÷ 3 = 8

© Houghton Mifflin Harcourt Publishing Company

72 UNIT 1 LESSON 17

Check Sheet 6: Mixed 3s, 4s, 0s, and 1s

CA CC Content Standards **3.0A.6, 3.0A.7**
Mathematical Practices **MP.5**

Name _____ Date _____

► (PATH to FLUENCY) Play *Multiplication Three-in-a-Row*

Read the rules for playing *Multiplication Three-in-a-Row*.
Then play the game with a partner.

> ### Rules for *Multiplication Three-in-a-Row*
>
> *Number of players:* 2
>
> *What You Will Need:* A set of multiplication Strategy Cards, *Three-in-a-Row* Game Grids for each player (see page 75)
>
> 1. Each player looks through the cards and writes any nine of the products in the squares of a Game Grid. A player may write the same product more than once.
>
> 2. Shuffle the cards and place them exercise side up in the center of the table.
>
> 3. Players take turns. On each turn, a player finds the answer to the multiplication on the top card and then turns the card over to check the answer.
>
> 4. If the answer is correct, the player looks to see if the product is on the game grid. If it is, the player puts an X through that grid square. If the answer is wrong, or if the product is not on the grid, the player does not mark anything. The player then puts the card problem side up on the bottom of the stack.
>
> 5. The first player to mark three squares in a row (horizontally, vertically, or diagonally) wins.

► PATH to FLUENCY **Play *Division Race***

Read the rules for playing *Division Race*. Then play the game with a partner.

Rules for *Division Race*

Number of players: 2

What You Will Need: a set of division Strategy Cards, the *Division Race* game board (see page 76), a different game piece for each player

1. Shuffle the cards and then place them exercise side up on the table.

2. Both players put their game pieces on "START."

3. Players take turns. On each turn, a player finds the answer to the division on the top card and then turns the card over to check the answer.

4. If the answer is correct, the player moves *forward* that number of spaces. If a player's answer is wrong, the player moves *back* a number of spaces equal to the correct answer. Players cannot move back beyond the "START" square. The player puts the card on the bottom of the stack.

5. If a player lands on a space with special instructions, he or she should follow those instructions.

6. The game ends when everyone lands on or passes the "End" square.

Name _____

Three-in-a-Row Game Grids **75**

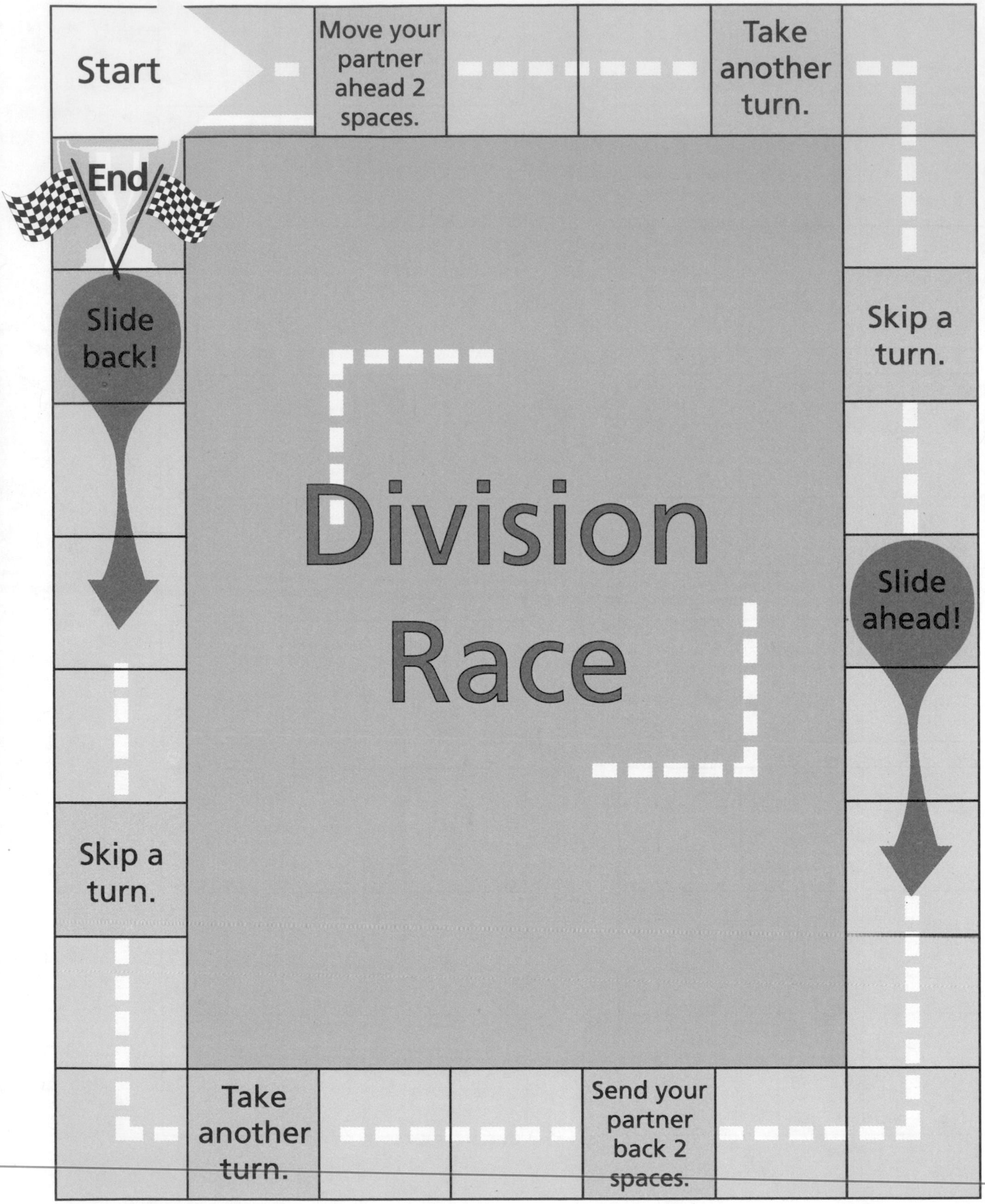

Start

Move your partner ahead 2 spaces.

Take another turn.

End

Slide back!

Skip a turn.

Division Race

Slide ahead!

Skip a turn.

Skip a turn.

Take another turn.

Send your partner back 2 spaces.

Division Race Game Board

► **PATH to FLUENCY** **Dashes 1–4**

Complete each Dash. Check your answers on page 81.

Dash 1 2s and 5s Multiplications	Dash 2 2s and 5s Divisions	Dash 3 9s and 10s Multiplications	Dash 4 9s and 10s Divisions
a. $2 \times 6 =$ _____	a. $18 / 2 =$ _____	a. $9 \times 10 =$ _____	a. $100 / 10 =$ _____
b. $9 * 5 =$ _____	b. $25 \div 5 =$ _____	b. $10 * 3 =$ _____	b. $9 \div 9 =$ _____
c. $7 \cdot 2 =$ _____	c. $8 / 2 =$ _____	c. $1 \cdot 9 =$ _____	c. $30 / 10 =$ _____
. $5 \times 8 =$ _____	d. $45 \div 5 =$ _____	d. $2 \times 10 =$ _____	d. $81 \div 9 =$ _____
e. $2 * 4 =$ _____	e. $16 / 2 =$ _____	e. $9 * 9 =$ _____	e. $70 / 10 =$ _____
f. $3 \cdot 5 =$ _____	f. $20 \div 5 =$ _____	f. $10 \cdot 6 =$ _____	f. $45 \div 9 =$ _____
g. $1 \times 2 =$ _____	g. $4 / 2 =$ _____	g. $4 \times 9 =$ _____	g. $10 / 10 =$ _____
h. $5 * 7 =$ _____	h. $40 \div 5 =$ _____	h. $10 \times 10 =$ _____	h. $54 \div 9 =$ _____
i. $2 \cdot 9 =$ _____	i. $20 / 2 =$ _____	i. $9 * 2 =$ _____	i. $50 / 10 =$ _____
j. $4 \times 5 =$ _____	j. $35 \div 5 =$ _____	j. $1 \cdot 10 =$ _____	j. $27 \div 9 =$ _____
k. $5 * 2 =$ _____	k. $6 / 2 =$ _____	k. $7 \times 9 =$ _____	k. $20 / 10 =$ _____
l. $5 \cdot 1 =$ _____	l. $15 \div 5 =$ _____	l. $10 * 5 =$ _____	l. $72 \div 9 =$ _____
m. $2 \times 2 =$ _____	m. $14 / 2 =$ _____	m. $9 \cdot 8 =$ _____	m. $40 / 10 =$ _____
n. $10 \times 5 =$ _____	n. $5 \div 5 =$ _____	n. $7 \times 10 =$ _____	n. $18 \div 9 =$ _____
o. $10 * 2 =$ _____	o. $10 / 2 =$ _____	o. $3 * 9 =$ _____	o. $60 / 10 =$ _____
p. $5 \cdot 6 =$ _____	p. $10 \div 5 =$ _____	p. $10 \cdot 4 =$ _____	p. $90 \div 9 =$ _____
q. $2 \times 3 =$ _____	q. $6 / 2 =$ _____	q. $9 \times 5 =$ _____	q. $90 / 10 =$ _____
r. $5 * 5 =$ _____	r. $30 \div 5 =$ _____	r. $8 * 10 =$ _____	r. $63 \div 9 =$ _____
s. $8 \cdot 2 =$ _____	s. $2 / 2 =$ _____	s. $6 \cdot 9 =$ _____	s. $80 / 10 =$ _____
t. $6 \times 5 =$ _____	t. $45 \div 5 =$ _____	t. $10 \times 9 =$ _____	t. $36 \div 9 =$ _____

► 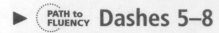 **Dashes 5–8**

Complete each Dash. Check your answers on page 81.

Dash 5 3s and 4s Multiplications	Dash 6 3s and 4s Divisions	Dash 7 0s and 1s Multiplications	Dash 8 1s and $n \div n$ Divisions
a. 3 × 9 = ____	a. 12 / 4 = ____	a. 0 × 6 = ____	a. 9 / 9 = ____
b. 4 * 2 = ____	b. 20 ÷ 4 = ____	b. 1 * 4 = ____	b. 8 ÷ 1 = ____
c. 6 • 3 = ____	c. 21 / 3 = ____	c. 4 • 0 = ____	c. 7 / 7 = ____
d. 10 × 4 = ____	d. 16 ÷ 4 = ____	d. 8 × 1 = ____	d. 6 ÷ 1 = ____
e. 3 * 1 = ____	e. 9 / 3 = ____	e. 0 * 2 = ____	e. 1 / 1 = ____
f. 4 • 1 = ____	f. 32 ÷ 4 = ____	f. 1 • 3 = ____	f. 4 ÷ 1 = ____
g. 10 × 3 = ____	g. 24 / 4 = ____	g. 9 × 0 = ____	g. 2 / 2 = ____
h. 5 * 4 = ____	h. 18 ÷ 3 = ____	h. 2 * 1 = ____	h. 2 ÷ 1 = ____
i. 3 • 3 = ____	i. 40 / 4 = ____	i. 0 • 8 = ____	i. 8 / 8 = ____
j. 4 × 4 = ____	j. 12 ÷ 3 = ____	j. 1 × 10 = ____	j. 9 ÷ 1 = ____
k. 8 * 3 = ____	k. 6 / 3 = ____	k. 7 * 0 = ____	k. 3 / 3 = ____
l. 7 • 4 = ____	l. 28 ÷ 4 = ____	l. 1 • 1 = ____	l. 5 ÷ 1 = ____
m. 3 × 2 = ____	m. 24 / 3 = ____	m. 0 × 0 = ____	m. 5 / 5 = ____
n. 4 * 9 = ____	n. 20 ÷ 4 = ____	n. 5 * 1 = ____	n. 10 / 10 = ____
o. 7 • 3 = ____	o. 27 / 3 = ____	o. 1 • 0 = ____	o. 7 ÷ 1 = ____
p. 3 × 4 = ____	p. 15 ÷ 3 = ____	p. 1 × 6 = ____	p. 4 / 4 = ____
q. 3 * 5 = ____	q. 27 / 3 = ____	q. 5 * 0 = ____	q. 10 ÷ 1 = ____
r. 4 • 6 = ____	r. 36 ÷ 4 = ____	r. 0 • 3 = ____	r. 6 / 6 = ____
s. 4 × 3 = ____	s. 8 / 4 = ____	s. 7 × 1 = ____	s. 3 ÷ 1 = ____
t. 8 * 4 = ____	t. 40 ÷ 4 = ____	t. 1 * 9 = ____	t. 1 / 1 = ____

► **PATH to FLUENCY** **Dashes 9–12**

Complete each Dash. Check your answers on page 82.

Dash 9 2s, 5s, 9s, 10s Multiplications	Dash 10 2s, 5s, 9s, 10s Divisions	Dash 11 3s, 4s, 0s, 1s Multiplications	Dash 12 3s, 4s, 1s Divisions
a. $4 \times 5 =$ _____	a. $8 / 2 =$ _____	a. $3 \times 0 =$ _____	a. $12 / 4 =$ _____
b. $10 \cdot 3 =$ _____	b. $50 \div 10 =$ _____	b. $4 \cdot 6 =$ _____	b. $5 \div 1 =$ _____
c. $8 * 9 =$ _____	c. $15 / 5 =$ _____	c. $9 * 1 =$ _____	c. $21 / 3 =$ _____
d. $6 \times 2 =$ _____	d. $63 \div 9 =$ _____	d. $3 \times 3 =$ _____	d. $1 \div 1 =$ _____
e. $5 \cdot 7 =$ _____	e. $90 / 10 =$ _____	e. $8 \cdot 4 =$ _____	e. $16 / 4 =$ _____
f. $10 * 5 =$ _____	f. $90 \div 9 =$ _____	f. $0 * 5 =$ _____	f. $9 \div 3 =$ _____
g. $8 \times 2 =$ _____	g. $35 / 5 =$ _____	g. $1 \times 6 =$ _____	g. $32 / 4 =$ _____
h. $6 \cdot 10 =$ _____	h. $14 \div 2 =$ _____	h. $4 \cdot 3 =$ _____	h. $8 \div 1 =$ _____
i. $9 * 3 =$ _____	i. $27 / 9 =$ _____	i. $7 * 4 =$ _____	i. $24 / 4 =$ _____
j. $2 \times 9 =$ _____	j. $45 / 5 =$ _____	j. $3 \times 7 =$ _____	j. $18 / 3 =$ _____
k. $5 \cdot 8 =$ _____	k. $10 \div 10 =$ _____	k. $0 \cdot 1 =$ _____	k. $10 \div 1 =$ _____
l. $10 * 7 =$ _____	l. $25 / 5 =$ _____	l. $10 * 1 =$ _____	l. $40 / 4 =$ _____
m. $5 \times 5 =$ _____	m. $54 \div 9 =$ _____	m. $4 \times 4 =$ _____	m. $12 \div 3 =$ _____
n. $1 \cdot 5 =$ _____	n. $6 / 2 =$ _____	n. $9 \cdot 3 =$ _____	n. $6 / 3 =$ _____
o. $9 * 6 =$ _____	o. $72 \div 9 =$ _____	o. $8 * 0 =$ _____	o. $4 \div 4 =$ _____
p. $10 \times 10 =$ _____	p. $40 / 5 =$ _____	p. $5 \times 4 =$ _____	p. $7 / 1 =$ _____
q. $4 \cdot 2 =$ _____	q. $80 \div 10 =$ _____	q. $1 \cdot 6 =$ _____	q. $28 \div 4 =$ _____
r. $10 * 8 =$ _____	r. $18 \div 2 =$ _____	r. $3 * 8 =$ _____	r. $24 \div 3 =$ _____
s. $3 \times 9 =$ _____	s. $36 / 9 =$ _____	s. $4 \times 9 =$ _____	s. $20 / 4 =$ _____
t. $9 \cdot 9 =$ _____	t. $30 \div 5 =$ _____	t. $0 \cdot 4 =$ _____	t. $27 \div 3 =$ _____

► **PATH to FLUENCY** **Dashes 9A–12A**

Complete each Dash. Check your answers on page 82.

Dash 9A 2s, 5s, 9s, 10s Multiplications	Dash 10A 2s, 5s, 9s, 10s Divisions	Dash 11A 3s, 4s, 0s, 1s Multiplications	Dash 12A 3s, 4s, 1s Divisions
a. 9×9 = ____	a. $30 / 5$ = ____	a. 0×4 = ____	a. $10 / 1$ = ____
b. $4 * 5$ = ____	b. $18 \div 2$ = ____	b. $4 * 9$ = ____	b. $40 \div 4$ = ____
c. $10 \cdot 3$ = ____	c. $40 / 5$ = ____	c. $3 \cdot 8$ = ____	c. $12 / 3$ = ____
d. 3×9 = ____	d. $6 \div 2$ = ____	d. 3×0 = ____	d. $6 \div 3$ = ____
e. $10 * 8$ = ____	e. $25 / 5$ = ____	e. $4 * 6$ = ____	e. $4 / 4$ = ____
f. $6 \cdot 2$ = ____	f. $45 \div 5$ = ____	f. $9 \cdot 1$ = ____	f. $7 \div 1$ = ____
g. 8×9 = ____	g. $14 / 2$ = ____	g. 3×3 = ____	g. $28 / 4$ = ____
h. $4 * 2$ = ____	h. $90 \div 9$ = ____	h. $8 * 4$ = ____	h. $24 \div 3$ = ____
i. $10 \cdot 10$ = ____	i. $63 / 9$ = ____	i. $0 \cdot 5$ = ____	i. $20 / 4$ = ____
j. 9×6 = ____	j. $50 \div 10$ = ____	j. 1×6 = ____	j. $27 \div 3$ = ____
k. $5 * 7$ = ____	k. $8 / 2$ = ____	k. $5 * 4$ = ____	k. $12 / 4$ = ____
l. $10 \cdot 5$ = ____	l. $15 \div 5$ = ____	l. $8 \cdot 0$ = ____	l. $5 \div 1$ = ____
m. 8×2 = ____	m. $90 / 10$ = ____	m. 9×3 = ____	m. $21 / 3$ = ____
n. $6 * 10$ = ____	n. $35 \div 5$ = ____	n. $4 * 4$ = ____	n. $1 \div 1$ = ____
o. $2 * 9$ = ____	o. $27 / 9$ = ____	o. $10 \cdot 1$ = ____	o. $16 / 4$ = ____
p. $9 \cdot 6$ = ____	p. $10 \div 10$ = ____	p. 4×3 = ____	p. $9 \div 3$ = ____
q. 1×5 = ____	q. $54 / 9$ = ____	q. $7 * 4$ = ____	q. $32 / 4$ = ____
r. $5 * 5$ = ____	r. $72 \div 9$ = ____	r. $3 \cdot 7$ = ____	r. $8 \div 1$ = ____
s. $10 \cdot 7$ = ____	s. $80 / 10$ = ____	s. 0×1 = ____	s. $24 / 4$ = ____
t. 5×8 = ____	t. $36 \div 9$ = ____	t. $10 * 1$ = ____	t. $18 \div 3$ = ____

► Answers to Dashes 1–8

Use this sheet to check your answers to the Dashes on pages 77 and 78.

Dash 1 2s and 5s ×	Dash 2 2s and 5s ÷	Dash 3 9s and 10s ×	Dash 4 9s and 10s ÷	Dash 5 3s and 4s ×	Dash 6 3s and 4s ÷	Dash 7 0s and 1s ×	Dash 8 1s and $n \div n$ ÷
a. 12	a. 9	a. 90	a. 10	a. 27	a. 3	a. 0	a. 1
b. 45	b. 5	b. 30	b. 1	b. 8	b. 5	b. 4	b. 8
c. 14	c. 4	c. 9	c. 3	c. 18	c. 7	c. 0	c. 1
d. 40	d. 9	d. 20	d. 9	d. 40	d. 4	d. 8	d. 6
e. 8	e. 8	e. 81	e. 7	e. 3	e. 3	e. 0	e. 1
f. 15	f. 4	f. 60	f. 5	f. 4	f. 8	f. 3	f. 4
g. 2	g. 2	g. 36	g. 1	g. 30	g. 6	g. 0	g. 1
h. 35	h. 8	h. 100	h. 6	h. 20	h. 6	h. 2	h. 2
i. 18	i. 10	i. 18	i. 5	i. 9	i. 10	i. 0	i. 1
j. 20	j. 7	j. 10	j. 3	j. 16	j. 4	j. 10	j. 9
k. 10	k. 3	k. 63	k. 2	k. 24	k. 2	k. 0	k. 1
l. 5	l. 3	l. 50	l. 8	l. 28	l. 7	l. 1	l. 5
m. 4	m. 7	m. 72	m. 4	m. 6	m. 8	m. 0	m. 1
n. 50	n. 1	n. 70	n. 2	n. 36	n. 5	n. 5	n. 1
o. 20	o. 5	o. 27	o. 6	o. 21	o. 9	o. 0	o. 7
p. 30	p. 2	p. 40	p. 10	p. 12	p. 5	p. 6	p. 1
q. 6	q. 3	q. 45	q. 9	q. 15	q. 9	q. 0	q. 10
r. 25	r. 6	r. 80	r. 7	r. 24	r. 9	r. 0	r. 1
s. 16	s. 1	s. 54	s. 8	s. 12	s. 2	s. 7	s. 3
t. 30	t. 9	t. 90	t. 4	t. 32	t. 10	t. 9	t. 0

Name _____

▶ Answers to Dashes 9–12, 9A–12A

Use this sheet to check your answers to the Dashes on pages 79 and 80.

Dash 9 ×	Dash 10 ÷	Dash 11 ×	Dash 12 ÷	Dash 9A ×	Dash 10A ÷	Dash 11A ×	Dash 12A ÷
a. 20	a. 4	a. 0	a. 3	a. 81	a. 6	a. 0	a. 10
b. 30	b. 5	b. 24	b. 5	b. 20	b. 9	b. 36	b. 10
c. 72	c. 3	c. 9	c. 7	c. 30	c. 8	c. 24	c. 4
d. 12	d. 7	d. 9	d. 1	d. 27	d. 3	d. 0	d. 2
e. 35	e. 9	e. 32	e. 4	e. 80	e. 5	e. 24	e. 1
f. 50	f. 10	f. 0	f. 3	f. 12	f. 9	f. 9	f. 7
g. 16	g. 7	g. 6	g. 8	g. 72	g. 7	g. 9	g. 7
h. 60	h. 7	h. 12	h. 8	h. 8	h. 10	h. 32	h. 8
i. 27	i. 3	i. 28	i. 6	i. 100	i. 7	i. 0	i. 5
j. 18	j. 9	j. 21	j. 6	j. 54	j. 5	j. 6	j. 9
k. 40	k. 1	k. 0	k. 10	k. 35	k. 4	k. 20	k. 3
l. 70	l. 5	l. 10	l. 10	l. 50	l. 3	l. 0	l. 5
m. 25	m. 6	m. 16	m. 4	m. 16	m. 9	m. 27	m. 7
n. 5	n. 3	n. 27	n. 2	n. 60	n. 7	n. 16	n. 1
o. 54	o. 8	o. 0	o. 1	o. 18	o. 3	o. 10	o. 4
p. 100	p. 8	p. 20	p. 7	p. 54	p. 1	p. 12	p. 3
q. 8	q. 8	q. 6	q. 7	q. 5	q. 6	q. 28	q. 8
r. 80	r. 9	r. 24	r. 8	r. 25	r. 8	r. 21	r. 8
s. 27	s. 4	s. 36	s. 5	s. 70	s. 8	s. 0	s. 6
t. 81	t. 6	t. 0	t. 9	t. 40	t. 4	t. 10	t. 6

© Houghton Mifflin Harcourt Publishing Company

Answers to Dashes 9–12, 9A–12A

▶ Solve Word Problems with 2s, 3s, 4s, 5s, and 9s

Write an equation and solve the problem. *Show your work.*

1. Toni counted 36 legs in the lion house at the zoo. How many lions were there?

   _____

2. One wall of an art gallery has a row of 5 paintings and a row of 9 paintings. How many paintings are on the wall?

   _____

3. Josh's muffin pan is an array with 4 rows and 6 columns. How many muffins can Josh make in the pan?

   _____

4. To get ready for the school spelling bee, Tanya studied 3 hours each night for an entire week. How many hours did she study?

   _____

5. The 14 trumpet players in the marching band lined up in 2 equal rows. How many trumpet players were in each row?

   _____

6. The Sunnyside Riding Stable has 9 horses. The owners are going to buy new horseshoes for all the horses. How many horseshoes are needed?

   _____

▶ Make Sense of Problems

Write an equation and solve the problem. *Show your work.*

7. Sadie plans to read 2 books every month for 6 months. How many books will she read during that time?

_____

8. A farmers' market sells pumpkins for $5 each. On Friday the market made $35 from the sale of pumpkins. How many pumpkins did the market sell on Friday?

_____

9. A keypad on Tim's phone has 21 buttons. There are 3 buttons in each row. How many rows of buttons are on the keypad?

_____

10. Paisley has a quilt that is made of different color squares. The quilt has 6 rows of 4 squares. How many squares are in the quilt?

_____

11. Each student collected 10 leaves for a group science project. If the group collected a total of 80 leaves, how many students are in the group?

_____

▶ Write a Word Problem

12. Write and solve a word problem that can be solved using the equation $4 \times 1 = n$.

_____

_____

Building Fluency with 0s, 1s, 2s, 3s, 4s, 5s, 9s, and 10s

Name _____ Date _____

CA CC Content Standards 3.OA.1, 3.OA.2, 3.OA.3, 3.OA.4, 3.OA.5 Mathematical Practices MP.1, MP.2, MP.4, MP.5

► (PATH to FLUENCY) **Math and Hobbies**

A hobby is something you do for fun. Owen's hobby is photography. He took pictures on a field trip and displayed them on a poster.

Solve.

1. How many photos did Owen display on the poster? Explain the different strategies you can use to find the answer. Write an equation for each.

_____

_____

_____

_____

2. What other ways could Owen have arranged the photos in an array on the poster?

_____

_____

► **PATH to FLUENCY** **What is Your Hobby?**

Carina asked some third graders, "What is your hobby?"
The answers are shown under the photos.

Photography
Eight more than dancing
said photography.

Dancing
Four third graders
said dancing.

Reading
Six less than photography said
reading.

Games
Eight third graders said
games.

3. **Use the information above to complete the chart below.**

What is Your Hobby?

Hobby	Number of Students
Dancing	
Photography	
Games	
Reading	

4. **Use the chart to complete the pictograph below.**

Hobbies

Dancing	
Photography	
Games	
Reading	

Each ☐ stands for 2 third graders.

5. **How many third graders answered Carina's question?**

_____

1. Write a multiplication equation for the array.

_____

2. Write the numbers that complete the pattern.

| 6 | 7 | 8 | 9 | 72 | 81 |

4 × 9 = 36

5 × 9 = 45

☐ × 9 = 54

7 × ☐ = 63

8 × 9 = ☐

3. Read the problem. Choose the type of problem it is.
   Then write an equation to solve the problem.

   Pala is drawing tulips on posters. She draws
   4 tulips each on 9 posters. How many tulips
   does Pala draw on the posters?

   The type of problem is

array multiplication
array division
equal groups multiplication

   Equation: _____

   _____ tulips

4. Draw a line to match the equation on the left with the unknown
   number on the right.

   $\frac{45}{5} = \blacksquare$ •   • 0

   $9 \times \blacksquare = 0$ •   • 5

   $\blacksquare \times 3 = 15$ •   • 8

   $\blacksquare \div 3 = 7$ •   • 9

   $72 \div \blacksquare = 9$ •   • 14

   $7 \times 2 = \blacksquare$ •   • 21

5. Write the number that completes the multiplication equation.

$$6 \times 4 = \boxed{} \times 6$$

$$7 \times 3 = (4 + 3) \times \boxed{}$$

$$5 \times (2 \times 4) = (\boxed{} \times \boxed{}) \times 4$$

6. Sydney wants to find the area of the large rectangle by adding the areas of the two small rectangles.

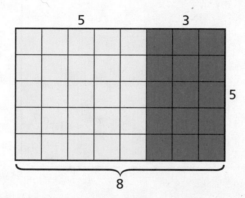

For numbers 6a–6d, choose Yes or No to tell whether or not Sydney could use the expression to find the area of the large rectangle.

6a. $(8 \times 5) + (5 \times 5)$ ○ Yes   ○ No

6b. $25 + 15$ ○ Yes   ○ No

6c. $(5 \times 5) + (3 \times 5)$ ○ Yes   ○ No

6d. $(5 \times 5) + (5 \times 3)$ ○ Yes   ○ No

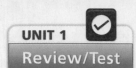
7. Look at the rectangle drawing.

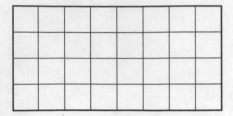

Part A

Write a word problem that can be solved using the drawing.

Part B

Solve the problem. Explain how to use the rectangle drawing to check your answer.

8. Select the situation which could be represented by the multiplication expression 5 × 7. Mark all that apply.

 Ⓐ total number of stamps on 5 pages with 7 stamps on each page

 Ⓑ total number of stamps when there are 5 stamps on each of 7 pages

 Ⓒ 5 stamps divided evenly onto 7 pages

 Ⓓ 5 more stamps than on a page with 7 stamps

Make a drawing for the problem. Then write an equation and solve it.

9. The 28 desks in Mr. Becker's class are arranged in 7 equal rows. How many desks are in each row?

10. Michelle's bookcase has 3 shelves. It holds 9 books on each shelf. How many books will fit in the bookcase?

11. Rami counts 6 birds sitting on each of 5 different wires. How many birds does Rami count?

12. Write the equation in the box for the multiplication property it shows.

$$9 \times 6 = 6 \times 9 \qquad 1 \times 10 = 10$$

$$0 \times 2 = 0 \qquad (3 \times 4) \times 5 = 3 \times (4 \times 5)$$

Associative Property	Commutative Property	Identity Property	Zero Property

13. Chloe buys 10 balloons for her sisters. She gives 5 balloons to each sister and has none left.

Part A

How many sisters does Chloe have? Write an equation and solve the problem.

Equation: _____

_____ sisters

Part B

Solve the problem in a different way. Tell how the ways are alike and different.

Family Letter

Content Overview

Dear Family,

In this unit, students learn multiplications and divisions for 6s, 7s, and 8s, while continuing to practice the rest of the basic multiplications and divisions covered in Unit 1.

Although students practice all the 6s, 7s, and 8s multiplications, they really have only six new multiplications to learn: 6×6, 6×7, 6×8, 7×7, 7×8, and 8×8. The lessons for these multiplications focus on strategies for finding the products using multiplications they know.

This unit also focuses on word problems. Students are presented with a variety of one-step and two-step word problems.

Here is an example of a two-step problem:

A roller coaster has 7 cars. Each car has 4 seats. If there were 3 empty seats, how many people were on the roller coaster?

Students use the language and context of each problem to determine which operation or operations—multiplication, division, addition, or subtraction—they must use to solve it. Students use a variety of methods to solve two-step word problems.

Please continue to help your child get faster on multiplications and divisions. Use all of the practice materials that your child has brought home. Your support is crucial to your child's learning.

Please call if you have any questions or comments.

Thank you.

Sincerely,
Your child's teacher

© Houghton Mifflin Harcourt Publishing Company

 CA CC

Unit 2 addresses the following standards from the *Common Core State Standards for Mathematics with California Additions*: 3.OA.1, 3.OA.2, 3.OA.3, 3.OA.4, 3.OA.5, 3.OA.6, 3.OA.7, 3.OA.8, 3.OA.9, 3.NBT.3, 3.MD.5, 3.MD.5a, 3.MD.5b, 3.MD.6, 3.MD.7, 3.MD.7a, 3.MD.7b and all Mathematical Practices

Estimada familia:

En esta unidad los estudiantes aprenden las multiplicaciones y divisiones con el 6, el 7 y el 8, mientras siguen practicando las demás multiplicaciones y divisiones que se presentaron en la Unidad 1.

Aunque los estudiantes practican todas las multiplicaciones con el 6, el 7 y el 8, en realidad sólo tienen que aprender seis multiplicaciones nuevas: 6×6, 6×7, 6×8, 7×7, 7×8 y 8×8. Las lecciones acerca de estas multiplicaciones se centran en estrategias para hallar los productos usando multiplicaciones que ya se conocen.

Esta unidad también se centra en problemas verbales. A los estudiantes se les presenta una variedad de problemas de uno y de dos pasos.

Este es un ejemplo de un problema de dos pasos:
Una montaña rusa tiene 7 carros. Cada carro tiene 7 asientos. Si hay 3 asientos vacíos. Cuántas personas había en la montaña rusa?

Los estudiantes aprovechan el lenguaje y el contexto de cada problema para determinar qué operación u operaciones deben usar para resolverlo: multiplicación, división, suma o resta. Los estudiantes usan una variedad de métodos para resolver problemas de dos pasos.

Por favor continúe ayudando a su niño a practicar las multiplicaciones y las divisiones. Use todos los materiales de práctica que su niño ha llevado a casa. Su apoyo es importante para el aprendizaje de su niño.

Si tiene alguna duda o pregunta, por favor comuníquese conmigo.

Atentamente,
El maestro de su niño

CA CC

En la Unidad 2 se aplican los siguientes estándares auxiliares, contenidos en los *Estándares estatales comunes de matemáticas con adiciones para California*: 3.OA.1, 3.OA.2, 3.OA.3, 3.OA.4, 3.OA.5, 3.OA.6, 3.OA.7, 3.OA.8, 3.OA.9, 3.NBT.3, 3.MD.5, 3.MD.5a, 3.MD.5b, 3.MD.6, 3.MD.7, 3.MD.7a, 3.MD.7b y todos los de prácticas matemáticas.

▶ **PATH to FLUENCY** **Explore Patterns with 6s**

What patterns do you see below?

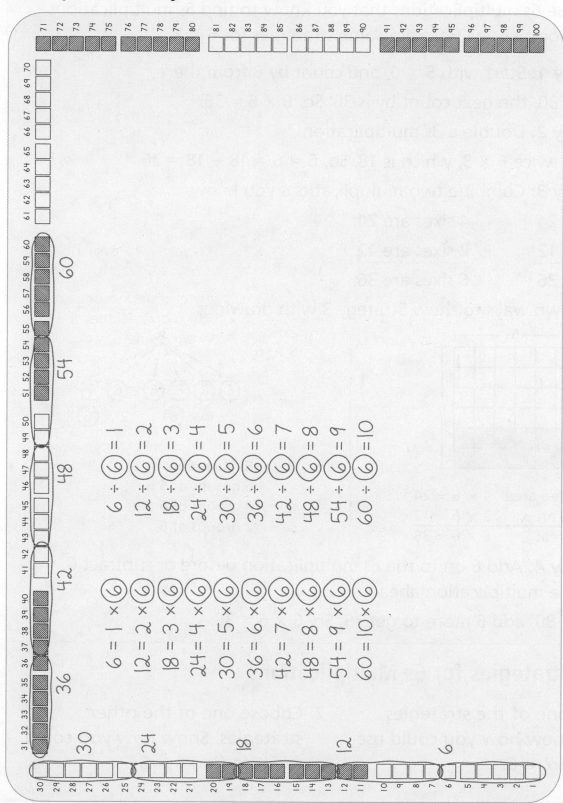

Name _____ Date _____

**PATH to
FLUENCY**

► **Strategies for Multiplying with 6**

You can use 6s multiplications that you know to find 6s multiplications that you don't know. Here are some strategies for 6 × 6.

- **Strategy 1:** Start with 5 × 6, and count by 6 from there.

  5 × 6 = 30, the next count by is 36. So, 6 × 6 = 36.

- **Strategy 2:** Double a 3s multiplication.

  6 × 6 is twice 6 × 3, which is 18. So, 6 × 6 = 18 + 18 = 36.

- **Strategy 3:** Combine two multiplications you know.

  4 × 6 = 24   4 sixes are 24.

  2 × 6 = 12   2 sixes are 12.
  _____   _____

  6 × 6 = 36   6 sixes are 36.

Here are two ways to show Strategy 3 with drawings.

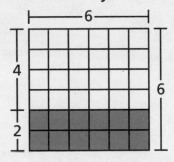

unshaded area: 4 × 6 = 24
shaded area: 2 × 6 = 12
total area: 6 × 6 = 36

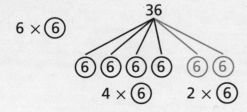

Explanation:
6 groups of 6 is
4 groups of 6 plus
2 groups of 6.

- **Strategy 4:** Add 6 on to the 6s multiplication before or subtract 6 from the multiplication ahead.

  5 × 6 = 30, add 6 more to get 36. So, 6 × 6 = 36.

► **Apply Strategies for 6s Multiplications**

1. Choose one of the strategies above. Show how you could use it to find 7 × 6.

2. Choose one of the other strategies. Show how you could use it to find 8 × 6.

Study Sheet C

6s

Count-bys	Mixed Up ×	Mixed Up ÷
1 × 6 = 6	10 × 6 = 60	54 ÷ 6 = 9
2 × 6 = 12	8 × 6 = 48	30 ÷ 6 = 5
3 × 6 = 18	2 × 6 = 12	12 ÷ 6 = 2
4 × 6 = 24	6 × 6 = 36	60 ÷ 6 = 10
5 × 6 = 30	4 × 6 = 24	48 ÷ 6 = 8
6 × 6 = 36	1 × 6 = 6	36 ÷ 6 = 6
7 × 6 = 42	9 × 6 = 54	6 ÷ 6 = 1
8 × 6 = 48	3 × 6 = 18	42 ÷ 6 = 7
9 × 6 = 54	7 × 6 = 42	18 ÷ 6 = 3
10 × 6 = 60	5 × 6 = 30	24 ÷ 6 = 4

7s

Count-bys	Mixed Up ×	Mixed Up ÷
1 × 7 = 7	6 × 7 = 42	70 ÷ 7 = 10
2 × 7 = 14	8 × 7 = 56	14 ÷ 7 = 2
3 × 7 = 21	5 × 7 = 35	28 ÷ 7 = 4
4 × 7 = 28	9 × 7 = 63	56 ÷ 7 = 8
5 × 7 = 35	4 × 7 = 28	42 ÷ 7 = 6
6 × 7 = 42	10 × 7 = 70	63 ÷ 7 = 9
7 × 7 = 49	3 × 7 = 21	21 ÷ 7 = 3
8 × 7 = 56	1 × 7 = 7	49 ÷ 7 = 7
9 × 7 = 63	7 × 7 = 49	7 ÷ 7 = 1
10 × 7 = 70	2 × 7 = 14	35 ÷ 7 = 5

8s

Count-bys	Mixed Up ×	Mixed Up ÷
1 × 8 = 8	6 × 8 = 48	16 ÷ 8 = 2
2 × 8 = 16	10 × 8 = 80	40 ÷ 8 = 5
3 × 8 = 24	7 × 8 = 56	72 ÷ 8 = 9
4 × 8 = 32	2 × 8 = 16	32 ÷ 8 = 4
5 × 8 = 40	4 × 8 = 32	8 ÷ 8 = 1
6 × 8 = 48	8 × 8 = 64	80 ÷ 8 = 10
7 × 8 = 56	5 × 8 = 40	64 ÷ 8 = 8
8 × 8 = 64	9 × 8 = 72	24 ÷ 8 = 3
9 × 8 = 72	3 × 8 = 24	56 ÷ 8 = 7
10 × 8 = 80	1 × 8 = 8	48 ÷ 8 = 6

Squares

Count-bys	Mixed Up ×	Mixed Up ÷
1 × 1 = 1	3 × 3 = 9	25 ÷ 5 = 5
2 × 2 = 4	9 × 9 = 81	4 ÷ 2 = 2
3 × 3 = 9	4 × 4 = 16	81 ÷ 9 = 9
4 × 4 = 16	6 × 6 = 36	9 ÷ 3 = 3
5 × 5 = 25	2 × 2 = 4	36 ÷ 6 = 6
6 × 6 = 36	7 × 7 = 49	100 ÷ 10 = 10
7 × 7 = 49	10 × 10 = 100	16 ÷ 4 = 4
8 × 8 = 64	1 × 1 = 1	49 ÷ 7 = 7
9 × 9 = 81	5 × 5 = 25	1 ÷ 1 = 1
10 × 10 = 100	8 × 8 = 64	64 ÷ 8 = 8

CA CC Content Standards 3.OA.1, 3.OA.2, 3.OA.3, 3.OA.4, 3.OA.6, 3.OA.7, 3.MD.5, 3.MD.5a, 3.MD.5b, 3.MD.6, 3.MD.7a, 3.MD.7b Mathematical Practices MP.1, MP.2, MP.4, MP.5

► **PATH to FLUENCY** Unknown Number Puzzles

Complete each Unknown Number puzzle.

1.

×	5	2	
	30		48
4		8	32
	45		72

2.

×		3	
6	30		42
4			28
	40	24	56

3.

×	4		8
9		81	
	12		24
	20	45	40

4.

×		3	
	60		20
6	36		
	18	9	6

5.

×	8		2
7		28	
	16	8	
	32	16	8

6.

×	9		
8		56	24
	54	42	18
5			15

7.

×	8		7
8		40	
	32	20	28
	24	15	

8.

×	3	4	
	27	36	81
7			63
			18

9.

×			10
8	48	16	
7	42	14	
		36	60

▶ Tiling and Multiplying to Find Area

Use inch tiles to find the area. Then label the side lengths and find the area using multiplication.

10.

Area: _____ _____

11.

Area: _____ _____

12.

Area: _____ _____

13.

Area: _____ _____

Solve Area Word Problems

► Draw Rectangles to Solve Area Word Problems

Draw a rectangle to help solve each problem. Label your answers with the correct units.

Show your work.

14. The mattress has a length of 7 feet and a width of 6 feet. What is the area of the mattress?

_____

15. The wading pool at Evans Park is shaped like a square with sides 8 feet long. What is the area of the wading pool?

_____

16. Milo's rug has a length of 5 feet and an area of 40 square feet. What is the width of his rug?

_____

17. Lana wants to enclose a garden plot. Each side of the garden will be 9 feet. What is the area of the garden?

_____

18. A picture has a length of 6 inches and a width of 8 inches. What is the area of the picture?

_____

19. A quilt square has sides that are 7 inches long. What is the area of the quilt square?

_____

► Draw a Picture to Solve a Problem

Draw a picture to help solve each problem.

20. Ana has a ribbon that is 18 inches long.
She cut the ribbon into 3 equal pieces.
Then she cut each of those pieces in half.
How many small pieces of ribbon are there?
How long is each piece?

_____

21. A sign is shaped like a square. Eva draws lines
on the sign to make 3 equal rectangles. Each
rectangle is 3 inches wide and 9 inches long.
What is the area of the square?

_____

22. Ty uses 20 feet of fencing to make a rectangular
garden. He divides the rectangle into 4 equal
squares all in one row. The side of each square
is 2 feet long. What is the area of the garden?

_____

23. Aaron is stacking cans in a grocery store. The
bottom row has 7 cans. Each row above has 1
fewer can. How many cans will be stacked in all?

_____

24. There are 4 cars in a row. Each car is 13 feet
long. There are 6 feet between each car. What
is the length from the front of the first car to
the back of the last car in the row?

_____

► **PATH to FLUENCY** **Check Sheet 7: 6s and 8s**

6s Multiplications	6s Divisions	8s Multiplications	8s Divisions
10 × 6 = 60	24 / 6 = 4	2 × 8 = 16	72 / 8 = 9
6 • 4 = 24	48 ÷ 6 = 8	8 • 10 = 80	16 ÷ 8 = 2
6 * 7 = 42	60 / 6 = 10	3 * 8 = 24	40 / 8 = 5
2 × 6 = 12	12 ÷ 6 = 2	9 × 8 = 72	8 ÷ 8 = 1
6 • 5 = 30	42 / 6 = 7	8 • 4 = 32	80 / 8 = 10
6 * 8 = 48	30 ÷ 6 = 5	8 * 7 = 56	48 ÷ 8 = 6
9 × 6 = 54	6 / 6 = 1	5 × 8 = 40	56 / 8 = 7
6 • 1 = 6	18 ÷ 6 = 3	8 • 6 = 48	24 ÷ 8 = 3
6 * 6 = 36	54 / 6 = 9	1 * 8 = 8	64 / 8 = 8
6 × 3 = 18	36 / 6 = 6	8 × 8 = 64	32 / 8 = 4
6 • 6 = 36	48 ÷ 6 = 8	4 • 8 = 32	80 ÷ 8 = 10
5 * 6 = 30	12 / 6 = 2	6 * 8 = 48	56 / 8 = 7
6 × 2 = 12	24 ÷ 6 = 4	8 × 3 = 24	8 ÷ 8 = 1
4 • 6 = 24	60 / 6 = 10	7 • 8 = 56	24 / 8 = 3
6 * 9 = 54	6 ÷ 6 = 1	8 * 2 = 16	64 ÷ 8 = 8
8 × 6 = 48	42 / 6 = 7	8 × 9 = 72	16 / 8 = 2
7 • 6 = 42	18 ÷ 6 = 3	8 • 1 = 8	72 ÷ 8 = 9
6 * 10 = 60	36 ÷ 6 = 6	8 * 8 = 64	32 ÷ 8 = 4
1 × 6 = 6	30 / 6 = 5	10 × 8 = 80	40 / 8 = 5
4 • 6 = 24	54 ÷ 6 = 9	5 • 8 = 40	48 ÷ 8 = 6

Check Sheet 7: 6s and 8s

Name

Date

CA CC Content Standards **3.OA.4, 3.OA.6, 3.OA.7, 3.OA.9**
Mathematical Practices **MP.2, MP.7, MP.8**

► **PATH to FLUENCY** **Explore Patterns with 8s**

What patterns do you see below?

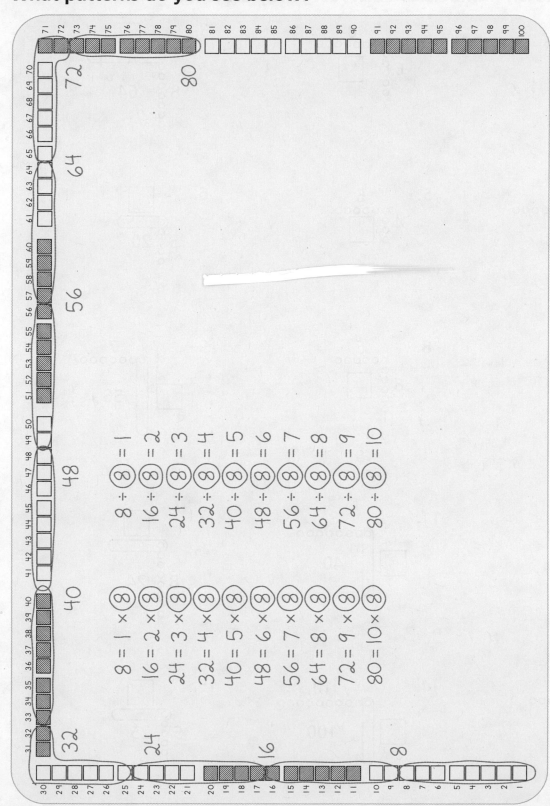

Name _____ Date _____

▶ PATH to FLUENCY **Fast-Array Drawings**

Find the unknown number for each Fast-Array drawing.

1. 6

42

2. 8
6 □

3. □
8 64

4. 9
□ 63

5. 6
4 □

6. □
5 20

7. □
9 45

8. 6
6 □

9. 7
□ 56

10. 7
7 □

11. 8
□ 40

12. □
8 24

13. 9
8 □

14. 10
□ 100

15. □
5 25

Multiply and Divide with 8

CA CC Content Standards **3.OA.1, 3.OA.2, 3.OA.3, 3.OA.4, 3.OA.6, 3.OA.7** Mathematical Practices **MP.1, MP.3, MP.4, MP.6**

► Identify the Type and Choose the Operation

Solve. Then circle what type it is and what operation you use.

1. Students in Mr. Till's class hung their paintings on the wall. They made 6 rows, with 5 paintings in each row. How many paintings did the students hang?

   _____

   Circle one: array   equal groups   area
   Circle one: multiplication   division

2. Write your own problem that is the same type as problem 1. _____

   _____

   _____

3. There are 8 goldfish in each tank at the pet store. If there are 56 goldfish in all, how many tanks are there?

   _____

   Circle one: array   equal groups   area
   Circle one: multiplication   division

4. Write your own problem that is the same type as problem 3. _____

   _____

   _____

5. Pierre built a rectangular pen for his rabbits. The pen is 4 feet wide and 6 feet long. What is the area of the pen? _____

   Circle one: array   equal groups   area
   Circle one: multiplication   division

▶ Identify the Type and Choose the Operation (continued)

6. Write your own problem that is the same type as problem 5. _____

_____

_____

7. Paulo arranged 72 baseball cards in 9 rows and a certain number of columns. Into how many columns did he arrange the cards? _____

Circle one: array   equal groups   area
Circle one: multiplication   division

8. Write your own problem that is the same type as Problem 7. _____

_____

_____

_____

9. The store sells bottles of juice in six-packs. Mr. Lee bought 9 six-packs for a picnic. How many bottles did he buy? _____

Circle one: array   equal groups   area
Circle one: multiplication   division

10. Write your own problem that is the same type as Problem 9. _____

_____

_____

_____

11. Math Journal Write an area multiplication problem. Draw a Fast Array to solve it.

Write Word Problems and Equations

▶ What's the Error?

Dear Math Students,

Today my teacher asked me to find the answer to 8 x 6. Here is what I wrote:

8 x 6 = 14

Is my answer correct? If not, please correct my work and tell me what I did wrong.

Your friend,
Puzzled Penguin

12. Write an answer to the Puzzled Penguin.

_____

_____

▶ Write and Solve Equations

Write an equation and solve the problem.

13. A large box of crayons holds 60 crayons. There are 10 crayons in each row. How many rows are there?

14. A poster covers 12 square feet. The poster is 4 feet long. How wide is the poster?

15. There are 7 groups of students with an equal number of students in each group working on a social studies project. There are 28 students working on the project. How many students are there in each group?

16. Amanda has 15 bracelets. She gave a number of bracelets to friends. She has 10 bracelets left. How many bracelets did she give to friends?

► Write and Solve Equations (continued)

Write an equation and solve the problem.

17. John has 24 baseball cards. He divided them equally among 6 friends. How many cards did each friend get?

_____

18. A third grade class of 24 students has 14 girls in it. How many boys are in the class?

_____

19. There are 16 pencils left in a container. Eight students will divide the pencils equally. How many pencils will each student get?

_____

20. Marc bought 18 golf balls. The golf balls were packaged in boxes of 6. How many boxes of golf balls did Marc buy?

_____

21. Lara keeps her DVDs in a case that has 10 sleeves. Each sleeve can hold 6 DVDs. How many DVDs can the case hold?

_____

22. Write a problem that can be solved using the equation $54 \div 6 = n$, where n is the number in each group. Then solve the problem.

_____

_____

Name _____ **Date** _____

CA CC Content Standards 3.OA.4, 3.OA.6, 3.OA.7, 3.OA.9 Mathematical Practices MP.2, MP.7, MP.8

► PATH to FLUENCY **Explore Patterns with 7s**

What patterns do you see below?

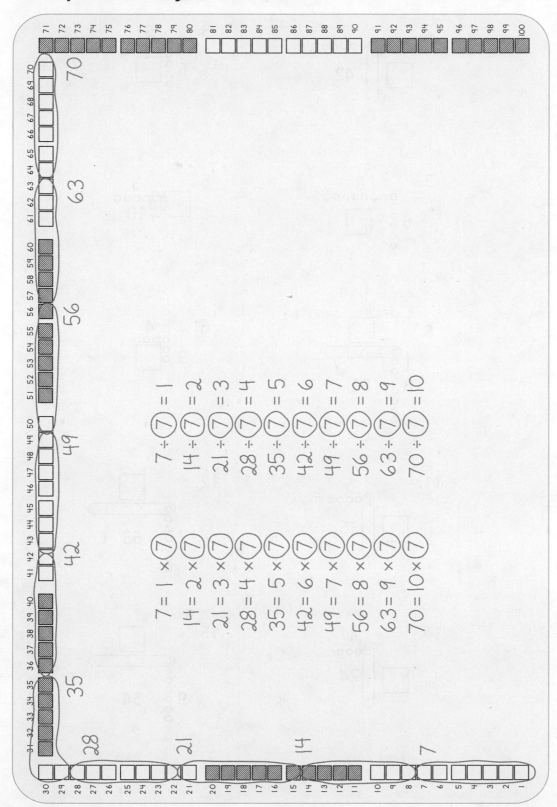

$7 \div 7 = 1$
$14 \div 7 = 2$
$21 \div 7 = 3$
$28 \div 7 = 4$
$35 \div 7 = 5$
$42 \div 7 = 6$
$49 \div 7 = 7$
$56 \div 7 = 8$
$63 \div 7 = 9$
$70 \div 7 = 10$

$7 = 1 \times 7$
$14 = 2 \times 7$
$21 = 3 \times 7$
$28 = 4 \times 7$
$35 = 5 \times 7$
$42 = 6 \times 7$
$49 = 7 \times 7$
$56 = 8 \times 7$
$63 = 9 \times 7$
$70 = 10 \times 7$

► PATH to FLUENCY **More Fast-Array Drawings**

Find the unknown number for each Fast-Array Drawing.

1. 7
    4 □

2. 7
    □ 42

3. 5
    6 □

4. □
    3 24

5. 8
    6 □

6. □ 5
    10

7. 6
    □ 36

8. □
    8 56

9. 4
    3 □

10. 7
    7 □

11. 5
    □ 35

12. □
    7 63

13. 6
    8 □

14. 4
    □ 24

15. □
    9 54

▶ PATH to FLUENCY **Check Sheet 8: 7s and Squares**

7s Multiplications	7s Divisions	Squares Multiplications	Squares Divisions
4 × 7 = 28	14 / 7 = 2	8 × 8 = 64	81 / 9 = 9
7 • 2 = 14	28 ÷ 7 = 4	10 • 10 = 100	4 ÷ 2 = 2
7 * 8 = 56	70 / 7 = 10	3 * 3 = 9	25 / 5 = 5
7 × 7 = 49	56 ÷ 7 = 8	9 × 9 = 81	1 ÷ 1 = 1
7 • 1 = 7	42 / 7 = 6	4 • 4 = 16	100 / 10 = 10
7 * 10 = 70	63 ÷ 7 = 9	7 * 7 = 49	36 ÷ 6 = 6
3 × 7 = 21	7 / 7 = 1	5 × 5 = 25	49 / 7 = 7
7 • 6 = 42	49 ÷ 7 = 7	6 • 6 = 36	9 ÷ 3 = 3
5 * 7 = 35	21 / 7 = 3	1 * 1 = 1	64 / 8 = 8
7 × 9 = 63	35 / 7 = 5	5 * 5 = 25	16 / 4 = 4
7 • 4 = 28	7 ÷ 7 = 1	1 • 1 = 1	100 ÷ 10 = 10
9 * 7 = 63	63 / 7 = 9	3 • 3 = 9	49 / 7 = 7
2 × 7 = 14	14 ÷ 7 = 2	10 × 10 = 100	1 ÷ 1 = 1
7 • 5 = 35	70 / 7 = 10	4 × 4 = 16	9 / 3 = 3
8 * 7 = 56	21 ÷ 7 = 3	9 * 9 = 81	64 ÷ 8 = 8
7 × 3 = 21	49 / 7 = 7	2 × 2 = 4	4 / 2 = 2
6 • 7 = 42	28 ÷ 7 = 4	6 * 6 = 36	81 ÷ 9 = 9
10 * 7 = 70	56 ÷ 7 = 8	7 × 7 = 49	16 ÷ 4 = 4
1 × 7 = 7	35 / 7 = 5	5 • 5 = 25	25 / 5 = 5
7 • 7 = 49	42 ÷ 7 = 6	8 • 8 = 64	36 ÷ 6 = 6

Check Sheet 8: 7s and Squares **113**

Check Sheet 8: 7s and Squares

Name _____ Date _____

CA CC Content Standards **3.OA.7, 3.OA.9, 3.MD.7b**
Mathematical Practices **MP.2, MP.7, MP.8**

►  **Explore Square Numbers**

Write an equation to show the area of each large square.

   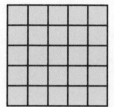

1. $1 \times 1 = 1$ **2.** _____   **3.** _____   **4.** _____

                                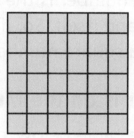

5. _____   **6.** _____

    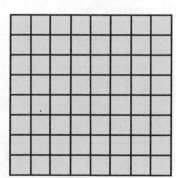

7. _____   **8.** _____

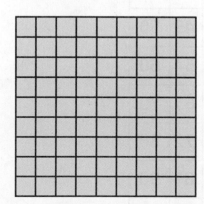   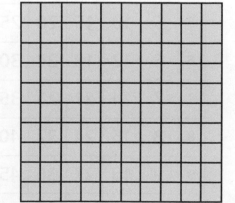

9. _____   **10.** _____

VOCABULARY
square numbers

▶ **Look for Patterns**

11. List the products in Exercises 1–10 in order.
Discuss the patterns you see with your class.

The numbers you listed in Exercise 11 are called
square numbers because they are the areas of
squares with whole-number lengths of sides.
A square number is the product of a whole
number and itself. So, if *n* is a whole number,
$n \times n$ is a square number.

▶ **Patterns on the Multiplication Table**

12. In the table below, circle the products that are
square numbers. Discuss the patterns you see
with your class.

X	1	2	3	4	5	6	7	8	9	10
1	1	2	3	4	5	6	7	8	9	10
2	2	4	6	8	10	12	14	16	18	20
3	3	6	9	12	15	18	21	24	27	30
4	4	8	12	16	20	24	28	32	36	40
5	5	10	15	20	25	30	35	40	45	50
6	6	12	18	24	30	36	42	48	54	60
7	7	14	21	28	35	42	49	56	63	70
8	8	16	24	32	40	48	56	64	72	80
9	9	18	27	36	45	54	63	72	81	90
10	10	20	30	40	50	60	70	80	90	100

► PATH to FLUENCY **Check Sheet 9: 6s, 7s, and 8s**

6s, 7s, and 8s Multiplications	6s, 7s, and 8s Multiplications	6s, 7s, and 8s Divisions	6s, 7s, and 8s Divisions
$1 \times 6 = 6$	$0 \times 8 = 0$	$24 / 6 = 4$	$54 / 6 = 9$
$6 \cdot 7 = 42$	$6 \cdot 2 = 12$	$21 \div 7 = 3$	$24 \div 8 = 3$
$3 * 8 = 24$	$4 * 7 = 28$	$16 / 8 = 2$	$14 / 7 = 2$
$6 \times 2 = 12$	$8 \times 3 = 24$	$24 \div 8 = 3$	$32 \div 8 = 4$
$7 \cdot 5 = 35$	$5 \cdot 6 = 30$	$14 / 7 = 2$	$18 / 6 = 3$
$8 * 4 = 32$	$7 * 2 = 14$	$30 \div 6 = 5$	$56 \div 7 = 8$
$6 \times 6 = 36$	$3 \times 8 = 24$	$35 / 7 = 5$	$40 / 8 = 5$
$8 \cdot 7 = 56$	$6 \cdot 4 = 24$	$24 \div 8 = 3$	$35 \div 7 = 5$
$9 * 8 = 72$	$0 * 7 = 0$	$18 / 6 = 3$	$12 / 6 = 2$
$6 \times 10 = 60$	$8 \times 1 = 8$	$12 / 6 = 2$	$21 / 7 = 3$
$7 \cdot 1 = 7$	$8 \cdot 6 = 48$	$42 \div 7 = 6$	$16 \div 8 = 2$
$8 * 3 = 24$	$7 * 9 = 63$	$56 / 8 = 7$	$42 / 6 = 7$
$5 \times 6 = 30$	$10 \times 8 = 80$	$49 \div 7 = 7$	$80 \div 8 = 10$
$4 \cdot 7 = 28$	$6 \cdot 10 = 60$	$16 / 8 = 2$	$36 / 6 = 6$
$2 * 8 = 16$	$3 * 7 = 21$	$60 \div 6 = 10$	$7 \div 7 = 1$
$7 \times 7 = 49$	$8 \times 4 = 32$	$54 / 6 = 9$	$64 / 8 = 8$
$7 \cdot 6 = 42$	$6 \cdot 5 = 30$	$8 \div 8 = 1$	$24 \div 6 = 4$
$8 * 8 = 64$	$7 * 4 = 28$	$28 \div 7 = 4$	$21 \div 7 = 3$
$9 \times 6 = 54$	$8 \times 8 = 64$	$72 / 8 = 9$	$49 / 7 = 7$
$10 \cdot 7 = 70$	$6 \cdot 9 = 54$	$56 \div 7 = 8$	$24 \div 8 = 3$

► PATH to FLUENCY **Check Sheet 10: 0s–10s**

0s–10s Multiplications	0s–10s Multiplications	0s–10s Divisions	0s–10s Divisions
9 × 0 = 0	9 × 4 = 36	9 / 1 = 9	90 / 10 = 9
1 • 1 = 1	5 • 9 = 45	12 ÷ 3 = 4	64 ÷ 8 = 8
2 * 3 = 6	6 * 10 = 60	14 / 2 = 7	15 / 5 = 3
1 × 3 = 3	7 × 3 = 21	20 ÷ 4 = 5	12 ÷ 6 = 2
5 • 4 = 20	5 • 3 = 15	10 / 5 = 2	14 / 7 = 2
7 * 5 = 35	4 * 1 = 4	48 ÷ 8 = 6	45 ÷ 9 = 5
6 × 9 = 54	7 × 5 = 35	35 / 7 = 5	8 / 1 = 8
4 • 7 = 28	6 • 3 = 18	60 ÷ 6 = 10	30 ÷ 3 = 10
1 * 8 = 8	8 * 7 = 56	81 / 9 = 9	16 / 4 = 4
9 × 8 = 72	5 × 8 = 40	20 / 10 = 2	8 / 2 = 4
2 • 10 = 20	9 • 9 = 81	16 ÷ 2 = 8	80 ÷ 10 = 8
0 * 7 = 0	9 * 10 = 90	30 / 5 = 6	36 / 4 = 9
4 × 1 = 4	0 × 0 = 0	49 ÷ 7 = 7	25 ÷ 5 = 5
2 • 4 = 8	1 • 0 = 0	60 / 6 = 10	42 / 7 = 6
10 * 3 = 30	1 * 6 = 6	30 ÷ 3 = 10	36 ÷ 6 = 6
8 × 4 = 32	7 × 2 = 14	8 / 1 = 8	90 / 9 = 10
5 • 8 = 40	6 • 3 = 18	16 ÷ 4 = 4	24 ÷ 8 = 3
4 * 6 = 24	4 * 5 = 20	16 ÷ 8 = 2	6 ÷ 2 = 3
7 × 6 = 42	6 × 6 = 36	40 / 10 = 4	9 / 3 = 3
1 • 8 = 8	10 • 7 = 70	36 ÷ 9 = 4	1 ÷ 1 = 1

© Houghton Mifflin Harcourt Publishing Company

▶ **PATH to FLUENCY** **Play Quotient Match and Division Blockout**

Read the rules for playing a game.
Then play the game with your partner.

Rules for Quotient Match

Number of players: 2 or 3

What each player will need: Division Strategy Cards for 6s, 7s, and 8s

1. Shuffle the cards. Put the division cards, without answers side up, on the table in 6 rows of 4.

2. Players take turns. On each turn, a player chooses three cards that he or she thinks have the same quotient and turns them over.

3. If all three cards do have the same quotient the player takes them. If the cards do not have the same quotient, the player turns them back over so the without answers side is up.

4. Play continues until no cards remain.

Rules for Division Blockout

Number of players: 3

What each player will need: Blockout Game Board (TRB M70), Division Strategy Cards for 6s, 7s, and 8s

1. Players do not write anything on the game board. The first row is for 6s, the second row for 7s, and the third row for 8s, as indicated in the gray column on the left.

2. Each player shuffles his or her Division Strategy Cards for 6s, 7s, 8s, making sure the division sides without answers are up.

3. Repeat Steps 2, 3, and 4 above. This time players will place the Strategy Cards in the appropriate row to indicate whether the unknown factor is 6, 7, or 8.

► (PATH to FLUENCY) **Play Multiplication Blockout**

Read the rules for playing *Multiplication Blockout*. Then play the game with your partner.

Rules for *Multiplication Block Out*

Number of players: 3

What each player will need: *Blockout* Game Board (TRB M70), Multiplication Strategy Cards for 6s, 7s, and 8s

1. Players choose any 5 factors from 2–9 and write them in any order in the gray spaces at the top of the game board. The players then write the products in the large white spaces. The result will be a scrambled multiplication table.

2. Once the table is complete, players cut off the gray row and gray column that show the factors so that only the products are showing. This will be the game board.

3. Each player shuffles his or her Multiplication Strategy Cards for 6s, 7s, and 8s, making sure the multiplication sides without answers are facing up.

4. One player says, "Go!" and everyone quickly places their Strategy Cards on the game board spaces showing the corresponding products. When a player's game board is completely filled, he or she shouts, "Blockout!"

5. Everyone stops and checks the player's work. If all the cards are placed correctly, that player is the winner. If the player has made a mistake, he or she sits out and waits for the next player to shout, "Blockout!"

▶ Solve Word Problems with 6s, 7s, 8s

Write an equation and solve the problem.

1. Terri counted 32 legs in the lion house at the zoo. How many lions were there?

2. Kyle saw 9 ladybugs while he was camping. Each one had 6 legs. How many legs did the 9 ladybugs have in all?

3. Adam walks 3 miles a day. How many miles does he walk in a week?

4. Nancy's dog Rover eats 6 cups of food a day. In 8 days, how many cups of food does Rover eat?

5. The school library has 72 books on the topic of weather. If 8 students shared the books equally, how many books would each student receive?

6. The 42 trumpet players in the marching band lined up in 6 equal rows. How many trumpet players were in each row?

► Solve Word Problems with 6s, 7s, and 8s (continued)

Write an equation and solve the problem.

7. Susan is having a party. She has 18 cups. She puts them in 6 equal stacks. How many cups are in each stack?

   _____

8. Regina made an array with 7 rows of 9 blocks. How many blocks are in the array?

   _____

9. Mr. Rodriguez plans to invite 40 students to a picnic. The invitations come in packs of 8. How many packs of invitations does Mr. Rodriguez need to buy?

   _____

10. A classroom has 7 rows of 4 desks. How many desks are there in the classroom?

    _____

11. Write a word problem for 48 ÷ 6 where 6 is the size of the group.

    _____

    _____

    _____

12. Write a word problem for 7 × 9 where 9 is the number of items in the collection.

    _____

    _____

    _____

Name _____ **Date** _____

CA CC Content Standards **3.OA.4, 3.OA.5, 3.OA.6, 3.OA.7, 3.OA.9** Mathematical Practices **MP.2**

► PATH to FLUENCY **Complete a Multiplication Table**

1. Look at the factors to complete the Multiplication Table. Leave blanks for the products you do not know.

✕	1	2	3	4	5	6	7	8	9	10
1										
2										
3										
4										
5										
6										
7										
8										
9										
10										

2. Write the multiplications you need to practice.

_____

_____

_____

_____

_____

Name _____ Date _____

► **PATH to FLUENCY** **Scrambled Multiplication Tables**

The factors are at the side and top of each table.
The products are in the white boxes.

Complete each table.

A

×									
6	30	54	60	42	24	18	12	48	36
2	10	18	20	14	8	6	4	16	12
10	50	90	100	70	40	30	20	80	60
8	40	72	80	56	32	24	16	64	48
5	25	45	50	35	20	15	10	40	30
1	5	9	10	7	4	3	2	8	6
9	45	81	90	63	36	27	18	72	54
4	20	36	40	28	16	12	8	32	24
7	35	63	70	49	28	21	14	56	42
3	15	27	30	21	12	9	6	24	18

B

×									
27	6	24	21	18	15	12	9	3	
36	8	32	28	24		16	12	4	40
9	2	8	7	6	5	4	3	1	10
18	4	16	14		10	8	6	2	20
	14	56	49	42		28	21	7	
72		64	56	48	40	32	24	8	80
45	10	40		30	25	20	15	5	
54	12	48	42	36	30	24	18	6	60
90		80	70	60		40	30	10	100
81	18	72		54	45	36	27	9	

C

×									
100		20		70	50		90		10
50	15		20	35		30		40	5
10	3		4	7		6	9		1
	9		12	21	15		27	24	
	6	4	8			12	18	16	2
	12	8	16	28	20		36	32	
90	27	18	36	63	45	54		72	
	18	12	24		30	36	54	48	6
	21		28	49		42		56	7
	24		32	56	40		72	64	8

D

×									
48		42	12	36		18	6		30
56	28		14		70	21		63	35
		70		60			10		50
	20	35		30		15	5	45	
32			8		40			36	
8	4		2			3	1		5
	8	14		12		6		18	10
64		56		48	80	24	8		40
72	36		18			27		81	
24		21		18	30		3	27	

Building Fluency with 0s–10s

Complete each Dash. Check your answers on page 129.

Dash 13 6s and 8s Multiplications	Dash 14 6s and 8s Divisions	Dash 15 7s and 8s Multiplications	Dash 16 7s and 8s Divisions
a. $6 \times 9 =$ _____	a. $72 / 8 =$ _____	a. $7 \times 3 =$ _____	a. $63 / 7 =$ _____
b. $8 * 2 =$ _____	b. $12 \div 6 =$ _____	b. $8 * 5 =$ _____	b. $80 \div 8 =$ _____
c. $4 \cdot 6 =$ _____	c. $16 / 8 =$ _____	c. $2 \cdot 7 =$ _____	c. $14 / 7 =$ _____
d. $7 \times 8 =$ _____	d. $24 \div 6 =$ _____	d. $1 \times 8 =$ _____	d. $16 \div 8 =$ _____
e. $6 * 1 =$ _____	e. $8 / 8 =$ _____	e. $7 * 9 =$ _____	e. $7 / 7 =$ _____
f. $8 \cdot 9 =$ _____	f. $6 \div 6 =$ _____	f. $8 \cdot 4 =$ _____	f. $48 \div 8 =$ _____
g. $3 \times 6 =$ _____	g. $40 / 8 =$ _____	g. $4 \times 7 =$ _____	g. $35 / 7 =$ _____
h. $4 * 8 =$ _____	h. $42 \div 6 =$ _____	h. $7 * 8 =$ _____	h. $32 \div 8 =$ _____
i. $6 \cdot 8 =$ _____	i. $24 / 8 =$ _____	i. $7 \cdot 1 =$ _____	i. $21 / 7 =$ _____
j. $8 \times 1 =$ _____	j. $18 \div 6 =$ _____	j. $8 \times 2 =$ _____	j. $8 \div 8 =$ _____
k. $2 * 6 =$ _____	k. $48 / 8 =$ _____	k. $5 * 7 =$ _____	k. $28 / 7 =$ _____
l. $3 \cdot 8 =$ _____	l. $48 \div 6 =$ _____	l. $9 \cdot 8 =$ _____	l. $40 \div 8 =$ _____
m. $6 \times 5 =$ _____	m. $64 / 8 =$ _____	m. $7 \times 6 =$ _____	m. $49 / 7 =$ _____
n. $8 * 8 =$ _____	n. $42 \div 6 =$ _____	n. $8 * 3 =$ _____	n. $72 \div 8 =$ _____
o. $6 \cdot 6 =$ _____	o. $56 / 8 =$ _____	o. $7 \cdot 7 =$ _____	o. $42 / 7 =$ _____
p. $5 \times 8 =$ _____	p. $30 \div 6 =$ _____	p. $8 \times 8 =$ _____	p. $24 \div 8 =$ _____
q. $6 * 7 =$ _____	q. $32 / 8 =$ _____	q. $7 * 0 =$ _____	q. $56 / 7 =$ _____
r. $8 \times 0 =$ _____	r. $54 \div 6 =$ _____	r. $6 \cdot 8 =$ _____	r. $64 \div 8 =$ _____
s. $0 * 6 =$ _____	s. $80 / 8 =$ _____	s. $8 \times 0 =$ _____	s. $70 / 7 =$ _____
t. $6 \cdot 10 =$ _____	t. $60 \div 6 =$ _____	t. $7 * 10 =$ _____	t. $56 \div 8 =$ _____

► **PATH to FLUENCY** Dashes 17–20

Complete each Dash. Check your answers on page 129.

Dash 17 6s and 7s Multiplications	Dash 18 6s and 7s Divisions	Dash 19 6s, 7s, 8s Multiplications	Dash 20 6s, 7s, 8s Divisions
a. $6 \times 6 =$ ___	a. $70 / 7 =$ ___	a. $7 \times 7 =$ ___	a. $21 / 7 =$ ___
b. $7 * 7 =$ ___	b. $60 \div 6 =$ ___	b. $6 \cdot 3 =$ ___	b. $16 \div 8 =$ ___
c. $3 \cdot 6 =$ ___	c. $28 / 7 =$ ___	c. $8 * 6 =$ ___	c. $54 / 6 =$ ___
d. $8 \times 7 =$ ___	d. $30 \div 6 =$ ___	d. $6 \times 6 =$ ___	d. $48 \div 8 =$ ___
e. $6 * 1 =$ ___	e. $42 / 7 =$ ___	e. $7 \cdot 6 =$ ___	e. $64 / 8 =$ ___
f. $7 \cdot 2 =$ ___	f. $24 \div 6 =$ ___	f. $4 * 7 =$ ___	f. $42 \div 6 =$ ___
g. $9 \times 6 =$ ___	g. $35 / 7 =$ ___	g. $9 \times 7 =$ ___	g. $56 / 7 =$ ___
h. $9 * 7 =$ ___	h. $12 \div 6 =$ ___	h. $6 \cdot 9 =$ ___	h. $72 \div 8 =$ ___
i. $6 \cdot 8 =$ ___	i. $7 / 7 =$ ___	i. $6 * 4 =$ ___	i. $18 / 6 =$ ___
j. $7 \times 3 =$ ___	j. $36 \div 6 =$ ___	j. $8 \times 8 =$ ___	j. $28 / 7 =$ ___
k. $7 * 6 =$ ___	k. $21 / 7 =$ ___	k. $7 \cdot 3 =$ ___	k. $56 \div 8 =$ ___
l. $1 \cdot 7 =$ ___	l. $48 \div 6 =$ ___	l. $8 * 7 =$ ___	l. $30 / 6 =$ ___
m. $6 \times 2 =$ ___	m. $63 / 7 =$ ___	m. $6 \times 7 =$ ___	m. $63 \div 7 =$ ___
n. $7 * 5 =$ ___	n. $6 \div 6 =$ ___	n. $3 \cdot 6 =$ ___	n. $32 / 8 =$ ___
o. $4 \cdot 6 =$ ___	o. $56 / 7 =$ ___	o. $2 * 7 =$ ___	o. $48 \div 6 =$ ___
p. $6 \times 7 =$ ___	p. $18 \div 6 =$ ___	p. $9 \times 8 =$ ___	p. $49 / 7 =$ ___
q. $6 * 5 =$ ___	q. $49 / 7 =$ ___	q. $5 \cdot 6 =$ ___	q. $36 \div 6 =$ ___
r. $7 \cdot 4 =$ ___	r. $42 \div 6 =$ ___	r. $7 * 8 =$ ___	r. $24 \div 8 =$ ___
s. $6 \times 10 =$ ___	s. $14 / 7 =$ ___	s. $3 \times 7 =$ ___	s. $42 / 7 =$ ___
t. $7 \times 10 =$ ___	t. $54 \div 6 =$ ___	t. $9 \cdot 6 =$ ___	t. $24 \div 6 =$ ___

► **PATH to FLUENCY** **Dashes 9B–12B**

Complete each multiplication and division Dash.
Check your answers on page 130.

Dash 9B 2s, 5s, 9s, 10s Multiplications	Dash 10B 2s, 5s, 9s, 10s Divisions	Dash 11B 0s, 1s, 3s, 4s Multiplications	Dash 12B 1s, 3s, 4s Divisions
a. 6 × 2 = _____	a. 18 / 2 = _____	a. 7 × 1 = _____	a. 2 / 1 = _____
b. 9 • 4 = _____	b. 25 ÷ 5 = _____	b. 0 • 6 = _____	b. 28 ÷ 4 = _____
c. 8 * 5 = _____	c. 70 / 10 = _____	c. 4 * 4 = _____	c. 3 / 3 = _____
d. 1 × 10 = _____	d. 54 ÷ 9 = _____	d. 7 × 3 = _____	d. 1 ÷ 1 = _____
e. 2 • 7 = _____	e. 50 / 5 = _____	e. 3 • 1 = _____	e. 40 / 4 = _____
f. 9 * 9 = _____	f. 81 ÷ 9 = _____	f. 4 * 7 = _____	f. 21 ÷ 3 = _____
g. 5 × 6 = _____	g. 8 / 2 = _____	g. 9 × 0 = _____	g. 5 / 1 = _____
h. 10 • 4 = _____	h. 90 ÷ 10 = _____	h. 1 • 1 = _____	h. 16 ÷ 4 = _____
i. 7 * 5 = _____	i. 35 / 5 = _____	i. 3 * 4 = _____	i. 15 / 3 = _____
j. 8 × 2 = _____	j. 27 / 9 = _____	j. 4 × 9 = _____	j. 6 / 1 = _____
k. 10 • 10 = _____	k. 2 ÷ 2 = _____	k. 8 • 1 = _____	k. 12 ÷ 4 = _____
l. 5 * 3 = _____	l. 36 / 9 = _____	l. 3 * 3 = _____	l. 27 / 3 = _____
m. 9 × 7 = _____	m. 45 ÷ 5 = _____	m. 0 × 4 = _____	m. 9 ÷ 1 = _____
n. 9 • 2 = _____	n. 14 / 2 = _____	n. 10 • 3 = _____	n. 8 / 4 = _____
o. 5 * 5 = _____	o. 20 ÷ 10 = _____	o. 6 * 4 = _____	o. 12 ÷ 3 = _____
p. 6 × 9 = _____	p. 9 / 9 = _____	p. 1 × 4 = _____	p. 3 / 1 = _____
q. 5 • 2 = _____	q. 20 ÷ 5 = _____	q. 3 • 6 = _____	q. 36 ÷ 4 = _____
r. 9 * 5 = _____	r. 45 ÷ 9 = _____	r. 4 * 8 = _____	r. 6 ÷ 3 = _____
s. 8 × 10 = _____	s. 5 / 5 = _____	s. 7 × 0 = _____	s. 4 / 1 = _____
t. 5 • 10 = _____	t. 4 ÷ 2 = _____	t. 5 • 3 = _____	t. 4 ÷ 4 = _____

Name _____

▶  **Dashes 9C–12C**

Complete each Dash. Check your answers on page 130.

Dash 9C 2s, 5, 9s, 10s Multiplications	Dash 10C 2s, 5, 9s, 10s Divisions	Dash 11C 0s, 1s, 3s, 4s Multiplications	Dash 12C 1s, 3s, 4s Divisions
a. 5 × 8 = ____	a. 36 ÷ 9 = ____	a. 0 × 7 = ____	a. 4 / 1 = ____
b. 9 * 9 = ____	b. 30 / 5 = ____	b. 1 * 4 = ____	b. 15 ÷ 3 = ____
c. 10 • 7 = ____	c. 18 ÷ 2 = ____	c. 3 • 6 = ____	c. 24 / 4 = ____
d. 4 × 5 = ____	d. 80 / 10 = ____	d. 4 × 9 = ____	d. 9 ÷ 1 = ____
e. 5 * 5 = ____	e. 40 ÷ 5 = ____	e. 8 * 0 = ____	e. 21 / 3 = ____
f. 10 • 3 = ____	f. 72 / 9 = ____	f. 7 * 1 = ____	f. 12 ÷ 4 = ____
g. 1 × 5 = ____	g. 6 ÷ 2 = ____	g. 4 • 3 = ____	g. 5 / 1 = ____
h. 3 * 9 = ____	h. 54 / 9 = ____	h. 4 × 4 = ____	h. 3 ÷ 3 = ____
i. 9 • 6 = ____	i. 25 ÷ 5 = ____	i. 0 * 5 = ____	i. 32 / 4 = ____
j. 10 × 8 = ____	j. 10 / 10 = ____	j. 1 • 6 = ____	j. 2 ÷ 1 = ____
k. 2 * 9 = ____	k. 45 ÷ 5 = ____	k. 3 × 2 = ____	k. 18 / 3 = ____
l. 6 • 2 = ____	l. 27 / 9 = ____	l. 4 * 7 = ____	l. 36 ÷ 4 = ____
m. 6 × 10 = ____	m. 14 ÷ 2 = ____	m. 1 • 0 = ____	m. 7 / 1 = ____
n. 8 * 9 = ____	n. 35 / 5 = ____	n. 2 × 1 = ____	n. 24 ÷ 3 = ____
o. 8 • 2 = ____	o. 90 ÷ 9 = ____	o. 9 * 3 = ____	o. 4 / 4 = ____
p. 4 × 2 = ____	p. 90 / 10 = ____	p. 2 • 4 = ____	p. 6 ÷ 1 = ____
q. 10 * 5 = ____	q. 63 ÷ 9 = ____	q. 0 × 3 = ____	q. 12 / 3 = ____
r. 10 • 10 = ____	r. 15 / 5 = ____	r. 1 * 1 = ____	r. 20 ÷ 4 = ____
s. 9 × 6 = ____	s. 50 ÷ 10 = ____	s. 3 • 9 = ____	s. 8 / 1 = ____
t. 5 * 7 = ____	t. 8 / 2 = ____	t. 4 × 5 = ____	t. 27 ÷ 3 = ____

© Houghton Mifflin Harcourt Publishing Company

128 UNIT 2 LESSON 8

Dashes 9C–12C

► PATH to FLUENCY **Answers to Dashes 13–20**

Use this sheet to check your answers to the Dashes on pages 125 and 126.

Dash 13 ×	Dash 14 ÷	Dash 15 ×	Dash 16 ÷	Dash 17 ×	Dash 18 ÷	Dash 19 ×	Dash 20 ÷
a. 54	a. 9	a. 21	a. 9	a. 36	a. 10	a. 49	a. 3
b. 16	b. 2	b. 40	b. 10	b. 49	b. 10	b. 18	b. 2
c. 24	c. 2	c. 14	c. 2	c. 18	c. 4	c. 48	c. 9
d. 56	d. 4	d. 8	d. 2	d. 56	d. 5	d. 36	d. 6
e. 6	e. 1	e. 63	e. 1	e. 6	e. 6	e. 42	e. 8
f. 72	f. 1	f. 32	f. 6	f. 14	f. 4	f. 28	f. 7
g. 18	g. 5	g. 28	g. 5	g. 54	g. 5	g. 63	g. 8
h. 32	h. 7	h. 56	h. 4	h. 63	h. 2	h. 54	h. 9
i. 48	i. 3	i. 7	i. 3	i. 48	i. 1	i. 24	i. 3
j. 8	j. 3	j. 16	j. 1	j. 21	j. 6	j. 64	j. 4
k. 12	k. 6	k. 35	k. 4	k. 42	k. 3	k. 21	k. 7
l. 24	l. 8	l. 72	l. 5	l. 7	l. 8	l. 56	l. 5
m. 30	m. 8	m. 42	m. 7	m. 12	m. 9	m. 42	m. 9
n. 64	n. 7	n. 24	n. 9	n. 35	n. 1	n. 18	n. 4
o. 36	o. 7	o. 49	o. 6	o. 24	o. 8	o. 14	o. 8
p. 40	p. 5	p. 64	p. 3	p. 42	p. 3	p. 72	p. 7
q. 42	q. 4	q. 0	q. 8	q. 30	q. 7	q. 30	q. 6
r. 0	r. 9	r. 48	r. 8	r. 28	r. 7	r. 56	r. 3
s. 0	s. 10	s. 0	s. 10	s. 60	s. 2	s. 21	s. 6
t. 60	t. 10	t. 70	t. 7	t. 70	t. 9	t. 54	t. 4

► PATH to FLUENCY **Answers to Dashes 9B–12C**

Use this sheet to check your answers to the Dashes on pages 127 and 128.

Dash 9B ×	Dash 10B ÷	Dash 11B ×	Dash 12B ÷	Dash 9C ×	Dash 10C ÷	Dash 11C ×	Dash 12C ÷
a. 12	a. 9	a. 7	a. 2	a. 40	a. 4	a. 0	a. 4
b. 36	b. 5	b. 0	b. 7	b. 81	b. 6	b. 4	b. 5
c. 40	c. 7	c. 16	c. 1	c. 70	c. 9	c. 18	c. 6
d. 10	d. 6	d. 21	d. 1	d. 20	d. 8	d. 36	d. 9
e. 14	e. 10	e. 3	e. 10	e. 25	e. 8	e. 0	e. 7
f. 81	f. 9	f. 28	f. 7	f. 30	f. 8	f. 7	f. 3
g. 30	g. 4	g. 0	g. 5	g. 5	g. 3	g. 12	g. 5
h. 40	h. 9	h. 1	h. 4	h. 27	h. 6	h. 16	h. 1
i. 35	i. 7	i. 12	i. 5	i. 54	i. 5	i. 0	i. 8
j. 16	j. 3	j. 36	j. 6	j. 80	j. 1	j. 6	j. 2
k. 100	k. 1	k. 8	k. 3	k. 18	k. 9	k. 6	k. 6
l. 15	l. 4	l. 9	l. 9	l. 12	l. 3	l. 28	l. 9
m. 63	m. 9	m. 0	m. 9	m. 60	m. 7	m. 0	m. 7
n. 18	n. 7	n. 30	n. 2	n. 72	n. 7	n. 2	n. 8
o. 25	o. 2	o. 24	o. 4	o. 16	o. 10	o. 27	o. 1
p. 54	p. 1	p. 4	p. 3	p. 8	p. 9	p. 8	p. 6
q. 10	q. 4	q. 18	q. 9	q. 50	q. 7	q. 0	q. 4
r. 45	r. 5	r. 32	r. 2	r. 100	r. 3	r. 1	r. 5
s. 80	s. 1	s. 0	s. 4	s. 54	s. 5	s. 27	s. 8
t. 50	t. 2	t. 15	t. 1	t. 35	t. 4	t. 20	t. 9

Name _____ **Date** _____

CA CC Content Standards **3.OA.1, 3.OA.2, 3.OA.3, 3.OA.4, 3.OA.6, 3.OA.7** Mathematical Practices **MP.1, MP.4**

► Choose the Operation

Write an equation and solve the problem.

1. Ernie helped his mother work in the yard for 3 days. He earned $6 each day. How much did he earn in all?

2. Ernie helped his mother work in the yard for 3 days. He earned $6 the first day, $5 the second day, and $7 the third day. How much did he earn in all?

3. Troy had $18. He gave $6 to each of his brothers and had no money left. How many brothers does Troy have?

4. Troy gave $18 to his brothers. He gave $4 to Raj, $7 to Darnell, and the rest to Jai. How much money did Jai get?

5. Jinja has 4 cousins. Grant has 7 more cousins than Jinja. How many cousins does Grant have?

6. Jinja has 4 cousins. Grant has 7 times as many cousins as Jinja. How many cousins does Grant have?

7. Camille has 15 fewer books than Jane has. Camille has 12 books. How many does Jane have?

8. Camille has 4 more books than Jane has. Camille has 15 books. How many books does Jane have?

► Write an Equation

Write an equation and solve the problem.

Show your work.

9. Luke had a $5 bill. He spent $3 on a sandwich. How much change did he get?

_____

10. Ramona is putting tiles on the kitchen floor. She will lay 8 rows of tiles, with 7 tiles in each row. How many tiles will Ramona use?

_____

11. Josh earned As on 6 tests last year. Jenna earned As on 6 times as many tests. How many As did Jenna earn?

_____

12. Sophie bought a stuffed animal for $3 and a board game for $7. How much money did Sophie spend?

_____

13. The Duarte family has 15 pets. Each of the 3 Duarte children care for the same number of pets. How many pets does each child care for?

_____

14. Ahmed spent $9 on a CD. Zal paid $6 more for the same CD at a different store. How much did Zal spend on the CD?

Equations and Word Problems

► Write the Question

Write a question for the given information and solve.

15. Anna read 383 pages this month. Chris read 416 pages.

Question: _____

Solution: _____

16. Marisol had 128 beads in her jewelry box. She gave away 56 of them.

Question: _____

Solution: _____

17. Louis put 72 marbles in 8 bags. He put the same number of marbles in each bag.

Question: _____

Solution: _____

18. Geoff planted 4 pots of seeds. He planted 6 seeds in each pot.

Question: _____

Solution: _____

19. Marly put 10 books on each of 5 shelves in the library.

Question: _____

Solution: _____

► Write the Problem

Write a problem that can be solved using the given equation. Then solve.

20. $9 \times 6 = \boxed{}$ Solution: _____

_____

_____

_____

21. $324 - 176 = \boxed{}$ Solution: _____

_____

_____

_____

22. $56 \div 7 = \boxed{}$ Solution: _____

_____

_____

_____

23. $459 + 535 = \boxed{}$ Solution: _____

_____

_____

_____

24. **Math Journal** Choose an operation. Write a word
    problem that involves that operation. Write an
    equation to solve your word problem.

CA CC Content Standards **3.OA.1, 3.OA.2, 3.OA.3, 3.OA.4, 3.OA.6, 3.OA.7, 3.OA.8** Mathematical Practices **MP.1, MP.3, MP.6, MP.8**

▶ Use Order of Operations

This exercise involves subtraction and multiplication:

$$10 - 3 \times 2$$

1. What do you get if you subtract first and then multiply? _____

2. What do you get if you multiply first and then subtract? _____

To make sure everyone has the same answer to problems like this one, people have decided that multiplication and division will be done *before* addition and subtraction. The answer you found in question 2 is correct.

If you want to tell people to add or subtract first, you must use parentheses. Parentheses mean "Do this first." For example, if you want people to subtract first in the exercise above, write it like this:

$$(10 - 3) \times 2$$

Find the answer.

3. $5 + 4 \times 2 =$ _____

4. $(9 - 3) \times 6 =$ _____

5. $8 \div 2 + 2 =$ _____

6. $6 \times (8 - 1) =$ _____

Rewrite each statement, using symbols and numbers instead of words.

7. Add 4 and 3, and multiply the total by 8. _____

8. Multiply 3 by 8, and add 4 to the total. _____

► **What's the Error?**

Dear Math Students,

Today I found the answer to 6 + 3 × 2.
Here is how I found the answer.

6 + 3 × 2

9 × 2 = 18

Is my answer correct? If not, please correct my work and tell me what I did wrong.

Your friend,
Puzzled Penguin

9. Write an answer to the Puzzled Penguin.

_____

_____

_____

Find the answer.

10. 4 + 3 × 5 = _____

11. 10 ÷ 2 + 3 = _____

12. 12 − 9 ÷ 3 = _____

13. 3 × 5 − 2 = _____

14. (4 + 3) × 5 = _____

15. 10 ÷ (2 + 3) = _____

16. (12 − 9) ÷ 3 = _____

17. 3 × (5 − 2) = _____

▶ Write First Step Questions

Write the first step question and answer.
Then solve the problem.

Show your work.

18. A roller coaster has 7 cars. Each car has 4 seats. If there were 3 empty seats, how many people were on the roller coaster?

_____

_____

19. Each week, Marta earns $10 babysitting. She always spends $3 and saves the rest. How much does she save in 8 weeks?

_____

_____

20. Abu bought 6 packs of stickers. Each pack had 8 stickers. Then Abu's friend gave him 10 more stickers. How many stickers does Abu have now?

_____

_____

21. Zoe made some snacks. She put 4 apple slices and 2 melon slices on each plate. She prepared 5 plates. How many slices of fruit did Zoe use in all?

_____

_____

22. Kyle ordered 8 pizzas for his party. Each pizza was cut into 8 slices. 48 of the slices were plain cheese, and the rest had mushrooms. How many slices of pizza had mushrooms?

_____

▶ Write First Step Questions (continued)

Write the first step question and answer.
Then solve the problem.

Show your work.

23. Nadia counted 77 birds on the pond. 53 were ducks, and the rest were geese. Then the geese flew away in 4 equal flocks. How many geese were in each flock?

_____

_____

24. Kagami baked 86 blueberry muffins. Her sisters ate 5 of them. Kagami divided the remaining muffins equally among 9 plates. How many muffins did she put on each plate?

_____

_____

25. Lucia had 42 plums. Jorge had 12 more plums than Lucia. Jorge divided his plums equally among 6 people. How many plums did each person get?

_____

_____

26. On his way to school, Kevin counted 5 mountain bikes and 3 road bikes. How many wheels were on the bikes altogether?

_____

_____

27. Juana has 21 shirts. Leslie had 7 less shirts than Juana, but then she bought 4 more. How many shirts does Leslie have now?

_____

Name

Date

CA CC Content Standards 3.0A.1, 3.0A.2, 3.0A.3, 3.0A.4, 3.0A.6, 3.0A.7, 3.0A.8 Mathematical Practices MP.1, MP.4

► Make Sense of Two Step Word Problems

Write an equation and solve the problem.

Show your work.

1. Nine hens laid 6 eggs each. Five of the eggs broke. How many eggs are left?

_____

2. There are 8 houses on Jeremiah's street. Each house has 1 willow tree, 6 apple trees, and 2 olive trees. How many trees are on Jeremiah's street in all?

_____

3. Tim has 9 marbles. Ryan has 3 fewer marbles than Tim. Leslie has 5 more marbles than Ryan. How many marbles does Leslie have?

_____

4. Mr. Helms has 2 stables with 4 horses in each stable. Ms. Martinez has 4 more horses than Mr. Helms. How many horses does Ms. Martinez have?

_____

5. Angela had $4. She bought 2 pumpkins for $1 each. How much money does Angela have now?

_____

6. Ahmad had $40. He bought an action figure for $5 and a backpack for $14. How much money does Ahmad have left?

_____

▶ **More Make Sense of Two Step Problems**

Write an equation and solve the problem.

Show your work.

7. In the locker room, there are 8 rows of 9 lockers. All of the lockers were full in the morning, but in the afternoon 6 were empty. How many lockers were full in the afternoon?

8. Anita received 3 postcards of zebras and 2 postcards of monkeys each month for 3 months. How many postcards is that?

9. The library has 2 books about the desert and 8 books about the rainforest. The books were divided into groups of 2. How many groups are there?

10. Each pack of pencils contains 8 pencils. Sahil bought 3 packs and divided them equally among 6 people. How many pencils did each person get?

11. James bought four 8-ounce bottles of water for a hiking trip. He drank 28 ounces. How many ounces of water are left?

12. Kaya has 20 photos of dogs and 30 photos of cats. She displayed an equal number of them on 10 posters for a fund raiser for an animal shelter. How many photos were on each poster?

CA CC Content Standards **3.OA.5, 3.OA.6, 3.OA.7, 3.NBT.3** Mathematical Practices **MP.5, MP.8**

► Multiply with Multiples of 10

When a number of ones is multiplied by 10, the ones become tens.

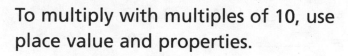

1 ten × 5 ones = 5 tens

$10 \times 5 =$ _____

To multiply with multiples of 10, use place value and properties.

$2 \times 3 \ = (2 \times 1) \times (3 \times 1) \ = (2 \times 3) \times (1 \times 1) \ = 6 \times 1 \ = 6$

$2 \times 30 = (2 \times 1) \times (3 \times 10) = (2 \times 3) \times (1 \times 10) = 6 \times 10 = 60$

Use a shortcut.

Find the basic multiplication product. Then multiply by 10.

2 × 30

$6 \times 10 = 60$

Multiply.

1. 6 × 40

$\times 10 =$ _____

2. 4 × 50

$\times 10 =$ _____

3. 70 × 8

$\times 10 =$ _____

4. 90 × 3

$\times 10 =$ _____

► Multiply Using Mental Math

Use a basic multiplication and mental math to complete.

5. $3 \times 4 =$ _____
    $3 \times 40 =$ _____

6. $1 \times 2 =$ _____
    $10 \times 2 =$ _____

7. $9 \times 8 =$ _____
    $9 \times 80 =$ _____

8. $2 \times 9 =$ _____
    $2 \times 90 =$ _____

9. $5 \times 5 =$ _____
    $5 \times 50 =$ _____

10. $3 \times 5 =$ _____
    $3 \times 50 =$ _____

11. $1 \times 1 =$ _____
    $10 \times 1 =$ _____

12. $2 \times 3 =$ _____
    $20 \times 3 =$ _____

13. $5 \times 6 =$ _____
    $5 \times 60 =$ _____

14. $2 \times 4 =$ _____
    $2 \times 40 =$ _____

15. $6 \times 3 =$ _____
    $6 \times 30 =$ _____

16. $9 \times 2 =$ _____
    $9 \times 20 =$ _____

17. $2 \times 30 =$ _____

18. $5 \times 40 =$ _____

19. $9 \times 60 =$ _____

20. $3 \times 80 =$ _____

21. $2 \times 70 =$ _____

22. $5 \times 90 =$ _____

23. $9 \times 50 =$ _____

24. $5 \times 20 =$ _____

25. $3 \times 30 =$ _____

26. $5 \times 80 =$ _____

27. $9 \times 90 =$ _____

28. $5 \times 60 =$ _____

29. $70 \times 5 =$ _____

30. $8 \times 50 =$ _____

31. $60 \times 4 =$ _____

32. Describe how to multiply a one-digit number and
    a multiple of 10. _____

► **PATH to FLUENCY** **Dashes 21–22, 19A–20A**

Complete each Dash. Check your answers on page 147.

Dash 21 2s, 3s, 4s, 5s, 9s Multiplications	Dash 22 2s, 3s, 4s, 5s, 9s Divisions	Dash 19A 6s, 7s, 8s Multiplications	Dash 20A 6s, 7s, 8s Divisions
a. $6 \times 3 =$ _____	a. $16 / 4 =$ _____	a. $9 \times 6 =$ _____	a. $24 \div 6 =$ _____
b. $4 \cdot 7 =$ _____	b. $54 \div 9 =$ _____	b. $7 * 7 =$ _____	b. $21 / 7 =$ _____
c. $8 * 2 =$ _____	c. $4 / 2 =$ _____	c. $3 \cdot 7 =$ _____	c. $42 \div 7 =$ _____
d. $5 \times 3 =$ _____	d. $28 \div 4 =$ _____	d. $6 \times 3 =$ _____	d. $16 / 8 =$ _____
e. $4 \cdot 4 =$ _____	e. $25 / 5 =$ _____	e. $7 * 8 =$ _____	e. $24 \div 8 =$ _____
f. $3 \cdot 9 =$ _____	f. $21 \div 3 =$ _____	f. $8 \cdot 6 =$ _____	f. $54 / 6 =$ _____
g. $9 \times 9 =$ _____	g. $40 / 4 =$ _____	g. $5 \times 6 =$ _____	g. $36 \div 6 =$ _____
h. $8 \cdot 9 =$ _____	h. $81 \div 9 =$ _____	h. $6 * 6 =$ _____	h. $48 / 8 =$ _____
i. $6 * 4 =$ _____	i. $35 / 5 =$ _____	i. $9 \cdot 8 =$ _____	i. $49 \div 7 =$ _____
j. $3 \times 3 =$ _____	j. $12 / 3 =$ _____	j. $7 \times 6 =$ _____	j. $64 / 8 =$ _____
k. $2 \cdot 7 =$ _____	k. $2 \div 2 =$ _____	k. $2 * 7 =$ _____	k. $48 \div 6 =$ _____
l. $8 \cdot 5 =$ _____	l. $63 / 9 =$ _____	l. $4 \cdot 7 =$ _____	l. $42 / 6 =$ _____
m. $4 \times 9 =$ _____	m. $36 \div 4 =$ _____	m. $3 \times 6 =$ _____	m. $32 \div 8 =$ _____
n. $9 \cdot 5 =$ _____	n. $18 / 2 =$ _____	n. $9 * 7 =$ _____	n. $56 / 7 =$ _____
o. $7 * 3 =$ _____	o. $9 \div 3 =$ _____	o. $6 \cdot 7 =$ _____	o. $63 \div 7 =$ _____
p. $2 \times 2 =$ _____	p. $36 / 9 =$ _____	p. $6 \times 9 =$ _____	p. $72 / 8 =$ _____
q. $8 \cdot 4 =$ _____	q. $40 \div 5 =$ _____	q. $8 * 7 =$ _____	q. $30 \div 6 =$ _____
r. $5 * 1 =$ _____	r. $12 \div 4 =$ _____	r. $6 \cdot 4 =$ _____	r. $18 / 6 =$ _____
s. $5 \times 5 =$ _____	s. $9 / 9 =$ _____	s. $7 \times 3 =$ _____	s. $56 \div 8 =$ _____
t. $6 \cdot 9 =$ _____	t. $14 \div 2 =$ _____	t. $8 * 8 =$ _____	t. $28 / 7 =$ _____

Name _____

► PATH to FLUENCY **Dashes 21A–22A, 19B–20B**

Complete each Dash. Check your answers on page 147.

Dash 21A 2s, 3s, 4s, 5s, 9s Multiplications	Dash 22A 2s, 3s, 4s, 5s, 9s Divisions	Dash 19B 6s, 7s, 8s Multiplications	Dash 20B 6s, 7s, 8s Divisions
a. $6 \times 9 =$ _____	a. $14 \div 2 =$ _____	a. $6 \times 2 =$ _____	a. $36 \div 6 =$ _____
b. $6 * 3 =$ _____	b. $16 / 4 =$ _____	b. $7 * 7 =$ _____	b. $63 / 7 =$ _____
c. $4 \cdot 7 =$ _____	c. $9 \div 9 =$ _____	c. $8 \cdot 5 =$ _____	c. $24 \div 8 =$ _____
d. $5 \times 5 =$ _____	d. $54 / 9 =$ _____	d. $4 \times 6 =$ _____	d. $18 / 6 =$ _____
e. $8 * 2 =$ _____	e. $12 \div 4 =$ _____	e. $3 * 7 =$ _____	e. $28 \div 7 =$ _____
f. $5 \cdot 1 =$ _____	f. $4 / 2 =$ _____	f. $1 \cdot 8 =$ _____	f. $48 / 8 =$ _____
g. $5 \times 3 =$ _____	g. $40 \div 5 =$ _____	g. $6 \times 9 =$ _____	g. $54 \div 6 =$ _____
h. $8 * 4 =$ _____	h. $28 / 4 =$ _____	h. $7 * 5 =$ _____	h. $42 / 7 =$ _____
i. $4 \cdot 4 =$ _____	i. $36 \div 9 =$ _____	i. $8 \cdot 3 =$ _____	i. $72 \div 8 =$ _____
j. $2 \times 2 =$ _____	j. $25 / 5 =$ _____	j. $4 \times 6 =$ _____	j. $6 / 6 =$ _____
k. $3 * 9 =$ _____	k. $9 \div 3 =$ _____	k. $9 * 7 =$ _____	k. $14 \div 7 =$ _____
l. $7 \cdot 3 =$ _____	l. $21 / 3 =$ _____	l. $8 \cdot 8 =$ _____	l. $56 / 8 =$ _____
m. $9 \times 9 =$ _____	m. $18 \div 2 =$ _____	m. $6 \times 1 =$ _____	m. $12 \div 6 =$ _____
n. $9 * 5 =$ _____	n. $40 / 4 =$ _____	n. $7 * 4 =$ _____	n. $7 / 7 =$ _____
o. $8 \cdot 9 =$ _____	o. $36 \div 4 =$ _____	o. $8 \cdot 6 =$ _____	o. $16 \div 8 =$ _____
p. $4 \times 9 =$ _____	p. $81 / 9 =$ _____	p. $7 \times 6 =$ _____	p. $30 / 6 =$ _____
q. $6 * 4 =$ _____	q. $63 \div 9 =$ _____	q. $2 * 7 =$ _____	q. $56 \div 7 =$ _____
r. $8 \cdot 5 =$ _____	r. $35 / 5 =$ _____	r. $9 \cdot 8 =$ _____	r. $8 / 8 =$ _____
s. $2 \times 7 =$ _____	s. $12 \div 3 =$ _____	s. $6 \times 5 =$ _____	s. $48 \div 6 =$ _____
t. $3 * 3 =$ _____	t. $2 / 2 =$ _____	t. $7 * 6 =$ _____	t. $21 / 7 =$ _____

Name _____

Complete each Dash. Check your answers on page 148.

Dash 21B 2s, 3s, 4s, 5s, 9s Multiplications	Dash 22B 2s, 3s, 4s, 5s, 9s Divisions	Dash 19C 6s, 7s, 8s Multiplications	Dash 20C 6s, 7s, 8s Divisions
a. 2 × 3 = ___	a. 8 ÷ 2 = ___	a. 6 × 8 = ___	a. 54 ÷ 6 = ___
b. 3 * 8 = ___	b. 18 / 3 = ___	b. 7 * 3 = ___	b. 49 / 7 = ___
c. 4 • 4 = ___	c. 12 ÷ 4 = ___	c. 8 • 6 = ___	c. 24 ÷ 8 = ___
d. 5 × 6 = ___	d. 25 / 5 = ___	d. 2 × 6 = ___	d. 6 / 6 = ___
e. 9 * 8 = ___	e. 63 ÷ 9 = ___	e. 8 * 7 = ___	e. 35 ÷ 7 = ___
f. 9 • 2 = ___	f. 16 / 2 = ___	f. 9 • 8 = ___	f. 72 / 8 = ___
g. 3 × 3 = ___	g. 3 ÷ 3 = ___	g. 6 × 4 = ___	g. 18 ÷ 6 = ___
h. 4 * 2 = ___	h. 28 / 4 = ___	h. 7 * 1 = ___	h. 28 / 7 = ___
i. 9 • 5 = ___	i. 45 ÷ 5 = ___	i. 8 • 3 = ___	i. 8 ÷ 8 = ___
j. 9 × 4 = ___	j. 27 / 9 = ___	j. 5 × 6 = ___	j. 30 / 6 = ___
k. 2 * 7 = ___	k. 12 ÷ 2 = ___	k. 9 * 7 = ___	k. 21 ÷ 7 = ___
l. 3 • 5 = ___	l. 12 / 3 = ___	l. 4 • 8 = ___	l. 40 / 8 = ___
m. 4 × 8 = ___	m. 20 ÷ 4 = ___	m. 6 × 6 = ___	m. 42 ÷ 6 = ___
n. 5 * 3 = ___	n. 40 / 5 = ___	n. 7 * 5 = ___	n. 63 / 7 = ___
o. 9 • 6 = ___	o. 54 ÷ 9 = ___	o. 8 • 8 = ___	o. 32 ÷ 8 = ___
p. 2 × 8 = ___	p. 2 / 2 = ___	p. 1 × 6 = ___	p. 36 / 6 = ___
q. 3 * 7 = ___	q. 9 ÷ 3 = ___	q. 2 * 7 = ___	q. 14 ÷ 7 = ___
r. 4 • 1 = ___	r. 36 / 4 = ___	r. 5 • 8 = ___	r. 56 / 8 = ___
s. 5 × 8 = ___	s. 15 ÷ 5 = ___	s. 6 × 9 = ___	s. 24 ÷ 6 = ___
t. 9 * 9 = ___	t. 9 / 9 = ___	t. 7 * 7 = ___	t. 42 / 7 = ___

► **PATH to FLUENCY** **Dashes 21C–22C, 19D–20D**

Complete each Dash. Check your answers on page 148.

Dash 21C 2s, 3s, 4s, 5s, 9s Multiplications	Dash 22C 2s, 3s, 4s, 5s, 9s Divisions	Dash 19D 6s, 7s, 8s Multiplications	Dash 20D 6s, 7s, 8s Divisions
a. $2 \times 9 =$ ___	a. $8 \div 2 =$ ___	a. $6 \times 9 =$ ___	a. $18 / 6 =$ ___
b. $3 * 7 =$ ___	b. $6 / 3 =$ ___	b. $7 * 6 =$ ___	b. $42 \div 7 =$ ___
c. $4 \cdot 5 =$ ___	c. $4 \div 4 =$ ___	c. $8 \cdot 2 =$ ___	c. $32 / 8 =$ ___
d. $5 \times 3 =$ ___	d. $20 / 5 =$ ___	d. $3 \times 6 =$ ___	d. $54 \div 6 =$ ___
e. $9 * 1 =$ ___	e. $63 \div 9 =$ ___	e. $4 * 7 =$ ___	e. $49 / 7 =$ ___
f. $1 \cdot 2 =$ ___	f. $16 / 2 =$ ___	f. $9 \cdot 8 =$ ___	f. $8 / 8 =$ ___
g. $4 \times 3 =$ ___	g. $15 \div 3 =$ ___	g. $6 \times 6 =$ ___	g. $30 \div 6 =$ ___
h. $4 * 1 =$ ___	h. $32 / 4 =$ ___	h. $7 * 2 =$ ___	h. $35 / 7 =$ ___
i. $7 \cdot 5 =$ ___	i. $30 \div 5 =$ ___	i. $8 \cdot 1 =$ ___	i. $48 \div 8 =$ ___
j. $9 \times 9 =$ ___	j. $45 / 9 =$ ___	j. $2 \times 6 =$ ___	j. $24 / 6 =$ ___
k. $2 * 3 =$ ___	k. $2 \div 2 =$ ___	k. $8 * 7 =$ ___	k. $14 \div 7 =$ ___
l. $3 \cdot 8 =$ ___	l. $21 / 3 =$ ___	l. $3 \cdot 8 =$ ___	l. $56 / 8 =$ ___
m. $4 \times 4 =$ ___	m. $12 \div 4 =$ ___	m. $6 \times 4 =$ ___	m. $6 \div 6 =$ ___
n. $5 * 2 =$ ___	n. $10 / 5 =$ ___	n. $7 * 5 =$ ___	n. $21 / 7 =$ ___
o. $9 \cdot 6 =$ ___	o. $9 \div 9 =$ ___	o. $8 \cdot 8 -$ ___	o. $40 \div 8 =$ ___
p. $6 \times 2 =$ ___	p. $12 / 2 =$ ___	p. $1 \times 6 =$ ___	p. $48 / 6 =$ ___
q. $9 * 3 =$ ___	q. $27 \div 3 =$ ___	q. $3 * 7 =$ ___	q. $56 \div 7 =$ ___
r. $6 \cdot 4 =$ ___	r. $20 / 4 =$ ___	r. $4 \cdot 8 =$ ___	r. $64 / 8 =$ ___
s. $5 \times 5 =$ ___	s. $40 \div 8 =$ ___	s. $6 \times 7 =$ ___	s. $36 \div 6 =$ ___
t. $3 * 9 =$ ___	t. $81 / 9 =$ ___	t. $7 * 7 =$ ___	t. $7 / 7 =$ ___

► Answers to Dashes 21–22, 19A–20B, 21A–22A

Use this sheet to check your answers to the Dashes on pages 143 and 144.

Dash 21 ×	Dash 22 ÷	Dash 19A ×	Dash 20A ÷	Dash 21A ×	Dash 22A ÷	Dash 19B ×	Dash 20B ÷
a. 18	a. 4	a. 54	a. 4	a. 54	a. 7	a. 12	a. 6
b. 28	b. 6	b. 49	b. 3	b. 18	b. 4	b. 49	b. 9
c. 16	c. 2	c. 21	c. 6	c. 28	c. 1	c. 40	c. 3
d. 15	d. 7	d. 18	d. 2	d. 25	d. 6	d. 24	d. 3
e. 16	e. 5	e. 56	e. 3	e. 16	e. 3	e. 21	e. 4
f. 27	f. 7	f. 48	f. 9	f. 5	f. 2	f. 8	f. 6
g. 81	g. 10	g. 30	g. 6	g. 15	g. 8	g. 54	g. 9
h. 72	h. 9	h. 36	h. 6	h. 32	h. 7	h. 35	h. 6
i. 24	i. 7	i. 72	i. 7	i. 16	i. 4	i. 24	i. 9
j. 9	j. 4	j. 42	j. 8	j. 4	j. 5	j. 24	j. 1
k. 14	k. 1	k. 14	k. 8	k. 27	k. 3	k. 63	k. 2
l. 40	l. 7	l. 28	l. 7	l. 21	l. 7	l. 64	l. 7
m. 36	m. 9	m. 18	m. 4	m. 81	m. 9	m. 6	m. 2
n. 45	n. 9	n. 63	n. 8	n. 45	n. 10	n. 28	n. 1
o. 21	o. 3	o. 42	o. 9	o. 72	o. 9	o. 48	o. 2
p. 4	p. 4	p. 54	p. 9	p. 36	p. 9	p. 42	p. 5
q. 32	q. 8	q. 56	q. 5	q. 24	q. 7	q. 14	q. 8
r. 5	r. 3	r. 24	r. 3	r. 40	r. 7	r. 72	r. 1
s. 25	s. 1	s. 21	s. 7	s. 14	s. 4	s. 30	s. 8
t. 54	t. 7	t. 64	t. 4	t. 9	t. 1	t. 42	t. 3

► Answers to Dashes 21B–22B, 19C–22C, 19D, 20D

Use this sheet to check your answers to the Dashes on pages 145 and 146.

Dash 21B ×	Dash 22B ÷	Dash 19C ×	Dash 20C ÷	Dash 21C ×	Dash 22C ÷	Dash 19D ×	Dash 20D ÷
a. 6	a. 4	a. 48	a. 9	a. 18	a. 4	a. 54	a. 3
b. 24	b. 6	b. 21	b. 7	b. 21	b. 2	b. 42	b. 6
c. 16	c. 3	c. 48	c. 3	c. 20	c. 1	c. 16	c. 4
d. 30	d. 5	d. 12	d. 1	d. 15	d. 4	d. 18	d. 9
e. 72	e. 7	e. 56	e. 5	e. 9	e. 7	e. 28	e. 7
f. 18	f. 8	f. 72	f. 9	f. 2	f. 8	f. 72	f. 1
g. 9	g. 1	g. 24	g. 3	g. 12	g. 5	g. 36	g. 5
h. 8	h. 7	h. 7	h. 4	h. 4	h. 8	h. 14	h. 5
i. 45	i. 9	i. 24	i. 1	i. 35	i. 6	i. 8	i. 6
j. 36	j. 3	j. 30	j. 5	j. 81	j. 5	j. 12	j. 4
k. 14	k. 6	k. 63	k. 3	k. 6	k. 1	k. 56	k. 2
l. 15	l. 4	l. 32	l. 5	l. 24	l. 7	l. 24	l. 7
m. 32	m. 5	m. 36	m. 7	m. 16	m. 3	m. 24	m. 1
n. 15	n. 8	n. 35	n. 9	n. 10	n. 2	n. 35	n. 3
o. 54	o. 6	o. 64	o. 4	o. 54	o. 1	o. 64	o. 5
p. 16	p. 1	p. 6	p. 6	p. 12	p. 6	p. 6	p. 8
q. 21	q. 3	q. 14	q. 2	q. 27	q. 9	q. 21	q. 8
r. 4	r. 9	r. 40	r. 7	r. 24	r. 5	r. 32	r. 8
s. 40	s. 3	s. 54	s. 4	s. 25	s. 5	s. 42	s. 6
t. 81	t. 1	t. 49	t. 6	t. 27	t. 9	t. 49	t. 1

Name _____ **Date** _____

CA CC Content Standards **3.0A.1, 3.0A.2, 3.0A.3, 3.0A.4, 3.0A.6, 3.0A.7, 3.0A.8** Mathematical Practices **MP.1, MP.2, MP.4, MP.5**

▶ Solve Two Step Word Problems

Write an equation and solve the problem.   *Show your work.*

1. Raul spent 10 minutes doing homework for each of 5 subjects and 15 minutes for another subject. How many minutes did Raul spend on his homework?

   _____

2. At Sonya's cello recital, there were 8 rows of chairs, with 6 chairs in each row. There was a person in each chair, and there were 17 more people standing. How many people were in the audience altogether?

   _____

3. Jana played a game with a deck of cards. She placed the cards on the floor in 3 rows of 10. If the deck has 52 cards, how many cards did Jana leave out?

   _____

4. Mukesh was making 7 salads. He opened a can of olives and put 6 olives on each salad. Then he ate the rest of the olives in the can. If there were 51 olives to start with, how many olives did Mukesh eat?

   _____

5. Peter wallpapered a wall that was 8 feet wide and 9 feet high. He had 28 square feet of wallpaper left over. How many square feet of wallpaper did he start with?

   _____

VOCABULARY
function table

► (PATH to FLUENCY) **What's My Rule?**

A **function table** is a table of ordered pairs. For every input number, there is only one output number. The rule describes what to do to the input number to get the output number.

Write the rule and then complete the function table.

6.

Rule: _____

Input	Output
7	12
8	___
___	54
6	36

7.

Rule: _____

Input	Output
81	9
45	5
72	___
___	7

8.

Rule: _____

Input	Output
4	28
8	56
6	___
7	___

9.

Rule: _____

Input	Output
32	8
8	2
___	3
24	___

10.

Rule: _____

Input	Output
21	7
27	9
___	6
15	___

11.

Rule: _____

Input	Output
5	25
___	40
9	___
3	15

► **PATH to FLUENCY** Play *Division Three-in-a-Row*

Rules for *Division Three-in-a-Row*

Number of players: 2
What You Will Need: Division Product Cards, one
Three-in-a-Row Game Grid for each player

1. Each player writes any nine quotients in the squares of a game grid. A player may write the same quotient more than once.

2. Shuffle the cards. Place them division side up in a stack in the center of the table.

3. Players take turns. On each turn, a player completes the division on the top card and then partners check the answer.

4. For a correct answer, if the quotient is on the game grid, the player puts an X through that grid square. If the answer is wrong, or if the quotient is not on the grid, the player doesn't mark anything. The player puts the card division side up on the bottom of the stack.

5. The first player to mark three squares in a row (horizontally, vertically, or diagonally) wins.

Name _____ **Date** _____

Three-in-a-Row Game Grids

2×2	$2 \bullet 3$	$2 * 4$	2×5
	Hint: What is $3 \cdot 2$?	Hint: What is $4 * 2$?	Hint: What is 5×2?

© Houghton Mifflin Harcourt Publishing Company

2×6	$2 \bullet 7$	$2 * 8$	2×9
Hint: What is 6×2?	Hint: What is $7 \cdot 2$?	Hint: What is $8 * 2$?	Hint: What is 9×2?

© Houghton Mifflin Harcourt Publishing Company

5×2	$5 \bullet 3$	$5 * 4$	5×5
Hint: What is 2×5?	Hint: What is $3 \cdot 5$?	Hint: What is $4 * 5$?	

© Houghton Mifflin Harcourt Publishing Company

5×6	$5 \bullet 7$	$5 * 8$	5×9
Hint: What is 6×5?	Hint: What is $7 \cdot 5$?	Hint: What is $8 * 5$?	Hint: What is 9×5?

© Houghton Mifflin Harcourt Publishing Company

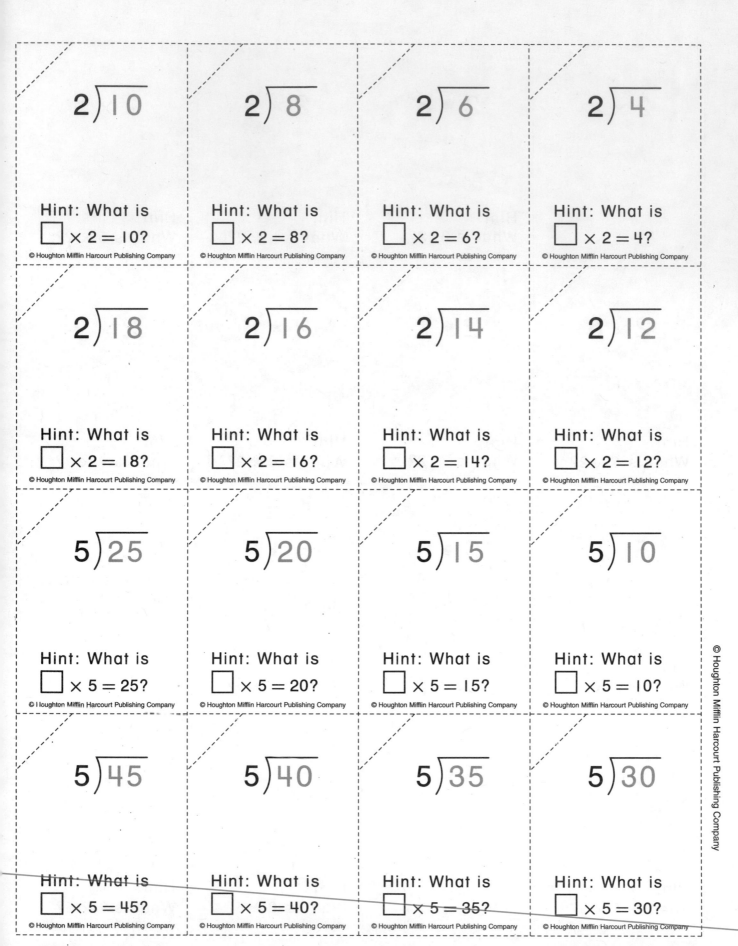

$2 \overline{)10}$

Hint: What is
$\square \times 2 = 10$?
© Houghton Mifflin Harcourt Publishing Company

$2 \overline{)8}$

Hint: What is
$\square \times 2 = 8$?
© Houghton Mifflin Harcourt Publishing Company

$2 \overline{)6}$

Hint: What is
$\square \times 2 = 6$?
© Houghton Mifflin Harcourt Publishing Company

$2 \overline{)4}$

Hint: What is
$\square \times 2 = 4$?
© Houghton Mifflin Harcourt Publishing Company

$2 \overline{)18}$

Hint: What is
$\square \times 2 = 18$?
© Houghton Mifflin Harcourt Publishing Company

$2 \overline{)16}$

Hint: What is
$\square \times 2 = 16$?
© Houghton Mifflin Harcourt Publishing Company

$2 \overline{)14}$

Hint: What is
$\square \times 2 = 14$?
© Houghton Mifflin Harcourt Publishing Company

$2 \overline{)12}$

Hint: What is
$\square \times 2 = 12$?
© Houghton Mifflin Harcourt Publishing Company

$5 \overline{)25}$

Hint: What is
$\square \times 5 = 25$?
© Houghton Mifflin Harcourt Publishing Company

$5 \overline{)20}$

Hint: What is
$\square \times 5 = 20$?
© Houghton Mifflin Harcourt Publishing Company

$5 \overline{)15}$

Hint: What is
$\square \times 5 = 15$?
© Houghton Mifflin Harcourt Publishing Company

$5 \overline{)10}$

Hint: What is
$\square \times 5 = 10$?
© Houghton Mifflin Harcourt Publishing Company

$5 \overline{)45}$

Hint: What is
$\square \times 5 = 45$?
© Houghton Mifflin Harcourt Publishing Company

$5 \overline{)40}$

Hint: What is
$\square \times 5 = 40$?
© Houghton Mifflin Harcourt Publishing Company

$5 \overline{)35}$

Hint: What is
$\square \times 5 = 35$?
© Houghton Mifflin Harcourt Publishing Company

$5 \overline{)30}$

Hint: What is
$\square \times 5 = 30$?
© Houghton Mifflin Harcourt Publishing Company

Product Cards: 2s, 5s, 9s

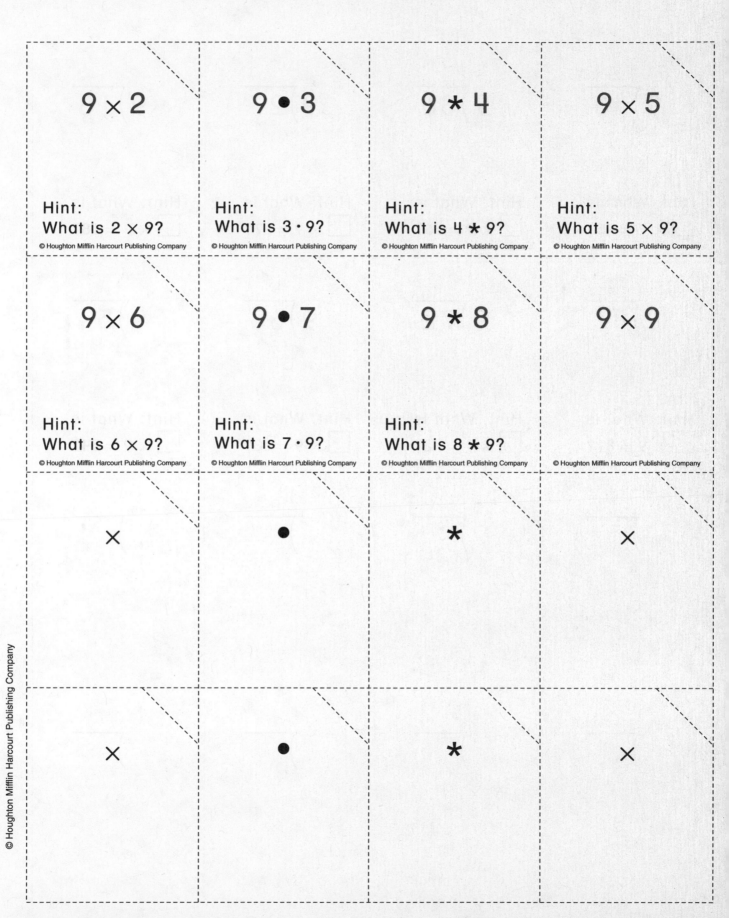

9×2	$9 \cdot 3$	$9 * 4$	9×5
Hint: What is 2×9?	**Hint:** What is $3 \cdot 9$?	**Hint:** What is $4 * 9$?	**Hint:** What is 5×9?
© Houghton Mifflin Harcourt Publishing Company	© Houghton Mifflin Harcourt Publishing Company	© Houghton Mifflin Harcourt Publishing Company	© Houghton Mifflin Harcourt Publishing Company
9×6	$9 \cdot 7$	$9 * 8$	9×9
Hint: What is 6×9?	**Hint:** What is $7 \cdot 9$?	**Hint:** What is $8 * 9$?	
© Houghton Mifflin Harcourt Publishing Company	© Houghton Mifflin Harcourt Publishing Company	© Houghton Mifflin Harcourt Publishing Company	© Houghton Mifflin Harcourt Publishing Company
×	•	*	×
×	•	*	×

You can write any numbers on the last 8 cards. Use them to practice difficult problems or if you lose a card.

$9\overline{)45}$

Hint: What is
☐ × 9 = 45?

$9\overline{)36}$

Hint: What is
☐ × 9 = 36?

$9\overline{)27}$

Hint: What is
☐ × 9 = 27?

$9\overline{)18}$

Hint: What is
☐ × 9 = 18?

$9\overline{)81}$

Hint: What is
☐ × 9 = 81?

$9\overline{)72}$

Hint: What is
☐ × 9 = 72?

$9\overline{)63}$

Hint: What is
☐ × 9 = 63?

$9\overline{)54}$

Hint: What is
☐ × 9 = 54?

You can write any numbers on the last 8 cards. Use them to practice difficult problems or if you lose a card.

Product Cards: 2s, 5s, 9s

3×2

Hint:
What is 2×3?
© Houghton Mifflin Harcourt Publishing Company

$3 \cdot 3$

© Houghton Mifflin Harcourt Publishing Company

$3 * 4$

Hint:
What is $4 * 3$?
© Houghton Mifflin Harcourt Publishing Company

3×5

Hint:
What is 5×3?
© Houghton Mifflin Harcourt Publishing Company

3×6

Hint:
What is 6×3?
© Houghton Mifflin Harcourt Publishing Company

$3 \cdot 7$

Hint:
What is $7 \cdot 3$?
© Houghton Mifflin Harcourt Publishing Company

$3 * 8$

Hint:
What is $8 * 3$?
© Houghton Mifflin Harcourt Publishing Company

3×9

Hint:
What is 9×3?
© Houghton Mifflin Harcourt Publishing Company

4×2

Hint:
What is 2×4?
© Houghton Mifflin Harcourt Publishing Company

$4 \cdot 3$

Hint:
What is $3 \cdot 4$?
© Houghton Mifflin Harcourt Publishing Company

$4 * 4$

© Houghton Mifflin Harcourt Publishing Company

4×5

Hint:
What is 5×4?
© Houghton Mifflin Harcourt Publishing Company

4×6

Hint:
What is 6×4?
© Houghton Mifflin Harcourt Publishing Company

$4 \cdot 7$

Hint:
What is $7 \cdot 4$?
© Houghton Mifflin Harcourt Publishing Company

$4 * 8$

Hint:
What is $8 * 4$?
© Houghton Mifflin Harcourt Publishing Company

4×9

Hint:
What is 9×4?
© Houghton Mifflin Harcourt Publishing Company

© Houghton Mifflin Harcourt Publishing Company

Product Cards: 3s, 4s

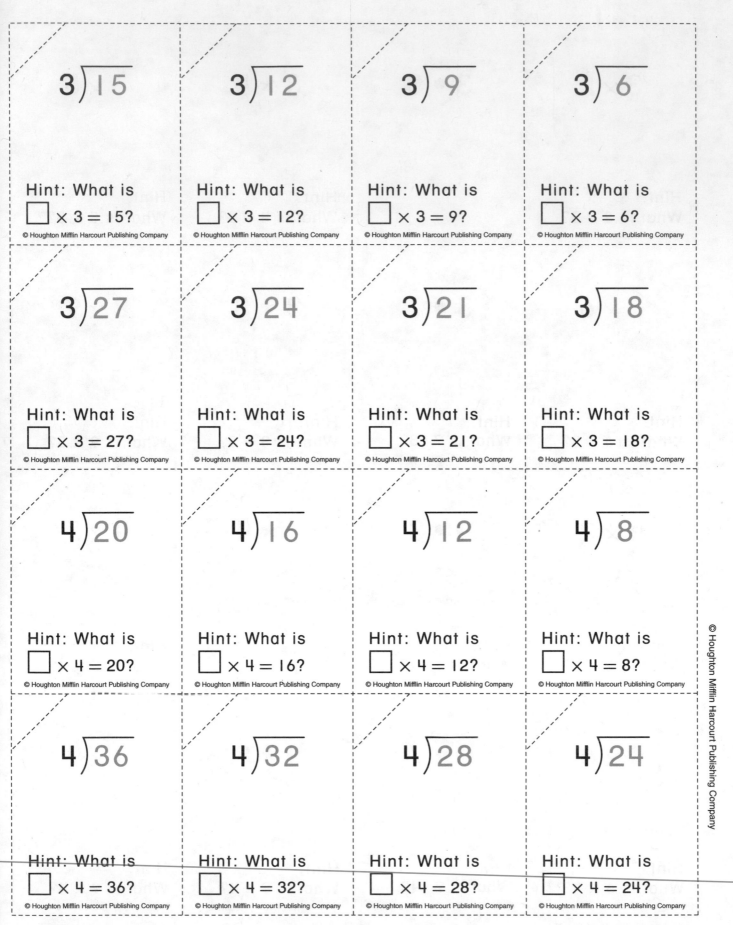

$3{\overline{\smash{)}15}}$ $3{\overline{\smash{)}12}}$ $3{\overline{\smash{)}9}}$ $3{\overline{\smash{)}6}}$

Hint: What is ☐ × 3 = 15?
© Houghton Mifflin Harcourt Publishing Company

Hint: What is ☐ × 3 = 12?
© Houghton Mifflin Harcourt Publishing Company

Hint: What is ☐ × 3 = 9?
© Houghton Mifflin Harcourt Publishing Company

Hint: What is ☐ × 3 = 6?
© Houghton Mifflin Harcourt Publishing Company

$3{\overline{\smash{)}27}}$ $3{\overline{\smash{)}24}}$ $3{\overline{\smash{)}21}}$ $3{\overline{\smash{)}18}}$

Hint: What is ☐ × 3 = 27?
© Houghton Mifflin Harcourt Publishing Company

Hint: What is ☐ × 3 = 24?
© Houghton Mifflin Harcourt Publishing Company

Hint: What is ☐ × 3 = 21?
© Houghton Mifflin Harcourt Publishing Company

Hint: What is ☐ × 3 = 18?
© Houghton Mifflin Harcourt Publishing Company

$4{\overline{\smash{)}20}}$ $4{\overline{\smash{)}16}}$ $4{\overline{\smash{)}12}}$ $4{\overline{\smash{)}8}}$

Hint: What is ☐ × 4 = 20?
© Houghton Mifflin Harcourt Publishing Company

Hint: What is ☐ × 4 = 16?
© Houghton Mifflin Harcourt Publishing Company

Hint: What is ☐ × 4 = 12?
© Houghton Mifflin Harcourt Publishing Company

Hint: What is ☐ × 4 = 8?
© Houghton Mifflin Harcourt Publishing Company

$4{\overline{\smash{)}36}}$ $4{\overline{\smash{)}32}}$ $4{\overline{\smash{)}28}}$ $4{\overline{\smash{)}24}}$

Hint: What is ☐ × 4 = 36?
© Houghton Mifflin Harcourt Publishing Company

Hint: What is ☐ × 4 = 32?
© Houghton Mifflin Harcourt Publishing Company

Hint: What is ☐ × 4 = 28?
© Houghton Mifflin Harcourt Publishing Company

Hint: What is ☐ × 4 = 24?
© Houghton Mifflin Harcourt Publishing Company

© Houghton Mifflin Harcourt Publishing Company

6×2

Hint:
What is 2×6?

$6 \cdot 3$

Hint:
What is $3 \cdot 6$?

$6 * 4$

Hint:
What is $4 * 6$?

6×5

Hint:
What is 5×6?

6×6

$6 \cdot 7$

Hint:
What is $7 \cdot 6$?

$6 * 8$

Hint:
What is $8 * 6$?

6×9

Hint:
What is 9×6?

7×2

Hint:
What is 2×7?

$7 \cdot 3$

Hint:
What is $3 \cdot 7$?

$7 * 4$

Hint:
What is $4 * 7$?

7×5

Hint:
What is 5×7?

7×6

Hint:
What is 6×7?

$7 \cdot 7$

$7 * 8$

Hint:
What is $8 * 7$?

7×9

Hint:
What is 9×7?

Product Cards: 6s, 7s, 8s

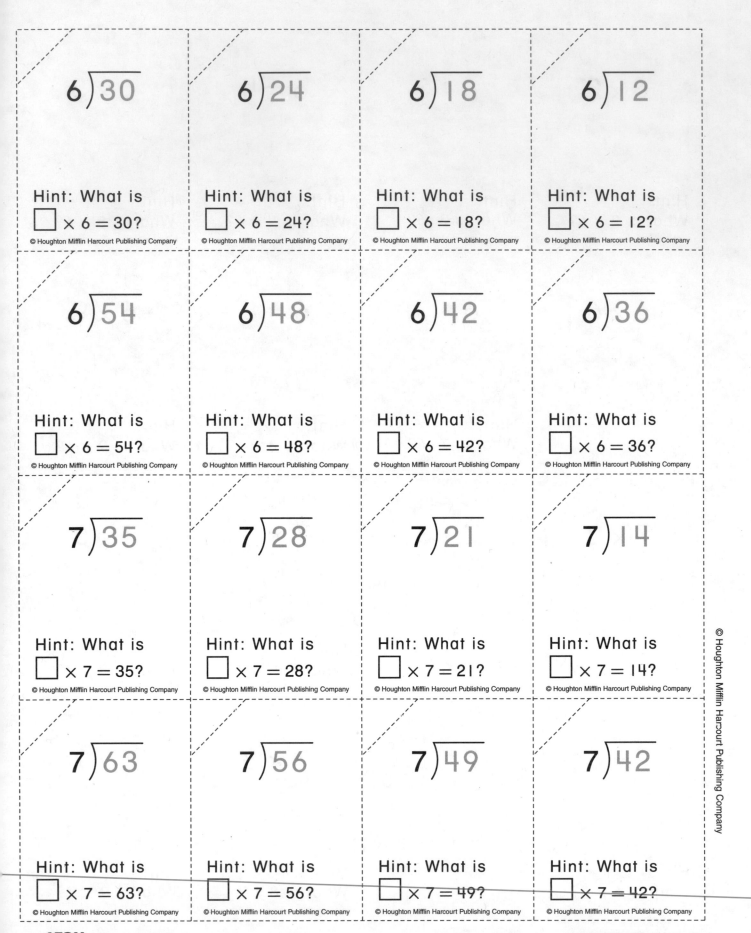

$6\overline{)30}$

Hint: What is
$\square \times 6 = 30$?

© Houghton Mifflin Harcourt Publishing Company

$6\overline{)24}$

Hint: What is
$\square \times 6 = 24$?

© Houghton Mifflin Harcourt Publishing Company

$6\overline{)18}$

Hint: What is
$\square \times 6 = 18$?

© Houghton Mifflin Harcourt Publishing Company

$6\overline{)12}$

Hint: What is
$\square \times 6 = 12$?

© Houghton Mifflin Harcourt Publishing Company

$6\overline{)54}$

Hint: What is
$\square \times 6 = 54$?

© Houghton Mifflin Harcourt Publishing Company

$6\overline{)48}$

Hint: What is
$\square \times 6 = 48$?

© Houghton Mifflin Harcourt Publishing Company

$6\overline{)42}$

Hint: What is
$\square \times 6 = 42$?

© Houghton Mifflin Harcourt Publishing Company

$6\overline{)36}$

Hint: What is
$\square \times 6 = 36$?

© Houghton Mifflin Harcourt Publishing Company

$7\overline{)35}$

Hint: What is
$\square \times 7 = 35$?

© Houghton Mifflin Harcourt Publishing Company

$7\overline{)28}$

Hint: What is
$\square \times 7 = 28$?

© Houghton Mifflin Harcourt Publishing Company

$7\overline{)21}$

Hint: What is
$\square \times 7 = 21$?

© Houghton Mifflin Harcourt Publishing Company

$7\overline{)14}$

Hint: What is
$\square \times 7 = 14$?

© Houghton Mifflin Harcourt Publishing Company

$7\overline{)63}$

Hint: What is
$\square \times 7 = 63$?

© Houghton Mifflin Harcourt Publishing Company

$7\overline{)56}$

Hint: What is
$\square \times 7 = 56$?

© Houghton Mifflin Harcourt Publishing Company

$7\overline{)49}$

Hint: What is
$\square \times 7 = 49$?

© Houghton Mifflin Harcourt Publishing Company

$7\overline{)42}$

Hint: What is
$\square \times 7 = 42$?

© Houghton Mifflin Harcourt Publishing Company

© Houghton Mifflin Harcourt Publishing Company

Product Cards: 6s, 7s, 8s

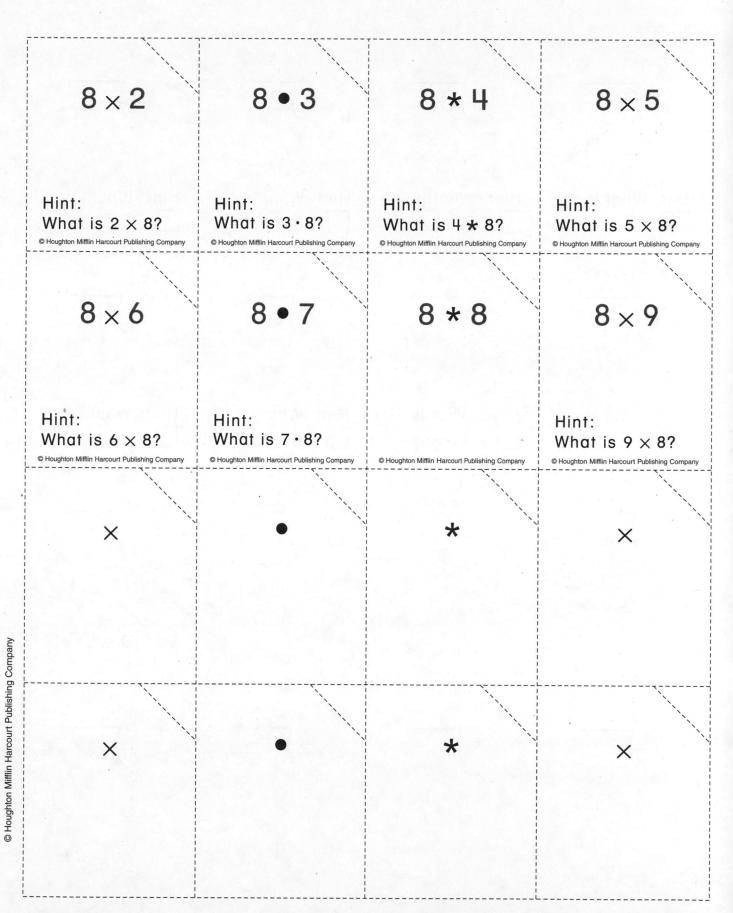

8 × 2

Hint:
What is 2 × 8?
© Houghton Mifflin Harcourt Publishing Company

8 • 3

Hint:
What is 3 • 8?
© Houghton Mifflin Harcourt Publishing Company

8 * 4

Hint:
What is 4 * 8?
© Houghton Mifflin Harcourt Publishing Company

8 × 5

Hint:
What is 5 × 8?
© Houghton Mifflin Harcourt Publishing Company

8 × 6

Hint:
What is 6 × 8?
© Houghton Mifflin Harcourt Publishing Company

8 • 7

Hint:
What is 7 • 8?
© Houghton Mifflin Harcourt Publishing Company

8 * 8

© Houghton Mifflin Harcourt Publishing Company

8 × 9

Hint:
What is 9 × 8?
© Houghton Mifflin Harcourt Publishing Company

×

•

*

×

×

•

*

×

© Houghton Mifflin Harcourt Publishing Company

You can write any numbers on the last 8 cards. Use them to practice difficult problems or if you lose a card.

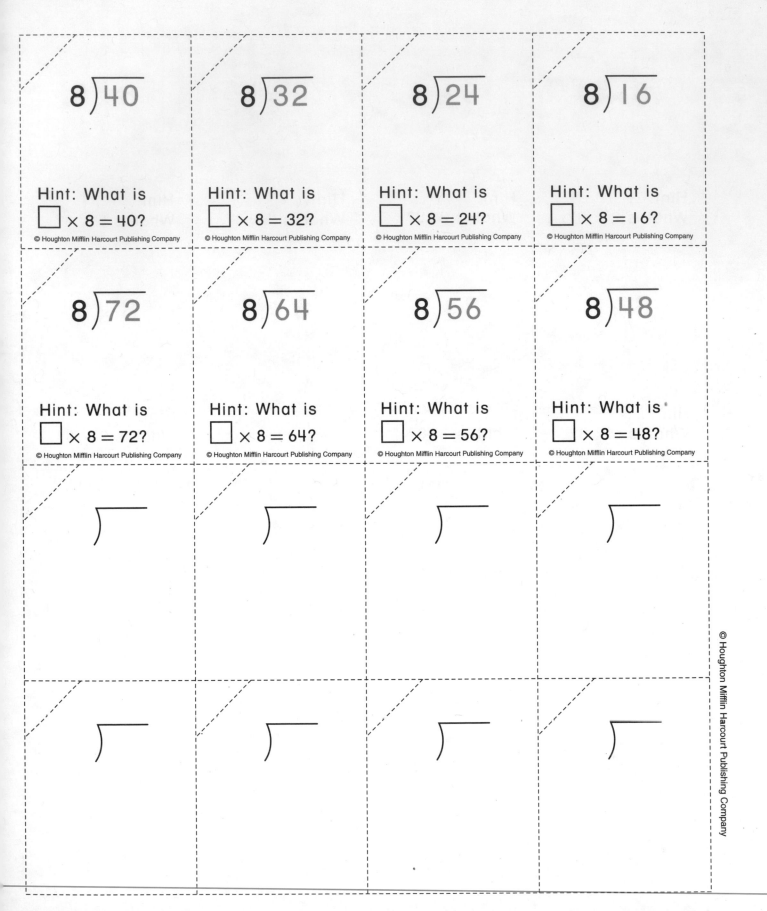

$8\overline{)40}$

Hint: What is
$\square \times 8 = 40$?

© Houghton Mifflin Harcourt Publishing Company

$8\overline{)32}$

Hint: What is
$\square \times 8 = 32$?

© Houghton Mifflin Harcourt Publishing Company

$8\overline{)24}$

Hint: What is
$\square \times 8 = 24$?

© Houghton Mifflin Harcourt Publishing Company

$8\overline{)16}$

Hint: What is
$\square \times 8 = 16$?

© Houghton Mifflin Harcourt Publishing Company

$8\overline{)72}$

Hint: What is
$\square \times 8 = 72$?

© Houghton Mifflin Harcourt Publishing Company

$8\overline{)64}$

Hint: What is
$\square \times 8 = 64$?

© Houghton Mifflin Harcourt Publishing Company

$8\overline{)56}$

Hint: What is
$\square \times 8 = 56$?

© Houghton Mifflin Harcourt Publishing Company

$8\overline{)48}$

Hint: What is
$\square \times 8 = 48$?

© Houghton Mifflin Harcourt Publishing Company

You can write any numbers on the last 8 cards. Use them to practice difficult problems or if you lose a card.

Product Cards: 6s, 7s, 8s

► **PATH to FLUENCY** **Diagnostic Checkup for Basic Multiplication**

1. $7 \times 5 =$ ___

2. $2 \times 3 =$ ___

3. $9 \times 9 =$ ___

4. $9 \times 6 =$ ___

5. $6 \times 2 =$ ___

6. $3 \times 0 =$ ___

7. $3 \times 4 =$ ___

8. $6 \times 8 =$ ___

9. $5 \times 9 =$ ___

10. $3 \times 3 =$ ___

11. $2 \times 9 =$ ___

12. $5 \times 7 =$ ___

13. $6 \times 10 =$ ___

14. $4 \times 1 =$ ___

15. $6 \times 4 =$ ___

16. $4 \times 8 =$ ___

17. $5 \times 2 =$ ___

18. $1 \times 3 =$ ___

19. $3 \times 9 =$ ___

20. $7 \times 6 =$ ___

21. $7 \times 2 =$ ___

22. $9 \times 0 =$ ___

23. $8 \times 9 =$ ___

24. $8 \times 7 =$ ___

25. $8 \times 10 =$ ___

26. $6 \times 3 =$ ___

27. $4 \times 4 =$ ___

28. $3 \times 8 =$ ___

29. $5 \times 5 =$ ___

30. $6 \times 0 =$ ___

31. $7 \times 9 =$ ___

32. $6 \times 6 =$ ___

33. $9 \times 2 =$ ___

34. $8 \times 3 =$ ___

35. $5 \times 4 =$ ___

36. $7 \times 7 =$ ___

37. $5 \times 10 =$ ___

38. $5 \times 1 =$ ___

39. $10 \times 9 =$ ___

40. $5 \times 6 =$ ___

41. $6 \times 5 =$ ___

42. $9 \times 3 =$ ___

43. $4 \times 2 =$ ___

44. $7 \times 8 =$ ___

45. $8 \times 2 =$ ___

46. $5 \times 0 =$ ___

47. $4 \times 9 =$ ___

48. $6 \times 7 =$ ___

49. $9 \times 5 =$ ___

50. $6 \times 1 =$ ___

51. $7 \times 4 =$ ___

52. $9 \times 8 =$ ___

53. $4 \times 10 =$ ___

54. $5 \times 3 =$ ___

55. $6 \times 9 =$ ___

56. $8 \times 6 =$ ___

57. $8 \times 5 =$ ___

58. $8 \times 0 =$ ___

59. $8 \times 4 =$ ___

60. $4 \times 7 =$ ___

61. $3 \times 5 =$ ___

62. $7 \times 3 =$ ___

63. $5 \times 9 =$ ___

64. $3 \times 6 =$ ___

65. $7 \times 10 =$ ___

66. $8 \times 1 =$ ___

67. $0 \times 4 =$ ___

68. $9 \times 7 =$ ___

69. $4 \times 5 =$ ___

70. $4 \times 3 =$ ___

71. $1 \times 9 =$ ___

72. $8 \times 8 =$ ___

► PATH to FLUENCY **Diagnostic Checkup for Basic Division**

1. 12 ÷ 2 = ___   2. 8 ÷ 1 = ___   3. 36 ÷ 9 = ___   4. 35 ÷ 7 = ___

5. 20 ÷ 5 = ___   6. 24 ÷ 3 = ___   7. 12 ÷ 4 = ___   8. 6 ÷ 6 = ___

9. 6 ÷ 2 = ___   10. 3 ÷ 3 = ___   11. 18 ÷ 9 = ___   12. 63 ÷ 7 = ___

13. 20 ÷ 10 = ___   14. 0 ÷ 1 = ___   15. 40 ÷ 4 = ___   16. 48 ÷ 8 = ___

17. 18 ÷ 2 = ___   18. 6 ÷ 3 = ___   19. 8 ÷ 4 = ___   20. 36 ÷ 6 = ___

21. 8 ÷ 2 = ___   22. 9 ÷ 1 = ___   23. 9 ÷ 9 = ___   24. 56 ÷ 7 = ___

25. 40 ÷ 5 = ___   26. 9 ÷ 3 = ___   27. 36 ÷ 4 = ___   28. 56 ÷ 8 = ___

29. 80 ÷ 10 = ___   30. 7 ÷ 1 = ___   31. 45 ÷ 9 = ___   32. 48 ÷ 6 = ___

33. 5 ÷ 5 = ___   34. 30 ÷ 3 = ___   35. 16 ÷ 4 = ___   36. 72 ÷ 8 = ___

37. 10 ÷ 2 = ___   38. 1 ÷ 1 = ___   39. 54 ÷ 9 = ___   40. 21 ÷ 7 = ___

41. 25 ÷ 5 = ___   42. 15 ÷ 3 = ___   43. 32 ÷ 4 = ___   44. 24 ÷ 8 = ___

45. 90 ÷ 10 = ___   46. 18 ÷ 3 = ___   47. 63 ÷ 9 = ___   48. 54 ÷ 6 = ___

49. 45 ÷ 5 = ___   50. 6 ÷ 1 = ___   51. 20 ÷ 4 = ___   52. 49 ÷ 7 = ___

53. 15 ÷ 5 = ___   54. 0 ÷ 3 = ___   55. 28 ÷ 4 = ___   56. 30 ÷ 6 = ___

57. 16 ÷ 2 = ___   58. 21 ÷ 3 = ___   59. 81 ÷ 9 = ___   60. 64 ÷ 8 = ___

61. 30 ÷ 5 = ___   62. 12 ÷ 3 = ___   63. 27 ÷ 9 = ___   64. 42 ÷ 7 = ___

65. 40 ÷ 10 = ___   66. 10 ÷ 1 = ___   67. 24 ÷ 4 = ___   68. 18 ÷ 6 = ___

69. 35 ÷ 5 = ___   70. 27 ÷ 3 = ___   71. 72 ÷ 9 = ___   72. 42 ÷ 6 = ___

► (PATH to FLUENCY) **Patterns With 10s, 5s, and 9s**

These multiplication tables help us see some patterns
that make recalling basic multiplications easier.

1. What pattern do you see in the
10s count-bys?

_____

2. Look at the 5s and the 10s together.
What patterns do you see?

_____

5's and 10s

×	1	2	3	4	5	6	7	8	9	10
1	1	2	3	4	5	6	7	8	9	10
2	2	4	6	8	10	12	14	16	18	20
3	3	6	9	12	15	18	21	24	27	30
4	4	8	12	16	20	24	28	32	36	40
5	5	10	15	20	25	30	35	40	45	50
6	6	12	18	24	30	36	42	48	54	60
7	7	14	21	28	35	42	49	56	63	70
8	8	16	24	32	40	48	56	64	72	80
9	9	18	27	36	45	54	63	72	81	90
10	10	20	30	40	50	60	70	80	90	100

3. Look at the 9s count-bys. How does
each 9s count-by relate to the
10s count-by in the next row?

_____

How could this pattern help you
remember the 9s count-bys?

_____

_____

9's

×	1	2	3	4	5	6	7	8	9	10
1	1	2	3	4	5	6	7	8	9	10
2	2	4	6	8	10	12	14	16	18	20
3	3	6	9	12	15	18	21	24	27	30
4	4	8	12	16	20	24	28	32	36	40
5	5	10	15	20	25	30	35	40	45	50
6	6	12	18	24	30	36	42	48	54	60
7	7	14	21	28	35	42	49	56	63	70
8	8	16	24	32	40	48	56	64	72	80
9	9	18	27	36	45	54	63	72	81	90
10	10	20	30	40	50	60	70	80	90	100

4. Look at the digits in each 9s product.
What is the sum of the digits in each
9s product?

_____

How could you use this knowledge to check
your answers when you multiply by 9?

_____

► PATH to FLUENCY **Patterns With Other Numbers**

On these grids, find patterns with 2s, 4s, 6s, and 8s.

5. Look at the ones digits in all the 2s, 4s, 6s, and 8s count-bys. What pattern do you see?

_____

6. Are the 2s, 4s, 6s, and 8s products even numbers or odd numbers?

_____

2's, 4's, 6's, 8's

×	1	2	3	4	5	6	7	8	9
1	1	2	3	4	5	6	7	8	9
2	2	4	6	8	10	12	14	16	18
3	3	6	9	12	15	18	21	24	27
4	4	8	12	16	20	24	28	32	36
5	5	10	15	20	25	30	35	40	45
6	6	12	18	24	30	36	42	48	54
7	7	14	21	28	35	42	49	56	63
8	8	16	24	32	40	48	56	64	72
9	9	18	27	36	45	54	63	72	81
10	10	20	30	40	50	60	70	80	90

On the multiplication table labeled Doubles, look for rows that have products that are double the product in other rows.

7. Name the factors that have products that are double the products of another factor.

_____

_____

_____

_____

Doubles

×	1	2	3	4	5	6	7	8	9
1	1	2	3	4	5	6	7	8	9
2	2	4	6	8	10	12	14	16	18
3	3	6	9	12	15	18	21	24	27
4	4	8	12	16	20	24	28	32	36
5	5	10	15	20	25	30	35	40	45
6	6	12	18	24	30	36	42	48	54
7	7	14	21	28	35	42	49	56	63
8	8	16	24	32	40	48	56	64	72
9	9	18	27	36	45	54	63	72	81
10	10	20	30	40	50	60	70	80	90

8. How can you find 6×8 if you know 3×8?

_____

Rewrite each list of numbers so that it is a count by list.

9. 4, 8, 12, 18, 20, 24, 28 _____

10. 18, 28, 36, 45, 54, 63, 70 _____

2-15
Class Activity
Name

Date

CA CC Content Standards 3.OA.3, 3.OA.4
Mathematical Practices MP.1, MP.2, MP.4, MP.5

► Math and Recipes

The animal keepers at zoos feed and care for the animals. The animal keepers consult a zoo nutritionist to decide what and how much to feed the animals. In the zoo kitchens there are recipes posted for each type of animal such as the one shown below.

Gorilla Zoo Stew	
32 carrots	8 yams
32 oranges	8 eggs
24 apples	16 bananas
64 ounces Monkey Chow	72 grapes
48 ounces primate-diet food	56 stalks of celery
8 heads lettuce, any variety	bales of hydroponic grass to taste
Toss all ingredients lightly. Divide among 8 trays.	
The recipe makes 8 gorilla servings.	

Write an equation and solve the problem.

1. How much of each ingredient is in 1 gorilla serving?

_____

_____

_____

2. How much of each ingredient in the Gorrilla Zoo Stew recipe is needed to serve 6 gorillas?

_____

_____

_____

► **Favorite Zoo Animals**

A third grade class took a field trip to a zoo. The students were asked to name their favorite zoo animal. The pictograph below shows the animals the students chose.

Favorite Zoo Animal

Bear	☺ ☺ ☺ ☺ ☺ ☺ ☺
Elephant	☺ ☺ ☺ ☺ ☺ ☺ ☺ ☺
Giraffe	☺ ☺ ☺ ☺
Gorilla	☺ ☺ ☺ ☺ ☺ ☺
Lion	☺ ☺

Each ☺ stands for 7 students

3. Use the information in the pictograph to complete the chart to show the number of students that chose each zoo animal.

Favorite Zoo Animal

Zoo Animal	Number of Students
Bear	
Elephant	
Giraffe	
Gorilla	
Lion	

Solve.

4. If 63 students chose a zebra as their favorite zoo animal, how many symbols would you use to show that on the pictograph?

Solve.

1. Write the numbers that complete the unknown number puzzle.

| 3 | 5 | 8 | 10 | 12 | 24 | 54 |

×	9		2
6		18	
	45	15	◯
	72	24	16

Explain how you found the number in the circle.

2. There are 56 books on a library cart. Each student helper puts 7 books on a shelf. How many student helpers are there?

For numbers 2a–2d, choose Yes or No to tell whether the equation could be used to solve the problem.

2a. $56 \times 7 = \boxed{}$ ○ Yes   ○ No

2b. $56 \div 7 = \boxed{}$ ○ Yes   ○ No

2c. $7 \times \boxed{} = 56$ ○ Yes   ○ No

2d. $7 \div \boxed{} = 56$ ○ Yes   ○ No

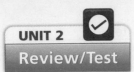

3. Raul makes a sign for the school fair. It has a length of 9 inches and a width of 8 inches. What is the area of the sign?

Draw a rectangle to help solve the problem. Label your drawing.

Write an equation to solve the problem.

Area of the sign: _____ square inches

4. For numbers 4a–4c, select True or False for each statement.

4a. The first step to solve $3 + 2 \times 4$ is $3 + 2$.

○ True   ○ False

4b. The first step to solve $5 \times 4 \div 2$ is 5×4

○ True   ○ False

4c. The first step to solve $(9 - 6) \div 3$ is $9 - 6$.

○ True   ○ False

5. Write a problem that can be solved using the given equation. Then solve.

$$7 \times 6 = \boxed{}$$

Solution: _____ tickets

6. Write the basic multiplication or division in the box that gives the unknown number. Use 8 or 9 for the unknown number.

$7 \times \boxed{} = 63$ $\qquad$ $36 \div 4 = \boxed{}$ $\qquad$ $24 \div \boxed{} = 3$

$4 \times \boxed{} = 32$ $\qquad$ $\boxed{} \times 9 = 72$ $\qquad$ $18 \div 2 = \boxed{}$

8	9

7. For numbers 7a–7d, choose Yes or No to tell whether the product is correct.

7a. $3 \times 30 = 900$ ○ Yes ○ No

7b. $5 \times 40 = 200$ ○ Yes ○ No

7c. $2 \times 40 = 800$ ○ Yes ○ No

7d. $9 \times 60 = 540$ ○ Yes ○ No

8. Carrie finds 7 seashells at the beach. Her brother finds 8 seashells. They divide the seashells equally among 3 people. How many seashells did each person get? Write an equation to solve the problem.

Equation: _____

_____ seashells

9. A toy store sells 7 different model cars. Each model car comes in 5 different colors. How many different model cars are there?

Part A

Solve the problem.

_____ different model cars

Part B

Choose the type of problem and the operation you use to solve.

The type is
| array |
| equal groups |
| area |

. The operation is
| multiplication |
| division |

.

Write another problem that is the same type.

```
┌─────────────────────────────────────────────┐
│                                             │
│                                             │
│                                             │
│                                             │
└─────────────────────────────────────────────┘
```

10. Write a question for the given information. Then write an equation and solve.

A museum has 297 visitors on Friday. It has 468 visitors on Saturday.

```
┌─────────────────────────────────────────────┐
│                                             │
│                                             │
│                                             │
└─────────────────────────────────────────────┘
```

Solution: _____ visitors

11. How can you use a pattern to find 6 × 9 if you know
3 × 9? Complete the given part of the multiplication
table to help you explain.

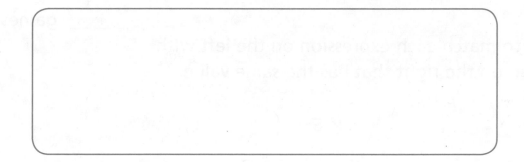

×	1	2	3	4	5	6	7	8	9
3									
6									

12. Select the equations that show square numbers.
Mark all that apply.

(A) 2 × 5 = 10   (D) 6 × 6 = 36

(B) 4 × 4 = 16   (E) 8 × 4 = 32

(C) 8 × 8 = 64   (F) 5 × 5 = 25

Draw a picture for one of the equations you chose.
Explain why it is a square number.

13. Read the problem. Write the first step question and answer.
Then write an equation to solve the problem.

A school buys games for 6 classrooms. It buys 3 board games,
4 puzzles games, and 1 video game for each classroom.
How many games does the school buy?

_____ games

14. Draw a line to match each expression on the left with
an expression on the right that has the same value.

7×40 •	• 5×6
$2 \times 4 \times 4$ •	• $7 \times 5 + 7 \times 2$
7×7 •	• $2 + 2$
$2 + 2 \times 4$ •	• 28×10
$5 \times 3 \times 2$ •	• 8×4
$8 \div 4 + 2$ •	• $2 + 8$

15. Choose the equations that make the statements true.

You know that
$3 \times 9 = 27$
$3 \times 5 = 15$
$8 \times 6 = 48$
$4 \times 7 = 28$
. So, you know that
$24 \div 3 = 8$
$18 \div 9 = 2$
$36 \div 6 = 6$
$48 \div 8 = 6$
.

Dear Family,

In this unit, students explore ways to measure things using the customary and metric systems of measurement.

The units of measure we will be working with include:

U.S. Customary System	**Metric System**
Length	**Length**
1 foot (ft) = 12 inches (in.) 1 yard (yd) = 3 feet (ft) 1 mile (mi) = 5,280 feet (ft)	1 meter (m) = 10 decimeters (dm) 1 meter (m) = 100 centimeters (cm) 1 decimeter (dm) = 10 centimeters (cm)
Capacity	**Capacity**
1 cup (c) = 8 fluid ounces (oz) 1 pint (pt) = 2 cups (c) 1 quart (qt) = 2 pints (pt) 1 gallon (gal) = 4 quarts (qt)	1 liter (L) = 1,000 milliliters (mL)
Weight	**Mass**
1 pound (lb) = 16 ounces (oz)	1 kilogram (kg) = 1,000 grams (g)

Students will solve problems that involve liquid volumes or masses given in the same unit by adding, subtracting, multiplying, or dividing and by using a drawing to represent the problem.

Students will also generate measurement data with halves and fourths of an inch such as hand spans and lengths of standing broad jumps and graph their data in a line plot.

You can help your child become familiar with these units of measure by working with measurements together. For example, you might estimate and measure the length of something in inches. You might use a measuring cup to explore how the cup can be used to fill pints, quarts, or gallons of liquid.

Thank you for helping your child learn important math skills. Please call if you have any questions or comments.

Sincerely,
Your child's teacher

© Houghton Mifflin Harcourt Publishing Company

 CA CC

Unit 3 addresses the following standards from the *Common Core State Standards for Mathematics with California Additions*: **3.OA.3, 3.NBT.2, 3.MD.1, 3.MD.2, 3.MD.3, 3.MD.4,** and for all Mathematical Practices.

Estimada familia:

En esta unidad los niños estudian cómo medir cosas usando el sistema usual de medidas y el sistema métrico decimal.

Las unidades de medida con las que trabajaremos incluirán:

Sistema usual	Sistema métrico decimal
Longitud	**Longitud**
1 pie (ft) = 12 pulgadas (pulg) 1 yarda (yd) = 3 pies (ft) 1 milla (mi) = 5,280 pies (ft)	1 metro (m) = 10 decímetros (dm) 1 metro (m) = 100 centímetros (cm) 1 decímetro (dm) = 10 centímetros (cm)
Capacidad	**Capacidad**
1 taza (tz) = 8 onzas líquidas (oz) 1 pinta (pt) = 2 tazas (tz) 1 cuarto (ct) = 2 pintas (pt) 1 galón (gal) = 4 cuartos (ct)	1 litro (L) = 1,000 mililitros (mL)
Peso	**Masa**
1 libra (lb) = 16 onzas (oz)	1 kilogramo (kg) = 1,000 gramos (g)

Los estudiantes resolverán problemas relacionados con volúmenes de líquido o masas, que se dan en la misma unidad, sumando, restando o dividiendo, y usando un dibujo para representar el problema.

También generarán datos de medidas, usando medios y cuartos de pulgada, de cosas tales como el palmo de una mano y la longitud de saltos largos, y representarán los datos en un diagrama de puntos.

Puede ayudar a que su niño se familiarice con estas unidades de medida midiendo con él diversas cosas. Por ejemplo, podrían estimar y medir la longitud de algo en pulgadas. Podrían usar una taza de medidas para aprender cómo se pueden llenar pintas, cuartos o galones con líquido.

Gracias por ayudar a su niño a aprender destrezas matemáticas importantes. Si tiene alguna duda o algún comentario, por favor comuníquese conmigo.

Atentamente,
El maestro de su niño

CA CC

En la Unidad 3 se aplican los siguientes estándares auxiliares, contenidos en los *Estándares estatales comunes de matemáticas con adiciones para California*: **3.OA.3, 3.NBT.2, 3.MD.1, 3.MD.2, 3.MD.3, 3.MD.4** y todos los de prácticas matemáticas.

VOCABULARY
line segment

▶ Units of Length

Circle length units and fractions of units to show the length of the **line segment**. Write the length.

1.

_____

2.

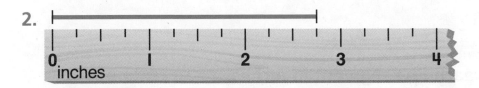

_____

3.

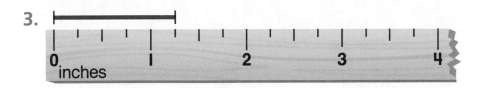

_____

4.

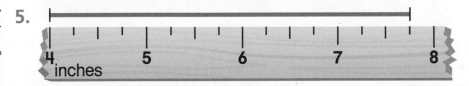

_____

5.

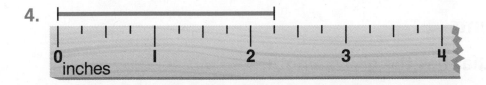

_____

6. Why is this ruler wrong?

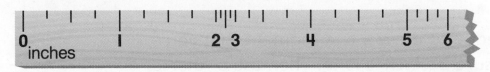

_____

_____

VOCABULARY
inch (in.)

▶ Estimate and Measure Length

Estimate the length of each line segment in inches.
Then measure it to the nearest $\frac{1}{2}$ inch.

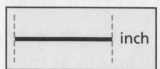
inch

7.

Estimate: _____ Actual: _____

8.

Estimate: _____ Actual: _____

Estimate the length of each line segment in inches.
Then measure it to the nearest $\frac{1}{4}$ inch.

9.

Estimate: _____ Actual: _____

▶ Draw Line Segments

Draw a line segment that has the given length.

10. 5 inches

11. $4\frac{1}{2}$ inches

12. $4\frac{3}{4}$ inches

13. Use a straightedge to draw a line segment that you
think will measure $2\frac{1}{2}$ inches long. Then use a ruler
to measure your line segment to the nearest $\frac{1}{4}$ inch.

_____

► Line Plots with Fractions

A **line plot** shows the frequency of data on a number line. In science class, students measured the lengths of leaves in a leaf collection. They measured the lengths to the nearest $\frac{1}{4}$ inch. The line plot shows the results.

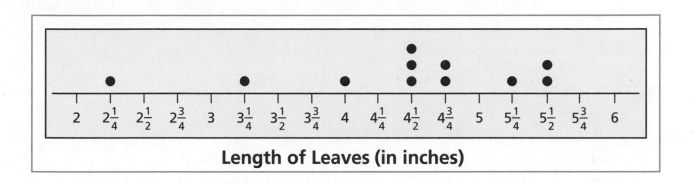

Length of Leaves (in inches)

Use the line plot to answer the questions.

14. How many leaves have a length of $4\frac{1}{2}$ inches? _____

15. How many leaves have a length that is less than 5 inches? _____

16. Write a question that can be answered using the line plot.

_____

_____

_____

▶ Make a Line Plot

Your teacher will ask each student to read his or her actual measure for the line segments you and your classmates drew with a straightedge on Student Activity Book page 168. Record the measures in the box below.

17. Use the measurement data from the box above to complete the line plot below.

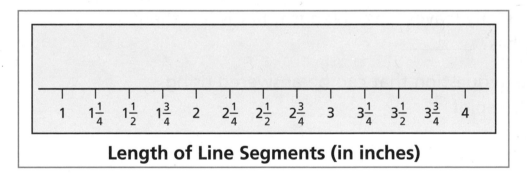

Length of Line Segments (in inches)

18. How many of the line segments have a measure of $2\frac{1}{2}$ inches?

_____

19. Which length appears the most often on the line plot?

Name _____ **Date** _____

CA CC Content Standards 3.OA.3, 3.MD.2
Mathematical Practices MP.1, MP.2, MP.3, MP.4, MP.6

> **VOCABULARY**
> liquid volume   cup (c)
> pint (pt)   quart (qt)
> gallon (gal)   fluid ounce
>   (fl oz)

► Choose the Unit

Choose the best unit to use to measure the liquid volume. Write *cup*, *pint*, *quart*, or *gallon*.

1. a carton of heavy cream

_____

2. a flower vase

_____

3. a swimming pool

_____

4. a wash tub

_____

► What's the Error?

Dear Math Students,

Today I had to choose the best unit to use to measure how much water is needed to fill a kitchen sink. I said the best unit to use is cups. Is my answer correct? If not, please correct my work and tell me what I did wrong.

Your friend,
Puzzled Penguin

5. Write an answer to Puzzled Penguin.

_____

_____

_____

6. Math Journal Think of a container. Choose the unit you would use to measure its capacity. Draw the container and write the name of the unit you chose. Explain why you chose that unit.

▶ Estimate Customary Units of Liquid Volume

Ring the better estimate.

7.

   2 cups

   2 quarts

8.

   5 cups

   5 gallons

9.

   1 pint

   1 gallon

10.

    1 cup

    1 pint

11.

    1 cup

    1 gallon

12.

    30 cups

    30 gallons

Solve.

13. Jamie makes a shopping list for a picnic with his four friends. He estimates that he'll need 5 quarts of lemonade for the group to drink. Do you think his estimate is reasonable? Explain.

_____

_____

► Use Drawings to Solve Problems

Use the drawing to represent and solve the problem.

14. A painter mixed 5 pints of yellow and 3 pints of blue paint to make green paint. How many pints of green paint did he make?

_____

15. Ryan bought a bottle of orange juice that had 16 fluid ounces. He poured 6 fluid ounces in a cup. How many fluid ounces are left in the bottle?

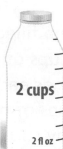

_____

16. A restaurant made 8 quarts of tea. They used all the tea to fill pitchers that hold 2 quarts each. How many pitchers were filled with tea?

_____

17. An ice cream machine makes 5 pints of ice cream in a batch. If 3 batches were made, how many pints of ice cream were made?

_____

18. Fran has a water jug that holds 24 quarts of water. She fills it with a container that holds 4 quarts. How many times must she fill the 4-quart container and pour it into the jug to fill the jug with 24 quarts?

_____

▶ Solve Problems

Use the drawing to represent and solve the problem.

Show Your Work.

19. Shanna bought 8 juice boxes filled with her favorite juice. Each box holds 10 fluid ounces. How many fluid ounces of her favorite juice did Shanna buy?

_____

20. Juana filled her punch bowl with 12 cups of punch. She gave some of her friends each a cup of punch. There are 7 cups of punch left in the bowl. How many cups did she give to friends?

_____

21. Mrs. Chavez made 20 quarts of pickles. She made 4 quarts each day. How many days did it take her to make the pickles?

_____

22. The sandwich shop began the day with 24 pints of apple cider. They sold 18 pints in the morning and the rest in the afternoon. How many pints of cider did they sell in the afternoon?

_____

23. A mid-sized aquarium holds 25 gallons of water and a large aquarium holds 35 gallons of water. How many gallons of water is needed to fill both aquariums?

▶ Choose the Appropriate Unit

**Choose the unit you would use to measure the
liquid volume of each. Write *mL* or *L*.**

1. a kitchen sink _____

2. a soup spoon _____

3. a teacup _____

4. a washing machine _____

Circle the better estimate.

5. a juice container   1 L   1 mL

6. a bowl of soup   500 L   500 mL

▶ Use Drawings to Represent Problems

**Use the drawing to represent and
solve the problem.**

7. There were 900 milliliters of water in a
pitcher. Terri poured 500 milliliters of
water into a bowl. How many milliliters
of water are left in the pitcher?

_____

8. Mr. Rojo put 6 liters of fuel into a gas
can that can hold 10 liters. Then he
added more liters to fill the can. How
many liters of fuel did he add to the can?

_____

9. Shelby needs to water each of her
3 plants with 200 milliliters of water. How
many milliliters of water does she need?

_____

► Make Sense of Problems Involving Liquid Volume

Use the drawing to represent and solve the problem.

10. The deli sold 24 liters of lemonade in 3 days. The same amount was sold each day. How many liters of lemonade did the deli sell each day?

_____

11. Tim has a bucket filled with 12 liters of water and a bucket filled with 20 liters of water. What is the total liquid volume of the buckets?

_____

12. Bella made a smoothie and gave her friend 250 milliliters. There are 550 milliliters left. How many milliliters of smoothie did Sara make?

_____

Solve. Use a drawing if you need to.

13. Diane has 36 cups of lemonade to divide equally among 4 tables. How many cups should she put at each table?

_____

14. Mr. Valle filled 7 jars with his famous barbeque sauce. Each jar holds 2 pints. How many pints of sauce did he have?

_____

► Choose the Appropriate Unit

Choose the unit you would use to measure the weight of each. Write *pound or ounce*.

1. a backpack full of books

_____

2. a couch

_____

3. a peanut

_____

4. a pencil

_____

Circle the better estimate.

5. a student desk   3 lb   30 lb

6. a television   20 oz   20 lb

7. a hamster   5 oz   5 lb

8. a slice of cheese   1 lb   1 oz

► Use Drawings to Represent Problems

Use the drawing to represent and solve the problem.

9. Selma filled each of 3 bags with 5 ounces of her favorite nuts. How many ounces of nuts did she use altogether to fill the bags?

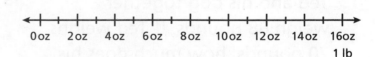

_____

10. Two apples together weigh 16 ounces. If one apple weighs 9 ounces, how much does the other apple weigh?

_____

► Use Drawings to Represent Problems (continued)

Use the drawing to represent and solve the problem.

11. Noah bought 16 ounces of turkey meat. If he uses 4 ounces to make a turkey patty, how many patties can he make?

12. A package of silver beads weighs 6 ounces and a package of wooden beads weighs 7 ounces more. How much does the package of wooden beads weigh?

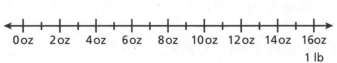

► Solve Word Problems

Solve. Use a drawing if you need to.

13. Ted and his dog together weigh 88 pounds. If Ted weighs 70 pounds, how much does his dog weigh?

14. Emma has 20 ounces of popcorn kernels in a bag. If she pops 4 ounces of kernels at a time, how many times can Emma pop corn?

15. Susan mailed 3 packages. Each package weighed 20 ounces. What was the total weight of the 3 packages?

16. Bailey caught two fish. The smaller fish weighs 14 ounces and the larger fish weighs 6 ounces more. How much does the larger fish weigh?

► Choose the Appropriate Unit

Choose the unit you would use to measure the mass of each. Write *gram* or *kilogram*.

17. an elephant

_____

18. a crayon

_____

19. a stamp

_____

20. a dog

_____

Circle the better estimate.

21. a pair of sunglasses	150 g	150 kg
22. a horse	6 kg	600 kg
23. a watermelon	40 g	4 kg
24. a quarter	500 g	5 g

► Use Drawings to Represent Problems

Use the drawing to represent and solve the problem.

25. Zach wants to buy 900 grams of pumpkin seed. The scale shows 400 grams. How many more grams does he need?

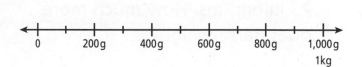

_____

26. Laura had 800 grams of fruit snacks. She put an equal amount into each of 4 containers. How many grams did she put in each container?

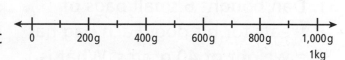

_____

▶ Solve Word Problems

Use the drawing to represent and solve the problem.

27. Nancy used 30 grams of strawberries and 45 grams of apples in her salad. How many grams of fruit altogether did she put in her salad?

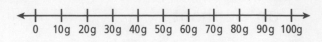

_____

28. Three people each donated a 20-kilogram bag of dog food to the animal shelter. How many kilograms of dog food was donated altogether?

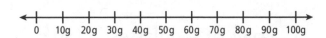

_____

Solve. Use a drawing if you need to.

29. Barry weighs 40 kilograms and his younger brother weighs 25 kilograms. How much more does Barry weigh?

_____

30. Jolie made 3 necklaces that have a total weight of 180 grams. If each necklace weighs the same, how much would each necklace weigh?

_____

31. Dan bought 6 small bags of treats for his dog. Each bag has a weight of 40 grams. What is the total weight of all the bags?

_____

32. Carrie has a dog and a cat. Together they have a mass of 21 kilograms. If the cat has a mass of 9 kilograms, what is the mass of Carrie's dog?

_____

Customary Units of Weight and Metric Units of Mass

▶ What's the Error?

Dear Math Students,

Today I had to solve this problem: *Toby bought 3 bags of chips. Each bag of chips weighs 50 grams. What is the weight of all 3 bags of chips? Here is how I solved the problem.*

$50 + 3 = 53$; 53 grams

Is my answer correct? If not, please correct my work and tell me what I did wrong. How do you know my answer is wrong?

Your friend,
Puzzled Penguin

33. Write an answer to the Puzzled Penguin.

_____

_____

_____

_____

Solve.   *Show your work.*

34. A tennis ball weighs 60 grams. A golf ball weighs 45 grams. How many grams do the tennis ball and golf ball weigh altogether?

35. How many more grams does the tennis ball weigh than the golf ball?

36. Gary bought 10 slices of ham at the deli. Each slice weighed 2 ounces. How many ounces of ham did Gary buy?

37. Sadie had 40 grams of sunflower seeds. She divided the seeds evenly among her 5 friends. How many grams did each friend get?

► Choose the Better Estimate

Circle the better estimate.

38.

200 grams

200 kilograms

39.

10 kilograms

10 grams

40.

3 ounces

3 pounds

41.

100 pounds

10 ounces

42.

100 pounds

1 ton

43.

1 kilogram

10 kilograms

Solve.

44. Suzie estimated the weights of objects and ordered them by the estimates of their weights. She explained that estimating them was easy since the smallest objects weighed the least and the largest objects weighed the most. Do you agree with Suzie?

CA CC Content Standards 3.OA.3, 3.MD.2
Mathematical Practices MP.1

Name _____ **Date** _____

► **Make Sense of Problems About Liquid Volume**

Solve. Use drawings if you need to.   *Show your work.*

1. Fran works in a science lab. She poured
   80 milliliters of liquid into each of 4 test tubes.
   How many milliliters of liquid did Fran pour into
   the test tubes altogether?

   _____

2. Nicholas wants to buy a bottle of shampoo.
   A large bottle has 375 milliliters of shampoo and
   a small bottle has 250 milliliters of shampoo.
   How many more milliliters of shampoo is in the
   larger bottle?

   _____

3. Allison used two containers of water to fill her
   aquarium. She used a container filled with 18 liters
   of water and another with 12 liters of water.
   What is the total liquid volume of the aquarium?

   _____

4. The coffee shop sold 28 liters of hot chocolate.
   If the same amount is sold each hour for 4 hours,
   how many liters of hot chocolate did the coffee
   shop sell each hour?

   _____

5. A recipe calls for 50 milliliters of milk. Eva has a
   spoon that holds 10 milliliters. How many times will
   Eva need to fill the spoon to follow the recipe?

   _____

► **Make Sense of Problems About Masses**

Solve. Use drawings if you need to.   *Show your work.*

6. A bag of green beans has a mass of 335 grams. A bag of peas has a mass of 424 grams. What is the total mass of both bags?

   _____

7. An average sized chicken egg has a mass of 60 grams. What would be the total mass of a half dozen eggs?

   _____

8. A kangaroo and her joey together have a mass of 75 kilograms. If the mother kangaroo has a mass of 69 kilograms, what is the mass of the joey?

   _____

9. Liam and 2 of his friends have backpacks. The backpacks have masses of 6 kilograms, 4 kilograms, and 5 kilograms. What is the total mass of the three backpacks?

   _____

10. Graham bought 4 bags of sunflower seeds. Each bag has 60 grams of seeds. Luke bought 3 bags of pumpkin seeds. Each bag has 80 grams of seeds. Who bought more grams of seeds, Graham or Luke? Explain.

    _____

Dear Family,

In math class, your child is beginning lessons about time. This topic is directly connected to home and community and involves skills your child will use often in everyday situations.

Students are reading time to the hour, half-hour, quarter-hour, five minutes, and minute, as well as describing the time before the hour and after the hour.

For example, you can read 3:49 both as after and before the hour.

Forty-nine minutes after three

Eleven minutes before four

Students will be using clocks to solve problems about elapsed time.

Help your child read time and find elapsed time. Ask your child to estimate how long it takes to do activities such as eating a meal, traveling to the store, or doing homework. Have your child look at the clock when starting an activity and then again at the end of the activity. Ask how long the activity took.

Your child will also learn to add and subtract time on a number line.

If you have any questions or comments, please call or write to me.

Sincerely,
Your child's teacher

CA CC

Unit 3 addresses the following standards from the *Common Core State Standards for Mathematics with California Additions*: **3.OA.3, 3.NBT.2, 3.MD.1, 3.MD.2, 3.MD.3, 3.MD.4**, and for all Mathematical Practices.

Estimada familia:

En la clase de matemáticas su niño está comenzando lecciones que le enseñan sobre la hora. Este tema se relaciona directamente con la casa y la comunidad, y trata de destrezas que su niño usará a menudo en situaciones de la vida diaria.

Los estudiantes leerán la hora, la media hora, el cuarto de hora, los cinco minutos y el minuto; también describirán la hora antes y después de la hora en punto.

Por ejemplo, 3:49 se puede leer de dos maneras:

Las tres y cuarenta y nueve   Once para las cuatro

Los estudiantes usarán relojes para resolver problemas acerca del tiempo transcurrido en diferentes situaciones.

Ayude a su niño a leer la hora y hallar el tiempo transcurrido. Pídale que estime cuánto tiempo tomarán ciertas actividades, tales como comer una comida completa, ir a la tienda o hacer la tarea. Pida a su niño que vea el reloj cuando comience la actividad y cuando la termine. Pregúntele cuánto tiempo tomó la actividad.

Su niño también aprenderá a sumar y restar tiempo en una recta numérica.

Si tiene alguna pregunta o algún comentario, por favor comuníquese conmigo.

Atentamente,
El maestro de su niño

© Houghton Mifflin Harcourt Publishing Company

CA CC

En la Unidad 3 se aplican los siguientes estándares auxiliares, contenidos en los *Estándares estatales comunes de matemáticas con adiciones para California*: 3.OA.3, 3.NBT.2, 3.MD.1, 3.MD.2, 3.MD.3, 3.MD.4 y todos los de prácticas matemáticas.

► Make an Analog Clock

Attach the clock hands to the clock face using a prong fastener.

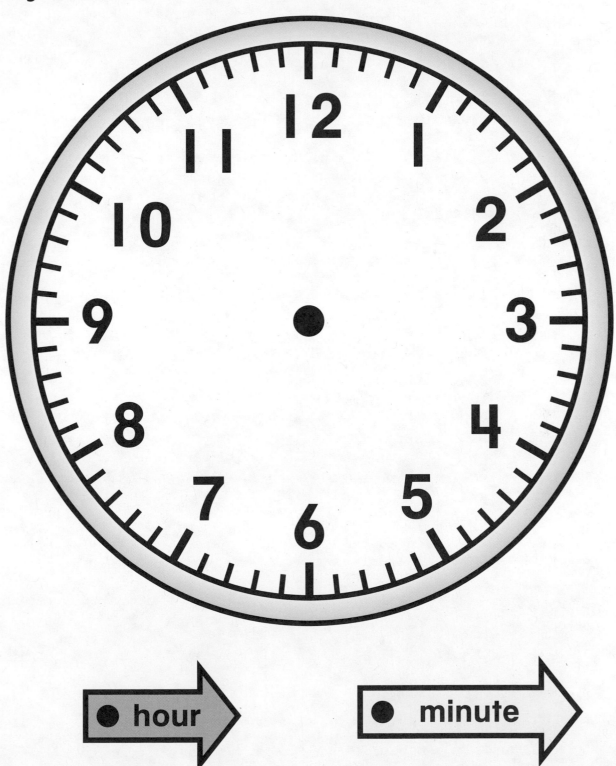

Paper Clock

Name _____   Date _____

CA CC Content Standards 3.MD.1
Mathematical Practices MP.5

▶ Time to 15 Minutes

Write the time on the digital clock. Then write how to say the time.

1.

2.

3.

4.

_____

Write the time on the digital clock. Write two ways to say the time.

5.

6.

7.

8.

_____

9.

10.

11.

12.

_____

▶ Show Time to 15 Minutes

Draw the hands on the analog clock. Write the time on the digital clock.

13. nine fifteen

14. half past seven

15. three o'clock

16. seven thirty

17. one forty-five

18. fifteen minutes after two

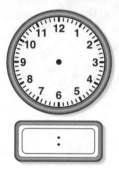

▶ Times of Daily Activities

19. Complete the table.

Time	Light or Dark	Part of the Day	Activity
3:15 A.M.			
8:00 A.M.			
2:30 P.M.			
6:15 P.M.			
8:45 P.M.			

► Time to 5 Minutes

Write the time on the digital clock. Then write how to say the time.

20.

[:]

_____

21.

[:]

_____

22.

[:]

_____

23.

[:]

_____

24.

[   ]

_____

25.

[   ]

_____

26.

[   ]

_____

27.

[   ]

_____

Write the time on the digital clock.

28. ten minutes after eight

[:]

29. seven twenty-five

[:]

30. eleven fifty

[:]

31. six forty

[   ]

32. five minutes after three

[   ]

33. four fifty-five

[   ]

► Time to 1 Minute

Write the time on the digital clock. Then write how to say the time.

34.

[:]

35.

[:]

36.

[:]

37.

[:]

38.

[ ]

39.

[ ]

40.

[ ]

41.

[ ]

Write the time on the digital clock.

42. ten fourteen

[:]

43. fifty-two minutes after eight

[:]

44. seven twenty-eight

[:]

45. nine thirty-one

[ ]

46. forty-six minutes after eleven

[ ]

47. thirty-seven minutes after 5

[ ]

► Times Before and After the Hour to 5 Minutes

Write the time as minutes *after* an hour and minutes *before* an hour.

1.

_____

_____

2.

_____

_____

3.

_____

_____

4.

_____

_____

5.

_____

_____

6.

_____

_____

7.

_____

_____

8.

_____

_____

9.

_____

_____

▶ Times Before and After the Hour to 1 Minute

Write the time as minutes *after* an hour and minutes *before* an hour.

10.

_____

_____

11.

_____

_____

12.

_____

_____

13.

_____

_____

14.

_____

_____

15.

_____

_____

16.

_____

_____

17.

_____

_____

18.

_____

_____

Name _____ Date _____

CA CC Content Standards **3.MD.1**
Mathematical Practices **MP.1**

► Elapsed Time in Minutes and Hours

1. Find the **elapsed time**.

Start Time	End Time	Elapsed Time
4:00 P.M.	7:00 P.M.	
7:45 A.M.	8:15 A.M.	
2:17 P.M.	7:17 P.M.	
11:00 A.M.	2:00 P.M.	
11:55 A.M.	4:25 P.M.	

2. Find the end time.

Start Time	Elapsed Time	End Time
1:00 P.M.	2 hours	
4:15 A.M.	4 hours	
4:55 P.M.	18 minutes	
2:15 A.M.	1 hour and 15 minutes	
11:55 A.M.	2 hours and 5 minutes	

3. Find the start time.

Start Time	Elapsed Time	End Time
	3 hours	4:15 P.M.
	15 minutes	2:45 P.M.
	2 hours and 35 minutes	11:55 A.M.
	1 hour and 20 minutes	3:42 A.M.

▶ Solve Problems About Elapsed Time on a Clock

Solve. Use your clock if you need to.

Show your work.

4. Loretta left her friend's house at 3:45 P.M. She had been there for 2 hours and 20 minutes. What time did she get there?

_____

5. Berto spent from 3:45 P.M. to 4:15 P.M. doing math homework and from 4:30 P.M. to 5:10 P.M. doing social studies homework. How much time did he spend on his math and social studies homework?

_____

6. Ed arrived at a biking trail at 9:00 A.M. He biked for 1 hour and 45 minutes. He spent 20 minutes riding home. What time did he get home?

_____

7. Vasco cleaned his room on Saturday. He started at 4:05 P.M. and finished at 4:30 P.M. For how long did he clean his room?

_____

8. Mario finished swimming at 10:45 A.M. He swam for 1 hour and 15 minutes. What time did he start?

_____

9. Eric has basketball practice from 3:30 P.M. to 4:15 P.M. He has violin practice at 5:30 P.M. Today basketball practice ended 30 minutes late and it takes Eric 15 minutes to walk to violin practice. Will he be on time? Explain.

_____

Elapsed Time

▶ Add Time

Solve using a number line.   *Show your work.*

1. Keisha went into a park at 1:30 P.M. She hiked for 1 hour 35 minutes. Then she went to the picnic area for 45 minutes and left the park. What time did Keisha leave the park?

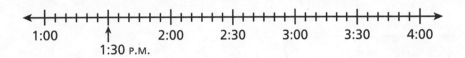

2. Loren arrived at the children's museum at 1:15 P.M. First, he spent 30 minutes looking at the dinosaur exhibit. Next, he watched a movie for 20 minutes. Then he spent 15 minutes in the museum gift shop. What time did Loren leave the museum? How long was he in the museum?

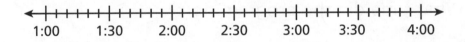

3. Caleb started working in the yard at 8:45 A.M. He raked for 1 hour 45 minutes and mowed for 45 minutes. Then he went inside. What time did he go inside? How long did he work in the yard?

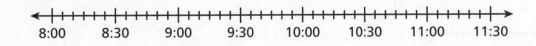

▶ Subtract Time

Solve using a number line.

4. Hank finished bowling at 7:15 P.M. He bowled for 2 hours 35 minutes. At what time did he start bowling?

5. Miguel has a job walking dogs. He finished walking the dogs at 7:10 P.M. He walked the dogs for 2 hours and 40 minutes. What time did Miguel start walking the dogs?

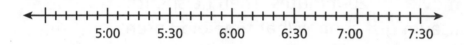

6. The school music program ended at 8:35 P.M. It lasted for 1 hour 50 minutes. What time did the program start?

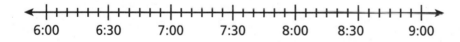

7. Lia took bread out of the oven at 3:15 P.M. It baked for 35 minutes. She spent 15 minutes measuring the ingredients and 15 minutes mixing the batter. What time did Lia start making the bread?

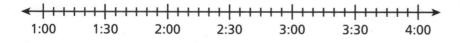

CA CC Content Standards 3.MD.1
Mathematical Practices MP.1, MP.3, MP.6

▶ Make Sense of Word Problems Involving Time Intervals

Solve. Use a clock or sketch a number line diagram if you need to.

Show your work.

1. Cory caught a train at 1:45 P.M. to go to his grandparents. The train trip lasted 35 minutes. Then he spent 10 minutes waiting for a cab and another 15 minutes riding in the cab. What time did Cory get to his grandparents' house?

_____

2. Hirva left home at 9:45 A.M. and returned home at 11:20 A.M. She spent 55 minutes at the gym and the rest of the time at the library. How much time did Hirva spend at the library?

_____

3. Diego arrived at soccer practice at 8:45 A.M. Practice lasted 45 minutes and then it took him 10 minutes to walk home. What time did Diego get home?

_____

4. Jan started working on her homework at 6:25 P.M. and she finished at 7:30 P.M. She spent 45 minutes on a book report and the rest of the time on math. How long did Jan spend on math?

_____

5. Shanna finished her chores at 4:25 P.M. She spent 35 minutes cleaning her room, 20 minutes bathing her dog, and 15 minutes folding clothes. What time did Shanna begin her chores?

▶ **What's the Error?**

Dear Math Students,

Today I was asked to find the time Jim got to the doctor's office if he woke up at 7:55 A.M., spent 45 minutes getting dressed, and then drove 20 minutes to the doctor's office.

Here is how I solved the problem.

From 7:55 on a clock, I counted up 45 minutes to 8:45, then I counted up 20 minutes to 9:05. Jim got to the doctor's office at 9:05 A.M.

Is my answer correct? If not, please correct my work and tell me what I did wrong. How do you know my answer is wrong?

Your friend,
Puzzled Penguin

6. Write an answer to the Puzzled Penguin.

_____

_____

_____

Solve.

7. Wayne left home at 3:50 P.M. to go to the park. It took 30 minutes to drive to the park. He spent 45 minutes at the park. What time did he leave the park?

_____

8. Leslie finished her project at 11:05 A.M. She spent 1 hour 10 minutes making a poster and 35 minutes writing a report. What time did Leslie start her project?

_____

Family Letter

Content Overview

Dear Family,

In the rest of the lessons in this unit, your child will be learning to show information in various ways. Students will learn to read and create pictographs and bar graphs. They will organize and display data in frequency tables and line plots. Students will also learn how to use graphs to solve real world problems.

Examples of pictographs, bar graphs, and line plots are shown below.

Birthday Cards Received

Bethany	✉ ✉ ✉ ✉
Raul	✉ ✉ ✉
Moishe	✉ ✉
Kirsten	✉ ✉ ✉ ✉

Each ✉ stands for 4 cards.

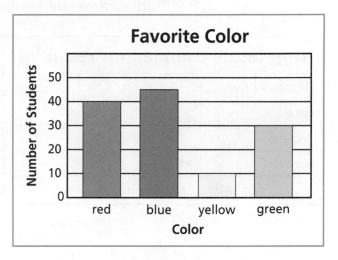

Favorite Color

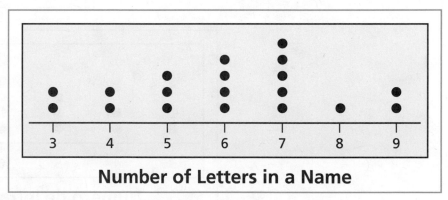

Number of Letters in a Name

Your child is learning how graphs are used in the world around us. You can help your child learn by sharing graphs that appear in newspapers, magazines, or online.

Thank you for helping your child learn how to read, interpret, and create graphs.

Sincerely,
Your child's teacher

CA CC

Unit 3 addresses the following standards from the *Common Core State Standards for Mathematics with California Additions*: 3.OA.3, 3.NBT.2, 3.MD.1, 3.MD.2, 3.MD.3, 3.MD.4, and for all Mathematical Practices.

Carta a la familia

Un vistazo general al contenido

Estimada familia:

Durante el resto de las lecciones de esta unidad, su niño aprenderá a mostrar información de varias maneras. Los estudiantes aprenderán a leer y a crear pictografías y gráficas de barras. Organizarán y mostrarán datos en tablas de frecuencia y en diagramas de puntos. También aprenderán cómo usar las gráficas para resolver problemas cotidianos.

Debajo se muestran ejemplos de pictografías, gráficas de barras y diagramas de puntos.

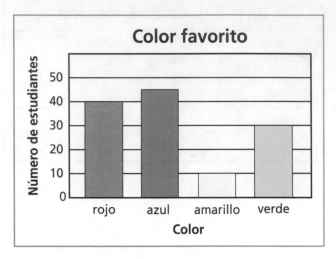

Su niño está aprendiendo cómo se usan las gráficas en la vida cotidiana. Puede ayudarlo mostrándole gráficas que aparezcan en periódicos, revistas o Internet.

Gracias por ayudar a su niño a aprender cómo leer, interpretar y crear gráficas.

Atentamente,
El maestro de su niño

 CA CC

© Houghton Mifflin Harcourt Publishing Company

En la Unidad 3 se aplican los siguientes estándares auxiliares, contenidos en los *Estándares estatales comunes de matemáticas con adiciones para California*: **3.OA.3, 3.NBT.2, 3.MD.1, 3.MD.2, 3.MD.3, 3.MD.4** y todos los de prácticas matemáticas.

Pictographs, Bar Graphs, and Line Plots

VOCABULARY
pictograph
key

► Read a Pictograph

A **pictograph** is a graph that uses pictures or symbols to represent data. The pictograph below shows the number of votes for favorite ice cream flavors. The **key** tells that each ice cream cone symbol stands for the way 4 students voted.

Favorite Ice Cream Flavors	
Peanut Butter Crunch	🍦 🍦
Cherry Vanilla	🍦 🍦 🍦
Chocolate	🍦 🍦 🍦 🍦 🍦

Each 🍦 stands for 4 votes.

Use the pictograph above to answer the questions.

1. How many votes were there for chocolate?

   _____

2. How many people in all voted for their favorite ice cream flavor?

   _____

3. How many votes were there for Cherry Vanilla?

   _____

4. How many people did not vote for chocolate?

   _____

5. How many fewer votes were there for Peanut Butter Crunch than Chocolate?

   _____

6. How many more people voted for Chocolate than for Peanut Butter Crunch and Cherry Vanilla combined?

   _____

▶ Make a Pictograph

7. Use the data about Kanye's CDs to make your own pictograph.

Kanye's CDs	
Type	**Number of CDs**
Jazz	12
Rap	16
Classical	4

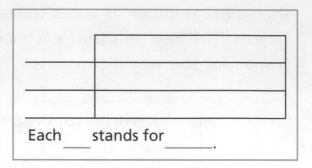

Each ___ stands for _____.

8. How many CDs in all does Kanye have?

_____

9. How many more rap CDs does Kanye have than classical?

_____

10. How many fewer jazz CDs does Kanye have than rap?

_____

11. How many pictures would you draw to show that Kanye has 9 Country and Western CDs?

_____

Read and Create Pictographs and Bar Graphs

► Read Bar Graphs

Look at this horizontal bar graph and answer the questions.

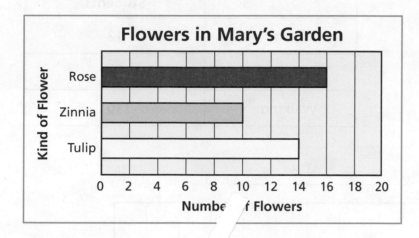

Flowers in Mary's Garden

Kind of Flower

Rose, Zinnia, Tulip

Number of Flowers — 0, 2, 4, 6, 8, 10, 12, 14, 16, 18, 20

12. What do the bars represent?

_____

_____

13. How many tulips are in Mary's garden?

_____

Look at this vertical bar graph and answer the questions.

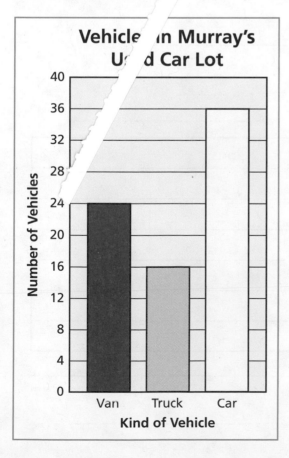

Vehicles in Murray's Used Car Lot

Number of Vehicles — 0, 4, 8, 12, 16, 20, 24, 28, 32, 36, 40

Van, Truck, Car

Kind of Vehicle

14. What do the bars represent?

_____

_____

_____

15. How many more vans than trucks are on Murray's Used Car Lot?

_____

► Create Bar Graphs

16. Use the information in this table to complete the horizontal bar graph.

Favorite Way to Exercise	
Activity	Number of Students
Biking	12
Swimming	14
Walking	10

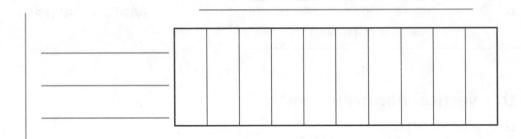

17. Use the information in this table to complete the vertical bar graph.

Favorite Team Sport	
Sport	Number of Students
Baseball	35
Soccer	60
Basketball	40

► **Solve Comparison Problems Using Data in Pictographs**

Use the pictograph below to answer the questions.

What Musical Instrument Do You Play?	
Guitar	♪ ♪ ♪ ♪ ♪
Drums	♪ ♪ ♪ ♪ ♪ ♪ ♪ ♪ ♪ ♪
Piano	♪ ♪ ♪ ♪ ♪ ♪ ♪
Violin	♪ ♪ ♪

Each ♪ = 4 students.

18. How many more students play guitar than violin?

_____

19. How many students do not play drums?

_____

20. Do more students play drums or guitar and violin combined?

_____

21. How many more students play guitar and piano combined than drums?

_____

22. Twelve fewer students play this instrument than drums.

_____

23. How many students in all were surveyed?

_____

▶ Solve Comparison Problems Using Data in Bar Graphs

Use the bar graph below to answer the questions.

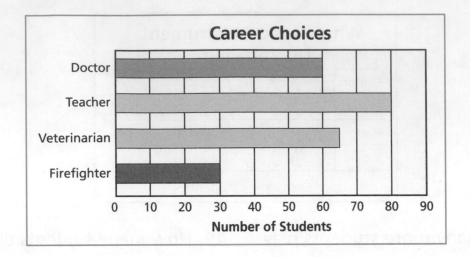

24. Twenty fewer students chose this career than teacher.

_____

25. Did more students choose veterinarian and firefighter combined or teacher?

_____

26. How many more students chose doctor than firefighter?

_____

27. How many students did not choose teacher?

_____

28. How many students in all were surveyed?

_____

29. How many more students chose doctor and firefighter combined than veterinarian?

_____

3-12

Class Activity

Name _____

Date _____

CA CC Content Standards **3.MD.3, 3.NBT.2**
Mathematical Practices **MP.1, MP.4**

▶ Horizontal Bar Graphs with Multidigit Numbers

Use this horizontal bar graph to answer the questions below.

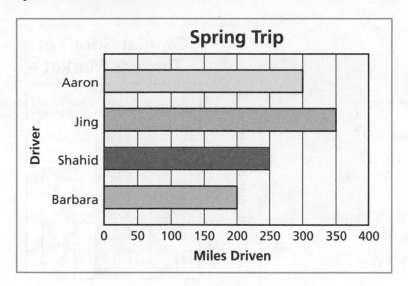

1. How many miles did Shahid drive?

_____

2. Who drove 100 more miles than Barbara?

_____

3. How many more miles did Aaron and
Barbara combined drive than Jing?

_____

4. How many more miles did Shahid and
Aaron combined drive than Barbara?

_____

5. How many fewer miles did Barbara drive than Jing?

_____

6. Write another question that can be answered
by using the graph.

_____

▶ Vertical Bar Graphs with Multidigit Numbers

Use the vertical bar graph at the right to answer the questions below.

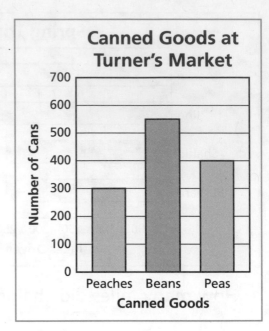

Canned Goods at Turner's Market

7. How many cans of peas are at Turner's Market?

_____

8. Are there more cans of beans or of peas and peaches combined?

_____

9. How many cans of beans and peaches are there altogether?

_____

10. How many more cans of beans are there than peas?

_____

11. How many fewer cans of peaches are there than peas and beans combined?

_____

12. Write another question that can be answered by using the graph.

_____

_____

_____

_____

Name   Date

► Create Bar Graphs with Multidigit Numbers

13. Use the information in this table to make a horizontal bar graph.

Joe's DVD Collection	
Type	DVDs
Comedy	60
Action	35
Drama	20

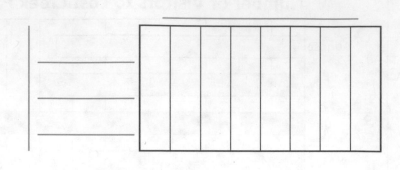

14. Use the information in this table to make a vertical bar graph.

Summer Bike Sales	
Type of Bike	Number Sold
Road Bike	200
Mountain Bike	600
Hybrid Bike	450

▶ Solve Problems Using Bar Graphs

Use the horizontal bar graph to answer the questions below.

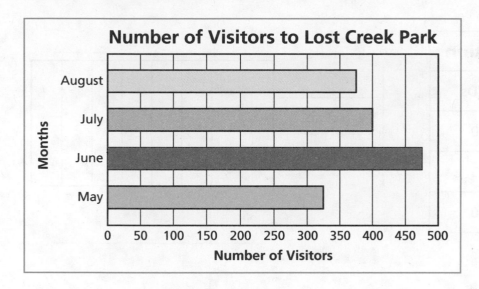

15. There were how many more visitors to Lost Creek Park in June than in May?

_____

16. How many visitors did the park have during the months of May and June combined?

_____

17. The park had how many more visitors in July than in August?

_____

18. Were there more visitors to the park in June or in May and August combined?

_____

19. Write another question that can be answered by using the graph.

_____

Read and Create Bar Graphs with Multidigit Numbers

Name_____ Date_____

CA CC Content Standards 3.MD.4
Mathematical Practices MP.1, MP.4

► Frequency Tables and Line Plots

The ages of some players on a basketball team can be shown in different ways.

A **tally chart** can be used to record and organize data.

A **frequency table** shows how many times events occur.

A **line plot** shows the frequency of data on a number line.

Tally Chart	
Age	Tally
7	I
8	III
9	IIIII
10	IIII
11	II

Frequency Table	
Age	Tally
7	1
8	3
9	5
10	4
11	2

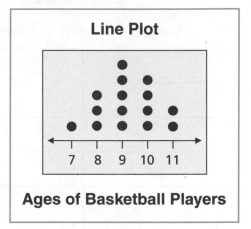

Ages of Basketball Players

► Make Sense of Data Displays

Use the data displays above to answer Exercises 1–4.

1. How many basketball players are 10 years old?

_____

2. Which age appears the most often?

_____

3. Are there more players younger than 9 or more players that are older than 9?

_____

4. Write another question that can be answered by using the data displays.

_____

_____

Name

Date

► Create Line Plots with Fractions

1. Measure the length of the hand spans of 10 classmates to the nearest $\frac{1}{2}$ inch. Have your classmates spread their fingers apart as far as possible, and measure from the tip of the thumb to the tip of the little finger. Record the data in the tally chart below and then make a frequency table.

Tally Chart	
Length	**Tally**

Frequency Table	
Length	**Tally**

2. Use the data to make a line plot.

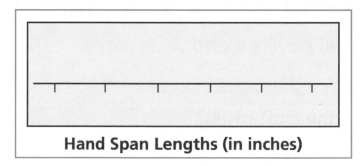

Hand Span Lengths (in inches)

3. Which length occurred the most often?

_____

4. Write a question that can be answered by using the data in the line plot.

_____

_____

Represent and Organize Data

CA CC Content Standards 3.MD.3, 3.MD.4, 3.OA.3
Mathematical Practices MP.1

▶ Solve Problems Using a Bar Graph

Five teams of students are riding their bikes after school
to raise money for the computer lab. Every completed
mile will earn the computer lab $2. The bar graph below
shows the number of miles completed in one week.

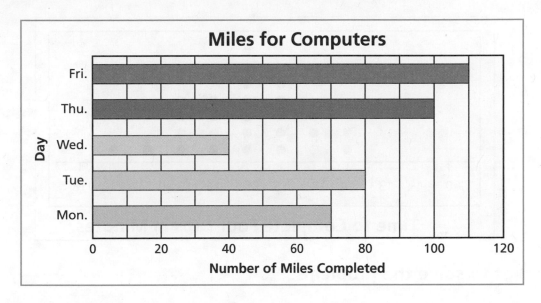

Use the bar graph to solve the problems.

1. How much money was earned
for the computer lab on Tuesday?

_____

2. How many fewer miles were
completed on Monday than on
Friday?

_____

3. How many miles in all did the
students ride?

_____

4. How many more miles did students
ride on Monday and Tuesday
combined than on Friday?

_____

5. There are four riders on each of
the five teams. If each student
completed the same number of
miles, how many miles did each
student ride on Wednesday?

_____

6. Did students ride more miles
on Monday and Wednesday
combined or on Thursday?

_____

▶ Solve Problems Using a Line Plot

The physical fitness coach asked her students to walk around a track four times. Four laps equal one mile. She recorded their times on the line plot below.

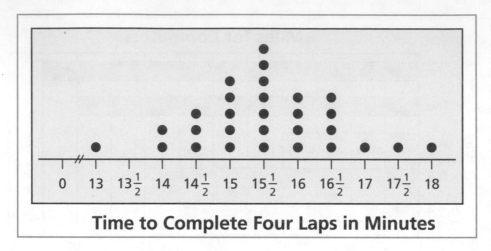

Time to Complete Four Laps in Minutes

Use the plot to solve the problems.

7. What is the difference between the greatest and the least amount of time students took to walk four laps?

8. Did more students complete the laps in 16 minutes or more or in $15\frac{1}{2}$ minutes or fewer?

9. How many students completed four laps in 16 minutes?

10. The coach recorded the times of how many students?

11. How many students completed four laps in fewer than 15 minutes?

12. Most students completed the laps between which two times?

3-15
Class Activity

Name

Date

CA CC Content Standards 3.MD.4
Mathematical Practices MP.1, MP.4

▶ Math and Sports

Many students take part in a track and field day at school each year. One event is the standing broad jump. In the standing broad jump, the jumper stands directly behind a starting line and then jumps. The length of the jump is measured from the starting line to the mark of the first part of the jumper to touch the ground.

Complete.

1. Your teacher will tell you when to do a standing broad jump. Another student should measure the length of your jump to the nearest $\frac{1}{2}$ foot and record it on a slip of paper.

2. Record the lengths of the students' jumps in the box below.

► How Far Can a Third Grader Jump?

To analyze how far a third grader can jump, the data needs to be organized and displayed.

3. Use the lengths of the students' jumps to complete the tally chart and the frequency table.

Tally Chart	
Length	**Tally**

Frequency Table	
Length	**Tally**

4. Make a line plot.

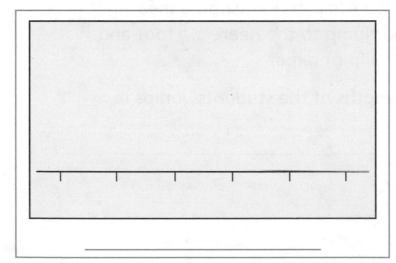

1. Matt's beach bucket contains 250 grams of sand. He adds 130 grams of sand to the bucket. How many grams of sand are in the bucket now?

_____ grams

2. For numbers 2a–2d, choose Yes or No to tell whether the words say the time on the clock.

2a. twenty-six minutes before eleven   ○ Yes   ○ No

2b. thirty-four minutes after twelve   ○ Yes   ○ No

2c. thirty-four minutes after eleven   ○ Yes   ○ No

2d. twenty-six minutes before twelve   ○ Yes   ○ No

3. Emma is eating a bowl of soup for dinner. She estimates the bowl holds 2 quarts of soup. Do you think Emma's estimate is reasonable? Why or why not?

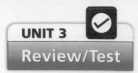
4. Kyle starts his homework at 6:30 P.M. He spends 35 minutes doing math homework and 40 minutes doing science homework. At what time does Kyle finish his homework? How much time does he spend on homework? Use the number line to help you.

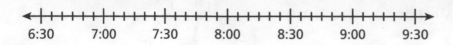

6:30   7:00   7:30   8:00   8:30   9:00   9:30

Kyle finishes his homework at _____ P.M.

He spends

| 1 hour 5 minutes |
| 1 hour 15 minutes | on homework.
| 1 hour 25 minutes |

5. Write the name of the object in the box that shows the unit you would use to measure the mass of the object.

| loaf of bread | watermelon | person |
| house key | lion | comb |

gram	kilogram

6. The bar graph shows the number of plants sold at a nursery.

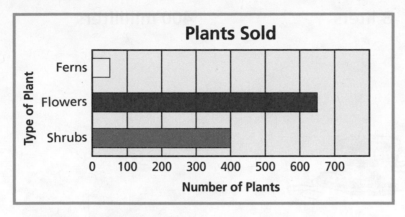

Plants Sold

How many more flowers does the nursery sell than ferns and shrubs combined?

_____ more flowers

Write and answer another question using data from the graph.

7. Estimate the length of the marker in inches. Then measure it to the nearest $\frac{1}{4}$ inch.

Estimate: _____ in.   Actual: _____ in.

8. Estimate the liquid volume of each object. Draw a line from the estimate to the object.

100 liters   3 liters   400 milliliters
  •   •   •

9. Tom measures the distances some softballs were thrown from home plate. The results are shown in the line plot. For numbers 9a–9d, select True or False for each statement.

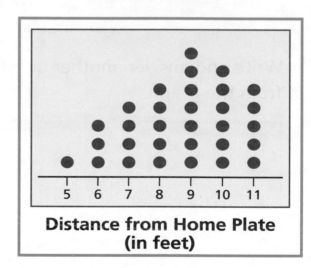

Distance from Home Plate (in feet)

9a. 8 softballs are thrown 5 feet.   ○ True   ○ False

9b. 13 softballs are thrown less than 9 feet.   ○ True   ○ False

9c. 11 softballs are thrown farther than 9 feet.   ○ True   ○ False

9d. 4 feet is the difference between the least and greatest distances thrown.   ○ True   ○ False

10. Use the data in the table to complete the pictograph and bar graph.

T-Shirt Sales			
Size	Small	Medium	Large
Number of Shirts	40	70	50

T-Shirt Sales

Small	
Medium	
Large	
Key:	

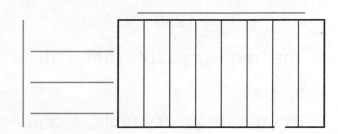

Which graph would you choose to show the data? Why?

11. Write the start time or end time to complete the chart.

8:48 A.M.	3:25 A.M.	12:5_ .M.
8:53 A.M.	3:35 P.M.	1:10 P.M.

Start Time	Elapsed Time	End Time
8:15 A.M.	38 minutes	
	55 minutes	4:20 A.M.
10:45 A.M.	2 hours 25 minutes	

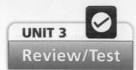
12. Billy needs 200 milliliters of lemonade to fill a small jar. How many milliliters of lemonade does he need to fill 6 jars of the same size?

Choose the measure to complete the sentence.

Billy needs
600
800
1200
milliliters of lemonade.

13. The frequency table shows the lengths of some books in a classroom.

Part A
Use the frequency table to complete the line plot.

Frequency Table	
Length (in inches)	Number of Books
5	2
$5\frac{1}{2}$	3
6	6
$6\frac{1}{2}$	5
7	8
$7\frac{1}{2}$	5
8	7

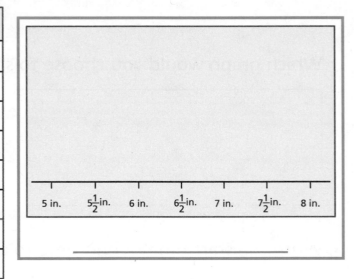

5 in. $5\frac{1}{2}$in.   6 in. $6\frac{1}{2}$in.   7 in. $7\frac{1}{2}$in.   8 in.

Part B
Most book lengths are between which two measures?

_____ inches and _____ inches

What if you measure three more book lengths at $7\frac{1}{2}$ inches and add the data to the line plot? How would your answer change?

Reference Tables

Table of Measures	
Metric	**Customary**
Length/Area	

Metric	Customary
1 meter (m) = 10 decimeters (dm)	1 foot (ft) = 12 inches (in.)
1 meter (m) = 100 centimeters (cm)	1 yard = 3 feet (ft)
1 decimeter (dm) = 10 centimeters (cm)	1 mile (mi) = 5,280 feet (ft)
1 square centimeter = 1 cm²	1 square inch = 1 in²
A metric unit for measuring area. It is the area of a square that is one centimeter on each side.	A customary unit for measuring area. It is the area of a square that is one inch on each side.

Liquid Volume	
1 liter (L) = 1,000 milliliters (mL)	1 tablespoon (tbsp) = $\frac{1}{2}$ fluid ounce (fl oz)
	1 cup (c) = 8 fluid ounces (fl oz)
	1 pint (pt) = 2 cups (c)
	1 quart (qt) = 2 pints (pt)
	1 gallon (gal) = 4 quarts (qt)

Reference Tables (continued)

Table of Units of Time

Time

1 minute (min) = 60 seconds (sec)

1 hour (hr) = 60 minutes

1 day = 24 hours

1 week (wk) = 7 days

1 month, about 30 days

1 year (yr) = 12 months (mo)
or about 52 weeks

1 year = 365 days

1 leap year = 366 days

Properties of Operations

Associative Property of Addition

$(a + b) + c = a + (b + c)$ $\qquad$ $(2 + 5) + 3 = 2 + (5 + 3)$

Commutative Property of Addition

$a + b = b + a$ $\qquad$ $4 + 6 = 6 + 4$

Identity Property of Addition

$a + 0 = 0 + a = a$ $\qquad$ $3 + 0 = 0 + 3 = 3$

Associative Property of Multiplication

$(a \cdot b) \cdot c = a \cdot (b \cdot c)$ $\qquad$ $(3 \cdot 5) \cdot 7 = 3 \cdot (5 \cdot 7)$

Commutative Property of Multiplication

$a \cdot b = b \cdot a$ $\qquad$ $6 \cdot 3 = 3 \cdot 6$

Identity Property of Multiplication

$a \cdot 1 = 1 \cdot a = a$ $\qquad$ $8 \cdot 1 = 1 \cdot 8 = 8$

Zero Property of Multiplication

$a \cdot 0 = 0 \cdot a = 0$ $\qquad$ $5 \cdot 0 = 0 \cdot 5 = 0$

Distributive Property of Multiplication over Addition

$a \cdot (b + c) = (a \cdot b) + (a \cdot c)$ $\qquad$ $2 \cdot (4 + 3) = (2 \cdot 4) + (2 \cdot 3)$

Problem Types

Addition and Subtraction Problem Types

	Result Unknown	Change Unknown	Start Unknown
Add to	Aisha had 274 stamps in her collection. Then her grandfather gave her 65 stamps. How many stamps does she have now? *Situation and solution equation:*[1] $274 + 65 = s$	Aisha had 274 stamps in her collection. Then her grandfather gave her some stamps. Now she has 339 stamps. How many stamps did her grandfather give her? *Situation equation:* $274 + s = 339$ *Solution equation:* $s = 339 - 274$	Aisha had some stamps in her collection. Then her grandfather gave her 65 stamps. Now she has 339 stamps. How many stamps did she have to start? *Situation equation* $s + 65 = 339$ *Solution equation:* $s = 339 - 65$
Take from	A store had 750 bottles of water at the start of the day. During the day, the store sold 490 bottles. How many bottles did they have at the end of the day? *Situation and solution equation:* $750 - 490 = b$	A store had 750 bottles of water at the start of the day. The store had 260 bottles left at the end of the day. How many bottles did the store sell? *Situation equation:* $750 - b = 260$ *Solution equation:* $b = 750 - 260$	A store had a number of bottles of water at the start of the day. The store sold 490 bottles of water. At the end of the day 260 bottles were left. How many bottles did the store have to start with? *Situation equation:* $b - 490 = 260$ *Solution equation:* $b = 260 + 490$

[1]A situation equation represents the structure (action) in the problem situation. A solution equation shows the operation used to find the answer.

	Total Unknown	Addend Unknown	Both Addends Unknown
Put Together/ Take Apart	A clothing store has 375 shirts with short sleeves and 148 shirts with long sleeves. How many shirts does the store have in all? *Math drawing:* s 375　　　148 *Situation and solution equation:* $375 + 148 = s$	Of the 523 shirts in a clothing store, 375 have short sleeves. The rest have long sleeves. How many shirts have long sleeves? *Math drawing:* 523 375　　　*l* *Situation equation:* $523 = 375 + l$ *Solution equation:* $l = 523 - 375$	A clothing store has 523 shirts. Some have short sleeves and some have long sleeves. How many of the shirts have short sleeves and how many have long sleeves? *Math drawing:* 523 s　　　*l* *Situation equation* $523 = s + l$

© Houghton Mifflin Harcourt Publishing Company

Problem Types continued

Addition and Subtraction Problem Types (continued)

	Difference Unknown	Greater Unknown	Smaller Unknown
Compare	At a zoo, the female black bear weighs 175 pounds. The male black bear weighs 260 pounds. How much more does the male black bear weigh than the female black bear? At a zoo, the female black bear weighs 175 pounds. The male black bear weighs 260 pounds. How much less does the female black bear weigh than the male black bear? *Math drawing:* 260 175 d *Situation equation:* $175 + d = 260$ or $d = 260 - 175$ *Solution equation:* $d = 260 - 175$	**Leading Language** At a zoo, the female black bear weighs 175 pounds. The male black bear weighs 85 pounds more than the female black bear. How much does the male black bear weigh? **Misleading Language** At a zoo, the female black bear weighs 175 pounds. The female black bear weighs 85 pounds less than the male black bear. How much does the male black bear weigh? *Math drawing:* m 175 85 *Situation and solution equation:* $175 + 85 = m$	**Leading Language** At a zoo, the male black bear weighs 260 pounds. The female black bear weighs 85 pounds less than the male black bear. How much does the female black bear weigh? **Misleading Language** At a zoo, the male black bear weighs 260 pounds. The male black bear weighs 85 pounds more than the female black bear. How much does the female black bear weigh? *Math drawing:* 260 f 85 *Situation equation* $f + 85 = 260$ or $f = 260 - 85$ *Solution equation:* $f = 260 - 85$

A comparison sentence can always be said in two ways. One way uses *more*, and the other uses *fewer* or *less*. Misleading language suggests the wrong operation. For example, it says *the female black bear weighs 85 pounds less than the male*, but you have to add 85 pounds to the female's weight to get the male's weight.

Multiplication and Division Problem Types

	Unknown Product	Group Size Unknown	Number of Groups Unknown
Equal Groups	A teacher bought 5 boxes of markers. There are 8 markers in each box. How many markers did the teacher buy? *Math drawing:* *Situation and solution equation:* $n = 5 \cdot 8$	A teacher bought 5 boxes of markers. She bought 40 markers in all. How many markers are in each box? *Math drawing:* *Situation equation:* $5 \cdot n = 40$ *Solution equation:* $n = 40 \div 5$	A teacher bought boxes of 8 markers. She bought 40 markers in all. How many boxes of markers did she buy? *Math drawing:* *Situation equation* $n \cdot 8 = 40$ *Solution equation:* $n = 40 \div 8$

Problem Types (continued)

	Unknown Product	Unknown Factor	Unknown Factor
Arrays	For the yearbook photo, the drama club stood in 3 rows of 7 students. How many students were in the photo in all? Math drawing: 7 3 OOOOOOO OOOOOOO OOOOOOO Situation and solution equation: $n = 3 \cdot 7$	For the yearbook photo, the 21 students in drama club, stood in 3 equal rows. How many students were in each row? Math drawing: n n — Total: 21 n Situation equation: $3 \cdot n = 21$ Solution equation: $n = 21 \div 3$	For the yearbook photo, the 21 students in drama club, stood in rows of 7 students. How many rows were there? Math drawing: 7 7 — Total: 21 7 Situation equation $n \cdot 7 = 21$ Solution equation: $n = 21 \div 7$
Area	The floor of the kitchen is 2 meters by 5 meters. What is the area of the floor? Math drawing: 5 2 [A] Situation and solution equation: $A = 5 \cdot 2$	The floor of the kitchen is 5 meters long. The area of the floor is 10 square meters. What is the width of the floor? Math drawing: 5 w [10] Situation equation: $5 \cdot w = 10$ Solution equation: $w = 10 \div 5$	The floor of the kitchen is 2 meters wide. The area of the floor is 10 square meters. What is the length of the floor? Math drawing: l 2 [10] Situation equation $l \cdot 2 = 10$ Solution equation: $l = 10 \div 2$

Vocabulary Activities

MathWord Power

► Word Review PAIRS

Work with a partner. Choose a word from a current unit or a review word from a previous unit. Use the word to complete one of the activities listed on the right. Then ask your partner if they have any edits to your work or questions about what you described. Repeat, having your partner choose a word.

Activities

► Give the meaning in words or gestures.

► Use the word in the sentence.

► Give another word that is related to the word in some way and explain the relationship.

► Crossword Puzzle PAIRS OR INDIVIDUALS

Create a crossword puzzle similar to the example below. Use vocabulary words from the unit. You can add other related words, too. Challenge your partner to solve the puzzle.

Across

1. _____ and subtraction are inverse operations.

2. To put amounts together

3. When you trade 10 ones for 1 ten, you _____.

4. The answer to an addition problem

Down

1. In 24 + 65 = 89, 24 is an _____.

3. A combination of the digits 0, 1, 2, 3, 4, 5, 6, 7, 8, and 9.

4. The operation that you can use to find out how much more one number is than another.

(Crossword grid)

- 4 Down/Across: s u m
- 1 Across: a d d i t i o n
- word: s u b t r a c t i o n
- word: a d d e n d
- 2 Across: a d d
- 3 Across: r e g r o u p
- 3 Down: n u m b e r

© Houghton Mifflin Harcourt Publishing Company

Vocabulary Activities (continued)

▶ Word Wall   PAIRS OR SMALL GROUPS

With your teacher's permission, start a word wall in your classroom. As you work through each lesson, put the math vocabulary words on index cards and place them on the word wall. You can work with a partner or a small group choosing a word and giving the definition.

▶ Word Web   INDIVIDUALS

Make a word web for a word or words you do not understand in a unit. Fill in the web with words or phrases that are related to the vocabulary word.

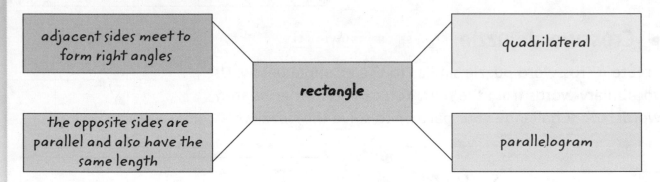

adjacent sides meet to form right angles		quadrilateral
	rectangle	
the opposite sides are parallel and also have the same length		parallelogram

▶ Alphabet Challenge   PAIRS OR INDIVIDUALS

Take an alphabet challenge. Choose 3 letters from the alphabet. Think of three vocabulary words for each letter. Then write the definition or draw an example for each word.

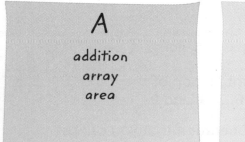

A
addition
array
area

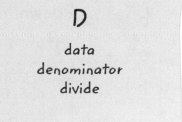

D
data
denominator
divide

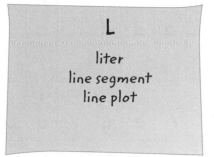

L
liter
line segment
line plot

▶ Concentration [PAIRS]

Write the vocabulary words and related words from a unit on index cards. Write the definitions on a different set of index cards. Mix up both sets of cards. Then place the cards facedown on a table in an array, for example, 3 by 3 or 3 by 4. Take turns turning over two cards. If one card is a word and one card is a definition that matches the word, take the pair. Continue until each word has been matched with its definition.

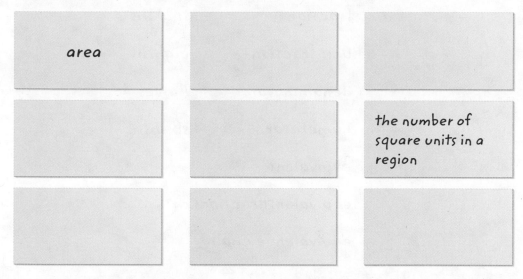

area		
		the number of square units in a region

▶ Math Journal [INDIVIDUALS]

As you learn new words, write them in your Math Journal. Write the definition of the word and include a sketch or an example. As you learn new information about the word, add notes to your definition.

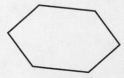

polygon: a closed plane figure with sides made of straight line segments.

In concave polygons, there exists a line segment with endpoints inside the polygon and a point on the line segment that is outside the polygon.

▶ What's the Word? PAIRS

Work together to make a poster or bulletin board display of the words in a unit. Write definitions on a set of index cards. Mix up the cards. Work with a partner, choosing a definition from the index cards. Have your partner point to the word on the poster and name the matching math vocabulary word. Switch roles and try the activity again.

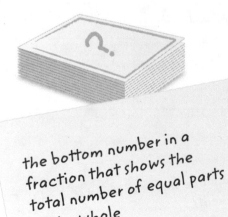

fraction   fourths

unit fraction   eighths

denominator   halves

numerator   sixths

equivalent

equivalent fractions

equivalence chain

thirds

the bottom number in a fraction that shows the total number of equal parts in the whole

Glossary

A

addend One of two or more numbers to be added together to find a sum.

Example: $8 + 4 = 12$

addend addend sum

addition A mathematical operation that combines two or more numbers.

Example: $23 + 52 = 75$

addend addend sum

adjacent (sides) Two sides of a figure that meet at a point.

Example: Sides a and b are adjacent.

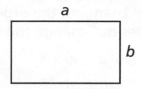

A.M. The time period between midnight and noon.

analog clock A clock with a face and hands.

angle A figure formed by two rays or two line segments that meet at an endpoint.

area The total number of square units that cover a figure.

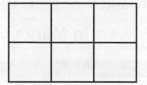

Example: The area of the rectangle is 6 square units.

array An arrangement of objects, pictures, or numbers in columns and rows.

Associative Property of Addition (Grouping Property of Addition)

The property which states that changing the way in which addends are grouped does not change the sum.

Example: $(2 + 3) + 1 = 2 + (3 + 1)$

$5 + 1 = 2 + 4$

$6 = 6$

Associative Property of Multiplication (Grouping Property of Multiplication)

The property which states that changing the way in which factors are grouped does not change the product.

Example: $(2 \times 3) \times 4 = 2 \times (3 \times 4)$

$6 \times 4 = 2 \times 12$

$24 = 24$

Glossary (continued)

axis (plural: **axes**) A reference line for a graph. A graph has 2 axes; one is horizontal and the other is vertical.

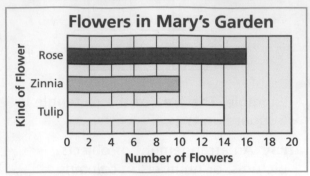

Flowers in Mary's Garden

bar graph A graph that uses bars to show data. The bars may be horizontal, as in the graph above, or vertical, as in the graph below.

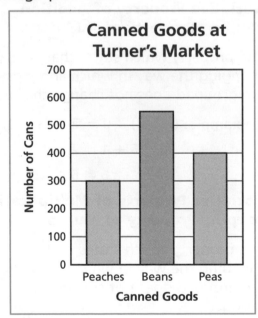

Canned Goods at Turner's Market

capacity The amount a container can hold.

centimeter (cm) A metric unit used to measure length.

100 centimeters = 1 meter

column A part of a table or array that contains items arranged vertically.

Commutative Property of Addition (Order Property of Addition) The property which states that changing the order of addends does not change the sum.

Example: $3 + 7 = 7 + 3$

$10 = 10$

Commutative Property of Multiplication (Order Property of Multiplication) The property which states that changing the order of factors does not change the product.

Example: $5 \times 4 = 4 \times 5$

$20 = 20$

comparison bars Bars that represent the greater amount, lesser amount, and difference in a comparison problem.

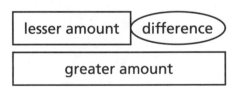

concave A polygon for which you can connect two points inside the polygon with a segment that passes outside the polygon.

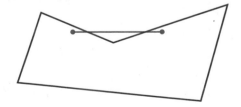

convex A polygon is convex if all of its diagonals are inside it.

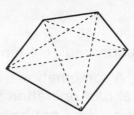

cup (c) A customary unit of measure used to measure capacity.

1 cup = 8 fluid ounces
2 cups = 1 pint
4 cups = 1 quart
16 cups = 1 gallon

D

data Pieces of information.

decagon A polygon with 10 sides.

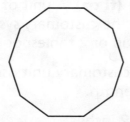

decimeter (dm) A metric unit used to measure length

1 decimeter = 10 centimeters

denominator The bottom number in a fraction that shows the total number of equal parts in the whole.

Example: $\frac{1}{3}$ denominator

diagonal A line segment that connects two corners of a figure and is not a side of the figure.

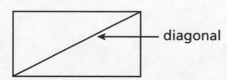
diagonal

difference The result of subtraction or of comparing.

digit Any of the symbols 0, 1, 2, 3, 4, 5, 6, 7, 8, 9.

digital clock A clock that displays the hour and minutes with numbers.

Distributive property You can multiply a sum by a number, or multiply each addend by the number and add the products; the result is the same.

Example:

$3 \times (2 + 4) = (3 \times 2) + (3 \times 4)$
$3 \times 6 \quad = \quad 6 \quad + \quad 12$
$18 \quad = \quad 18$

dividend The number that is divided in division.

Examples:

$12 \div 3 = 4$ $3\overline{)12}^{\,4}$

dividend   dividend

division The mathematical operation that separates an amount into smaller equal groups to find the number of groups or the number in each group.

Example: $12 \div 3 = 4$ is a division number sentence.

divisor The number that you divide by in division.

Example: $12 \div 3 = 4$ $3\overline{)12}^{\,4}$

divisor   divisor

Glossary (continued)

E

elapsed time The time that passes between the beginning and the end of an activity.

endpoint The point at either end of a line segment or the beginning point of a ray.

endpoint   endpoint   endpoint

equation A mathematical sentence with an equals sign.

Examples: $11 + 22 = 33$
$75 - 25 = 50$

equivalent Equal, or naming the same amount.

equivalent fractions Fractions that name the same amount.

Example: $\frac{1}{2}$ and $\frac{2}{4}$

equivalent fractions

estimate About how many or about how much.

even number A whole number that is a multiple of 2. The ones digit in an even number is 0, 2, 4, 6, or 8.

expanded form A number written to show the value of each of its digits.

Examples:
$347 = 300 + 40 + 7$
$347 = 3$ hundreds $+ 4$ tens $+ 7$ ones

expression A combination of numbers, variables, and/or operation signs. An expression does not have an equals sign.

Examples: $4 + 7$ $a - 3$

F

factors Numbers that are multiplied to give a product.

Example: $4 \times 5 = 20$

factor   factor   product

fluid ounce (fl oz) A unit of liquid volume in the customary system that equals $\frac{1}{8}$ cup or 2 tablespoons.

foot (ft) A customary unit used to measure length.

1 foot $= 12$ inches

fraction A number that names part of a whole or part of a set.

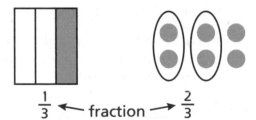

$\frac{1}{3}$ ← fraction → $\frac{2}{3}$

frequency table A table that shows how many times each event, item, or category occurs.

Frequency Table	
Age	Tally
7	1
8	3
9	5
10	4
11	2

function table A table of ordered pairs that shows a function.

For every input number, there is only one possible output number.

Rule: add 2	
Input	Output
1	3
2	4
3	5
4	6

G

gallon (gal) A customary unit used to measure capacity.

1 gallon = 4 quarts = 8 pints = 16 cups

gram (g) A metric unit of mass. One paper clip has a mass of about 1 gram.

1,000 grams = 1 kilogram

greater than (>) A symbol used to compare two numbers.

Example: 6 > 5
6 *is greater than* 5.

group To combine numbers to form new tens, hundreds, thousands, and so on.

H

height A vertical distance, or how tall something is.

hexagon A polygon with six sides.

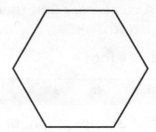

horizontal Extending in two directions, left and right.

horizontal bar graph A bar graph with horizontal bars.

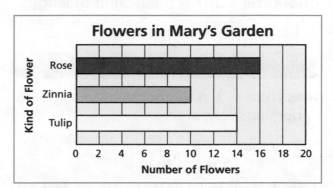

I

Identity Property of Addition If 0 is added to a number, the sum equals that number.

Example: 3 + 0 = 3

Identity Property of Multiplication The product of 1 and any number equals that number.

Example: 10 × 1 = 10

© Houghton Mifflin Harcourt Publishing Company

Glossary (continued)

improper fraction A fraction in which the numerator is equal to or is greater than the denominator. Improper fractions are equal to or greater than 1. $\frac{5}{5}$ and $\frac{8}{3}$ are improper fractions.

inch (in.) A customary unit used to measure length.

12 inches = 1 foot

K
---

key A part of a map, graph, or chart that explains what symbols mean.

kilogram (kg) A metric unit of mass.

1 kilogram = 1,000 grams

kilometer (km) A metric unit of length.

1 kilometer = 1,000 meters

L
---

less than (<) A symbol used to compare numbers.

Example: 5 < 6
5 *is less than* 6.

line A straight path that goes on forever in opposite directions.

line plot A diagram that shows frequency of data on a number line. Also called a *dot plot*.

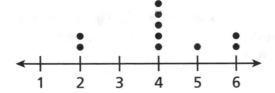

line segment A part of a line. A line segment has two endpoints.

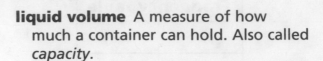

liquid volume A measure of how much a container can hold. Also called *capacity*.

liter (L) A metric unit used to measure capacity.

1 liter = 1,000 milliliters

M
---

mass The amount of matter in an object.

mental math A way to solve problems without using pencil and paper or a calculator.

meter (m) A metric unit used to measure length.

1 meter = 100 centimeters

method A procedure, or way, of doing something.

mile (mi) A customary unit of length.

1 mile = 5,280 feet

milliliter (mL) A metric unit used to measure capacity.

1,000 milliliters = 1 liter

mixed number A whole number and a fraction.

$1\frac{3}{4}$ is a mixed number.

multiple A number that is the product of the given number and any whole number.

multiplication A mathematical operation that combines equal groups.

Example: $4 \times 3 = 12$

factor   factor   product

$3 + 3 + 3 + 3 = 12$

4 times

N

number line A line on which numbers are assigned to lengths.

numerator The top number in a fraction that shows the number of equal parts counted.

Example: $\frac{1}{3}$ numerator

O

octagon A polygon with eight sides.

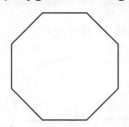

odd number A whole number that is not a multiple of 2. The ones digit in an odd number is 1, 3, 5, 7, or 9.

opposite sides Sides of a polygon that are across from each other; they do not meet at a point.

Example: Sides *a* and *c* are opposite.

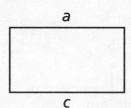

Order of operations A set of rules that state the order in which the operations in an expression should be done.

STEP 1: Perform operations inside parentheses first.

STEP 2: Multiply and divide from left to right.

STEP 3: Add and subtract from left to right.

ounce (oz) A customary unit used to measure weight.

16 ounces = 1 pound

P

parallel lines Two lines that are the same distance apart.

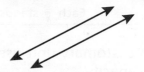

parallelogram A quadrilateral with both pairs of opposite sides parallel.

pentagon A polygon with five sides.

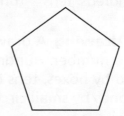

Glossary (continued)

perimeter The distance around a figure.

Example:

Perimeter = 3 cm + 5 cm + 3 cm + 5 cm = 16 cm

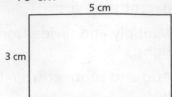

pictograph A graph that uses pictures or symbols to represent data.

Favorite Ice Cream Flavors	
Peanut Butter Crunch	
Cherry Vanilla	
Chocolate	
	Each stands for 4 votes.

pint (pt) A customary unit used to measure capacity.

1 pint = 2 cups

place value The value assigned to the place that a digit occupies in a number.

9   6   2
↑   ↑   ↑
hundreds   tens   ones

place value drawing A drawing that represents a number. Hundreds are represented by boxes, tens by vertical lines, and ones by small circles.

P.M. The time period between noon and midnight.

polygon A closed plane figure with sides made up of straight line segments.

pound (lb) A customary unit used to measure weight.

1 pound = 16 ounces

product The answer when you multiply numbers.

Example: 4 × 7 = 28

factor   factor   product

proof drawing A drawing used to show that an answer is correct.

$$\begin{array}{r} 249 \\ + 386 \\ \underline{11} \\ 635 \end{array}$$

Q

quadrilateral A polygon with four sides.

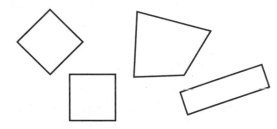

quart (qt) A customary unit used to measure capacity.

1 quart = 4 cups

quotient The answer when you divide numbers.

Examples:

$35 \div 7 = 5$

$$5 \leftarrow \text{quotient}$$
$$7\overline{)35}$$

quotient

ray A part of a line that has one endpoint and goes on forever in one direction.

rectangle A parallelogram that has 4 right angles.

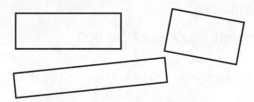

rhombus A parallelogram with equal sides.

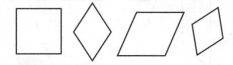

right angle An angle that measures 90°.

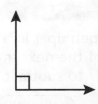

round To find about how many or how much by expressing a number to the nearest ten, hundred, thousand, and so on.

row A part of a table or array that contains items arranged horizontally.

scale An arrangement of numbers in order with equal intervals.

side (of a figure) One of the line segments that make up a polygon.

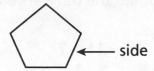
side

simplify To write an equivalent fraction with a smaller numerator and denominator.

situation equation An equation that shows the action or the relationship in a problem.

Example: 35 + *n* = 40

solution equation An equation that shows the operation to perform in order to solve the problem.

Example: *n* = 40 − 35

square A rectangle with four sides of the same length.

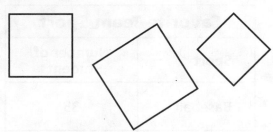

square number The product of a whole number and itself.

Example: 4 × 4 = 16

square number

Glossary (continued)

square unit A unit of area equal to the area of a square with one-unit sides.

standard form The name of a number written using digits.

Example: 1,829

subtract To find the difference of two numbers.

Example: 18 − 11 = 7

subtraction A mathematical operation on two numbers that gives the difference.

Example: 43 − 40 = 3

sum The answer when adding two or more addends.

Example: 37 + 52 = 89

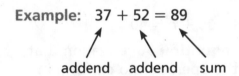

addend   addend   sum

T

table An easy-to-read arrangement of data, usually in rows and columns.

Favorite Team Sport	
Sport	**Number of Students**
Baseball	35
Soccer	60
Basketball	40

tally marks Short line segments drawn in groups of 5. Each mark, including the slanted mark, stands for 1 unit.

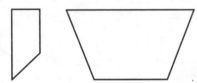 means 13
5   5   3

total The answer when adding two or more addends. The sum of two or more numbers.

Example: 672 + 228 = 900

addend   addend   total
sum

trapezoid A quadrilateral with exactly one pair of parallel sides.

triangle A polygon with three sides.

U

ungroup To open up 1 in a given place to make 10 of the next smaller place value in order to subtract.

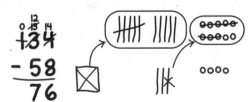

unit fraction A fraction whose numerator is 1. It shows one equal part of a whole.

Example: $\frac{1}{4}$

unit square A square whose area is 1 square unit.

variable A letter or symbol used to represent an unknown number in an algebraic expression or equation.

Example: $2 + n$

n is a variable.

Venn diagram A diagram that uses circles to show the relationship among sets of objects.

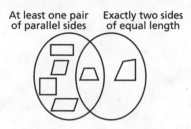

At least one pair of parallel sides   Exactly two sides of equal length

vertex A point where sides, rays, or edges meet.

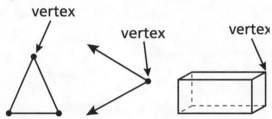

vertex

vertex

vertex

vertical Extending in two directions, up and down.

vertical bar graph A bar graph with vertical bars.

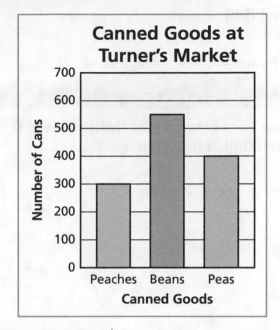

Canned Goods at Turner's Market

weight The measure of how heavy something is.

word form A name of a number written using words instead of digits.

Example: Nine hundred eighty-four

Y

yard (yd) A customary unit used to measure length.

1 yard = 3 feet = 36 inches

Z

Zero Property of Multiplication If 0 is multiplied by a number, the product is 0.

Example: $3 \times 0 = 0$

California Common Core Standards for Mathematical Content

3.OA Operations and Algebraic Thinking

Represent and solve problems involving multiplication and division.

3.OA.1	Interpret products of whole numbers, e.g., interpret 5×7 as the total number of objects in 5 groups of 7 objects each.	Unit 1 Lessons 1, 2, 3, 4, 5, 6, 7, 8, 9, 10, 12, 13, 14, 16, 18, 19; Unit 2 Lessons 2, 4, 7, 9, 10, 11, 13, 15
3.OA.2	Interpret whole-number quotients of whole numbers, e.g., interpret $56 \div 8$ as the number of objects in each share when 56 objects are partitioned equally into 8 shares, or as a number of shares when 56 objects are partitioned into equal shares of 8 objects each.	Unit 1 Lessons 4, 5, 6, 7, 9, 10, 12, 13, 14, 15, 16, 17, 18, 19; Unit 2 Lessons 2, 4, 7, 9, 10, 11, 13, 15
3.OA.3	Use multiplication and division within 100 to solve word problems in situations involving equal groups, arrays, and measurement quantities, e.g., by using drawings and equations with a symbol for the unknown number to represent the problem.	Unit 1 Lessons 2, 3, 4, 5, 6, 7, 9, 10, 12, 13, 14, 16, 18, 19; Unit 2 Lessons 2, 4, 7, 9, 10, 11, 13, 15; Unit 3 Lessons 2, 3, 4, 5, 14; Unit 5 Lessons 2, 3, 7, 8, 9, 11
3.OA.4	Determine the unknown whole number in a multiplication or division equation relating three whole numbers.	Unit 1 Lessons 1, 4, 5, 6, 7, 8, 9, 10, 11, 12, 13, 14, 16, 18, 19; Unit 2 Lessons 1, 2, 3, 4, 5, 6, 7, 8, 9, 10, 11, 13, 14, 15; Unit 5 Lessons 2, 3

Understand properties of multiplication and the relationship between multiplication and division.

3.OA.5	Apply properties of operations as strategies to multiply and divide.	Unit 1 Lessons 3, 6, 11, 12, 14, 15, 19; Unit 2 Lessons 1, 8, 12, 15
3.OA.6	Understand division as an unknown-factor problem.	Unit 1 Lessons 4, 5, 6, 7, 8, 9, 10, 11, 12, 13, 14, 15, 16, 17, 18; Unit 2 Lessons 1, 2, 3, 4, 5, 6, 7, 8, 9, 10, 11, 12, 13, 14

Multiply and divide within 100.

3.OA.7	Fluently multiply and divide within 100, using strategies such as the relationship between multiplication and division or properties of operations. By the end of Grade 3, know from memory all products of two one-digit numbers.	Unit 1 Lessons 1, 2, 3, 4, 5, 6, 7, 8, 9, 10, 11, 12, 13, 14, 15, 16, 17, 18, 19; Unit 2 Lessons 1, 2, 3, 4, 5, 6, 7, 8, 9, 10, 11, 12, 13, 14, 15

Solve problems involving the four operations, and identify and explain patterns in arithmetic.

3.OA.8	Solve two-step word problems using the four operations. Represent these problems using equations with a letter standing for the unknown quantity. Assess the reasonableness of answers using mental computation and estimation strategies including rounding.	Unit 2 Lessons 9, 10, 11, 13; Unit 3 Lesson 17; Unit 4 Lesson 17; Unit 5 Lessons 7, 8, 9, 10, 11

3.OA.9	Identify arithmetic patterns (including patterns in the addition table or multiplication table), and explain them using properties of operations.	Unit 1 Lessons 1, 5, 6, 7, 8, 10, 12, 15, 19; Unit 2 Lessons 1, 3, 5, 6, 8, 14, 15; Unit 4 Lesson 17

3.NBT Number and Operations in Base Ten

Use place value understanding and properties of operations to perform multi-digit arithmetic.

3.NBT.1	Use place value understanding to round whole numbers to the nearest 10 or 100.	Unit 4 Lessons 1, 2, 3, 4, 5, 6, 10, 17, 18; Unit 5 Lesson 4
3.NBT.2	Fluently add and subtract within 1000 using strategies and algorithms based on place value, properties of operations, and/or the relationship between addition and subtraction.	Unit 3 Lessons 11, 12; Unit 4 Lessons 1, 2, 3, 4, 5, 6, 7, 8, 9, 10, 11, 12, 13, 14, 15, 16, 17, 18; Unit 5 Lessons 1, 2, 3, 4, 5, 6, 8, 9, 10, 11
3.NBT.3	Multiply one-digit whole numbers by multiples of 10 in the range 10–90 (e.g., 9×80, 5×60) using strategies based on place value and properties of operations.	Unit 2 Lesson 12

3.NF Number and Operations–Fractions

Develop understanding of fractions as numbers.

3.NF.1	Understand a fraction $\frac{1}{b}$ as the quantity formed by 1 part when a whole is partitioned into b equal parts; understand a fraction $\frac{a}{b}$ as the quantity formed by a parts of size $\frac{1}{b}$.	Unit 7 Lessons 1, 2, 9
3.NF.2	Understand a fraction as a number on the number line; represent fractions on a number line diagram.	Unit 7 Lesson 2, 3, 4, 8
3.NF.2a	Represent a fraction $\frac{1}{b}$ on a number line diagram by defining the interval from 0 to 1 as the whole and partitioning it into b equal parts. Recognize that each part has size $\frac{1}{b}$ and that the endpoint of the part based at 0 locates the number $\frac{1}{b}$ on the number line.	Unit 7 Lessons 2, 3, 4, 8
3.NF.2b	Represent a fraction $\frac{a}{b}$ on a number line diagram by marking off a lengths $\frac{1}{b}$ from 0. Recognize that the resulting interval has size $\frac{a}{b}$ and that its endpoint locates the number $\frac{1}{b}$ on the number line.	Unit 7 Lessons 2, 3, 4, 8
3.NF.3	Explain equivalence of fractions in special cases, and compare fractions by reasoning about their size.	Unit 7 Lessons 4, 5, 6, 7, 8, 9
3.NF.3a	Understand two fractions as equivalent (equal) if they are the same size, or the same point on a number line.	Unit 7 Lessons 6, 7, 8, 9
3.NF.3b	Recognize and generate simple equivalent fractions, e.g., $\frac{1}{2} = \frac{2}{4}$, $\frac{4}{6} = \frac{2}{3}$. Explain why the fractions are equivalent, e.g., by using a visual fraction model.	Unit 7 Lessons 6, 7, 8, 9
3.NF.3c	Express whole numbers as fractions, and recognize fractions that are equivalent to whole numbers.	Unit 7 Lesson 3, 4, 7, 8

| 3.NF.3d | Compare two fractions with the same numerator or the same denominator by reasoning about their size. Recognize that comparisons are valid only when the two fractions refer to the same whole. Record the results of comparisons with the symbols >, =, or <, and justify the conclusions, e.g., by using a visual fraction model. | Unit 7 Lessons 4, 5, 8, 9 |

3.MD Measurement and Data

Solve problems involving measurement and estimation of intervals of time, liquid volumes, and masses of objects.

| 3.MD.1 | Tell and write time to the nearest minute and measure time intervals in minutes. Solve word problems involving addition and subtraction of time intervals in minutes, e.g., by representing the problem on a number line diagram. | Unit 3 Lessons 6, 7, 8, 9, 10, 15 |
| 3.MD.2 | Measure and estimate liquid volumes and masses of objects using standard units of grams (g), kilograms (kg), and liters (l). Add, subtract, multiply, or divide to solve one-step word problems involving masses or volumes that are given in the same units, e.g., by using drawings (such as a beaker with a measurement scale) to represent the problem. | Unit 3 Lessons 2, 3, 4, 5 |

Represent and interpret data.

| 3.MD.3 | Draw a scaled picture graph and a scaled bar graph to represent a data set with several categories. Solve one- and two-step "how many more" and "how many less" problems using information presented in scaled bar graphs. | Unit 3 Lessons 11, 12, 14 |
| 3.MD.4 | Generate measurement data by measuring lengths using rulers marked with halves and fourths of an inch. Show the data by making a line plot, where the horizontal scale is marked off in appropriate units—whole numbers, halves, or quarters. | Unit 3 Lessons 1, 13, 14, 15 |

Geometric measurement: understand concepts of area and relate area to multiplication and to addition.

3.MD.5	Recognize area as an attribute of plane figures and understand concepts of area measurement.	Unit 1 Lesson 11; Unit 2 Lesson 2; Unit 6 Lessons 5, 7
3.MD.5a	A square with side length 1 unit, called "a unit square," is said to have "one square unit" of area, and can be used to measure area.	Unit 1 Lesson 11; Unit 2 Lesson 2; Unit 6 Lessons 5, 7
3.MD.5b	A plane figure that can be covered without gaps or overlaps by n unit squares is said to have an area of n square units.	Unit 1 Lesson 11; Unit 2 Lesson 2; Unit 6 Lessons 5, 7

3.MD.6	Measure areas by counting unit squares (square cm, square m, square in, square ft, and improvised units).	Unit 1 Lesson 11; Unit 6 Lessons 5, 6, 10
3.MD.7	Relate area to the operations of multiplication and addition.	Unit 1 Lesson 11, 12, 14; Unit 2 Lessons 2, 6, 8; Unit 6 Lessons 5, 6, 7, 8, 9,11
3.MD.7a	Find the area of a rectangle with whole-number side lengths by tiling it, and show that the area is the same as would be found by multiplying the side lengths.	Unit 1 Lesson 11; Unit 2 Lesson 2; Unit 6 Lessons 5, 6
3.MD.7b	Multiply side lengths to find areas of rectangles with whole number side lengths in the context of solving real world and mathematical problems, and represent whole-number products as rectangular areas in mathematical reasoning.	Unit 1 Lessons 11, 12, 14; Unit 2 Lessons 2, 6; Unit 6 Lessons 5, 6, 7, 8, 9
3.MD.7c	Use tiling to show in a concrete case that the area of a rectangle with whole-number side lengths a and $b + c$ is the sum of $a \times b$ and $a \times c$. Use area models to represent the distributive property in mathematical reasoning.	Unit 1 Lessons 11, 12, 14; Unit 6 Lesson 6
3.MD.7d	Recognize area as additive. Find areas of rectilinear figures by decomposing them into non-overlapping rectangles and adding the areas of the non-overlapping parts, applying this technique to solve real world problems.	Unit 1 Lesson 11; Unit 2 Lessons 2, 6, 8; Unit 6 Lessons 6, 8, 9, 11

Geometric measurement: recognize perimeter as an attribute of plane figures and distinguish between linear and area measures.

3.MD.8	Solve real world and mathematical problems involving perimeters of polygons, including finding the perimeter given the side lengths, finding an unknown side length, and exhibiting rectangles with the same perimeter and different areas or with the same area and different perimeters.	Unit 6 Lessons 5, 6, 7, 9, 11

3.G Geometry

Reason with shapes and their attributes.

CC.3.G.1	Understand that shapes in different categories (e.g., rhombuses, rectangles, and others) may share attributes (e.g., having four sides), and that the shared attributes can define a larger category (e.g., quadrilaterals). Recognize rhombuses, rectangles, and squares as examples of quadrilaterals, and draw examples of quadrilaterals that do not belong to any of these subcategories.	Unit 6 Lessons 1, 2, 3, 4, 11
CC.3.G.2	Partition shapes into parts with equal areas. Express the area of each part as a unit fraction of the whole.	Unit 6 Lesson 1; Unit 7 Lessons 1, 2, 9

California Common Core Standards for Mathematical Practice

MP.1 Make sense of problems and persevere in solving them.

Mathematically proficient students start by explaining to themselves the meaning of a problem and looking for entry points to its solution. They analyze givens, constraints, relationships, and goals. They make conjectures about the form and meaning of the solution and plan a solution pathway rather than simply jumping into a solution attempt. They consider analogous problems, and try special cases and simpler forms of the original problem in order to gain insight into its solution. They monitor and evaluate their progress and change course if necessary. Older students might, depending on the context of the problem, transform algebraic expressions or change the viewing window on their graphing calculator to get the information they need. Mathematically proficient students can explain correspondences between equations, verbal descriptions, tables, and graphs or draw diagrams of important features and relationships, graph data, and search for regularity or trends. Younger students might rely on using concrete objects or pictures to help conceptualize and solve a problem. Mathematically proficient students check their answers to problems using a different method, and they continually ask themselves, "Does this make sense?" They can understand the approaches of others to solving complex problems and identify correspondences between different approaches.

Unit 1 Lessons 3, 4, 5, 6, 7, 9, 10, 12, 13, 14, 16, 18, 19

Unit 2 Lessons 1, 2, 4, 7, 9, 10, 11, 13, 15

Unit 3 Lessons 2, 3, 4, 5, 6, 8, 9, 10, 11, 12, 13, 14, 15

Unit 4 Lessons 3, 4, 5, 6, 7, 8, 9, 10, 11, 12, 13, 14, 15, 16, 17, 18

Unit 5 Lessons 1, 2, 3, 4, 6, 7, 8, 9, 10, 11

Unit 6 Lessons 6, 9, 11

Unit 7 Lessons 2, 3, 7, 8, 9

MP.2 Reason abstractly and quantitatively.

Mathematically proficient students make sense of quantities and their relationships in problem situations. They bring two complementary abilities to bear on problems involving quantitative relationships: the ability to *decontextualize*—to abstract a given situation and represent it symbolically and manipulate the representing symbols as if they have a life of their own, without necessarily attending to their referents—and the ability to *contextualize*, to pause as needed during the manipulation process in order to probe into the referents for the symbols involved. Quantitative reasoning entails habits of creating a coherent representation of the problem at hand; considering the units involved; attending to the meaning of quantities, not just how to compute them; and knowing and flexibly using different properties of operations and objects.

Unit 1 Lessons 1, 2, 3, 5, 6, 7, 8, 10, 11, 12, 19

Unit 2 Lessons 1, 2, 3, 5, 6, 8, 13, 15

Unit 3 Lessons 1, 2, 3, 4, 8, 12, 13, 15

Unit 4 Lessons 1, 2, 5, 6, 9, 11, 12, 13, 14, 15, 16, 17, 18

Unit 5 Lessons 1, 2, 3, 4, 8, 11

Unit 6 Lessons 1, 5, 6, 7, 8, 9, 11

Unit 7 Lessons 1, 2, 3, 4, 5, 6, 7, 8, 9

MP.3 Construct viable arguments and critique the reasoning of others.

Mathematically proficient students understand and use stated assumptions, definitions, and previously established results in constructing arguments. They make conjectures and build a logical progression of statements to explore the truth of their conjectures. They are able to analyze situations by breaking them into cases, and can recognize and use counterexamples. They justify their conclusions, communicate them to others, and respond to the arguments of others. They reason inductively about data, making plausible arguments that take into account the context from which the data arose. Mathematically proficient students are also able to compare the effectiveness of two plausible arguments, distinguish correct logic or reasoning from that which is flawed, and—if there is a flaw in an argument—explain what it is. Elementary students can construct arguments using concrete referents such as objects, drawings, diagrams, and actions. Such arguments can make sense and be correct, even though they are not generalized or made formal until later grades. Later, students learn to determine domains to which an argument applies. Students at all grades can listen or read the arguments of others, decide whether they make sense, and ask useful questions to clarify or improve the arguments.

Unit 1 Lessons 1, 2, 3, 4, 5, 6, 7, 8, 9, 10, 11, 12, 13, 14, 15, 16, 18, 19

Unit 2 Lessons 1, 2, 3, 4, 5, 6, 8, 9, 10, 11, 12, 13, 14, 15

Unit 3 Lessons 1, 2, 3, 4, 5, 6, 7, 8, 9, 10, 12, 13, 14, 15

Unit 4 Lessons 1, 2, 3, 4, 5, 6, 7, 8, 9, 10, 11, 12, 13, 14, 15, 16, 17, 18

Unit 5 Lessons 1, 2, 3, 4, 5, 6, 7, 8, 9, 10, 11

Unit 6 Lessons 1, 2, 3, 4, 5, 6, 7, 8, 9, 10, 11

Unit 7 Lessons 1, 2, 3, 4, 5, 6, 7, 8, 9

MP.4 Model with mathematics.

Mathematically proficient students can apply the mathematics they know to solve problems arising in everyday life, society, and the workplace. In early grades, this might be as simple as writing an addition equation to describe a situation. In middle grades, a student might apply proportional reasoning to plan a school event or analyze a problem in the community. By high school, a student might use geometry to solve a design problem or use a function to describe how one quantity of interest depends on another. Mathematically proficient students who can apply what they know are comfortable making assumptions and approximations to simplify a complicated situation, realizing that these may need revision later. They are able to identify important quantities in a practical situation and map their relationships using such tools as diagrams, two-way tables, graphs, flowcharts and formulas. They can analyze those relationships mathematically to draw conclusions. They routinely interpret their mathematical results in the context of the situation and reflect on whether the results make sense, possibly improving the model if it has not served its purpose.

Unit 1 Lessons 1, 2, 3, 4, 5, 6, 7, 8, 9, 10, 12, 13, 14, 16, 18, 19

Unit 2 Lessons 2, 4, 7, 9, 11, 13, 15

Unit 3 Lessons 2, 3, 4, 5, 6, 8, 9, 10, 11, 12, 13, 15

Unit 4 Lessons 3, 4, 7, 8, 9, 10, 11, 12, 14, 17, 18

Unit 5 Lessons 1, 2, 3, 4, 8, 9, 10, 11

Unit 6 Lessons 6, 9, 10, 11

Unit 7 Lessons 3, 8, 9

MP.5 Use appropriate tools strategically.

Mathematically proficient students consider the available tools when solving a mathematical problem. These tools might include pencil and paper, concrete models, a ruler, a protractor, a calculator, a spreadsheet, a computer algebra system, a statistical package, or dynamic geometry software. Proficient students are sufficiently familiar with tools appropriate for their grade or course to make sound decisions about when each of these tools might be helpful, recognizing both the insight to be gained and their limitations. For example, mathematically proficient high school students analyze graphs of functions and solutions generated using a graphing calculator. They detect possible errors by strategically using estimation and other mathematical knowledge. When making mathematical models, they know that technology can enable them to visualize the results of varying assumptions, explore consequences, and compare predictions with data. Mathematically proficient students at various grade levels are able to identify relevant external mathematical resources, such as digital content located on a website, and use them to pose or solve problems. They are able to use technological tools to explore and deepen their understanding of concepts.

Unit 1 Lessons 1, 2, 3, 4, 5, 6, 7, 8, 9, 10, 11, 12, 13, 14, 15, 16, 17, 18, 19

Unit 2 Lessons 1, 2, 3, 4, 5, 6, 7, 8, 9, 10, 11, 12, 13, 14, 15

Unit 3 Lessons 1, 2, 3, 4, 6, 7, 8, 9, 10, 13, 15

Unit 4 Lessons 1, 2, 3, 4, 5, 6, 7, 8, 13, 17, 18

Unit 5 Lessons 1, 2, 3, 4, 11

Unit 6 Lessons 1, 3, 4, 5, 6, 10, 11

Unit 7 Lessons 1, 2, 3, 5, 6, 7, 9

MP.6 Attend to precision.

Mathematically proficient students try to communicate precisely to others. They try to use clear definitions in discussion with others and in their own reasoning. They state the meaning of the symbols they choose, including using the equal sign consistently and appropriately. They are careful about specifying units of measure, and labeling axes to clarify the correspondence with quantities in a problem. They calculate accurately and efficiently, express numerical answers with a degree of precision appropriate for the problem context. In the elementary grades, students give carefully formulated explanations to each other. By the time they reach high school they have learned to examine claims and make explicit use of definitions.

Unit 1 Lessons 1, 2, 3, 4, 5, 6, 7, 8, 9, 10, 11, 12, 13, 14, 15, 16, 18, 19

Unit 2 Lessons 1, 2, 3, 4, 5, 6, 7, 8, 9, 10, 11, 12, 13, 14, 15

Unit 3 Lessons 1, 2, 3, 4, 5, 6, 7, 8, 9, 10, 11, 12, 13, 14, 15

Unit 4 Lessons 1, 2, 3, 4, 5, 6, 7, 8, 9, 10, 11, 12, 13, 14, 15, 16, 17, 18

Unit 5 Lessons 1, 2, 3, 4, 5, 6, 7, 8, 9, 10, 11

Unit 6 Lessons 1, 2, 3, 4, 5, 6, 7, 8, 9, 10, 11

Unit 7 Lessons 1, 2, 3, 4, 5, 6, 7, 8, 9

MP.7 Look for and make use of structure.

Mathematically proficient students look closely to discern a pattern or structure. Young students, for example, might notice that three and seven more is the same amount as seven and three more, or they may sort a collection of shapes according to how many sides the shapes have. Later, students will see 7×8 equals the well remembered $7 \times 5 + 7 \times 3$, in preparation for learning about the distributive property. In the expression $x^2 + 9x + 14$, older students can see the 14 as 2×7 and the 9 as $2 + 7$. They recognize the significance of an existing line in a geometric figure and can use the strategy of drawing an auxiliary line for solving problems. They also can step back for an overview and shift perspective. They can see complicated things, such as some algebraic expressions, as single objects or as being composed of several objects. For example, they can see $5 - 3(x - y)^2$ as 5 minus a positive number times a square and use that to realize that its value cannot be more than 5 for any real numbers x and y.

Unit 1 Lessons 1, 2, 4, 5, 6, 7, 8, 10, 11, 12, 13, 15, 19

Unit 2 Lessons 1, 3, 5, 6, 14, 15

Unit 3 Lessons 2, 15

Unit 4 Lessons 1, 2, 3, 4, 11, 14, 16, 17, 18

Unit 5 Lessons 1, 2, 3, 4, 5, 8, 11

Unit 6 Lessons 1, 2, 3, 4, 5, 8, 10, 11

Unit 7 Lessons 1, 2, 3, 6, 9

MP.8 Look for and express regularity in repeated reasoning.

Mathematically proficient students notice if calculations are repeated, and look both for general methods and for shortcuts. Upper elementary students might notice when dividing 25 by 11 that they are repeating the same calculations over and over again, and conclude they have a repeating decimal. By paying attention to the calculation of slope as they repeatedly check whether points are on the line through (1, 2) with slope 3, middle school students might abstract the equation $(y - 2)/(x - 1) = 3$. Noticing the regularity in the way terms cancel when expanding $(x - 1)(x + 1)$, $(x - 1)$ $(x^2 + x + 1)$, and $(x - 1)(x^3 + x^2 + x + 1)$ might lead them to the general formula for the sum of a geometric series. As they work to solve a problem, mathematically proficient students maintain oversight of the process, while attending to the details. They continually evaluate the reasonableness of their intermediate results.

Unit 1 Lessons 1, 2, 3, 5, 7, 8, 10, 11, 12, 19

Unit 2 Lessons 1, 2, 3, 5, 6, 10, 12, 14, 15

Unit 3 Lessons 1, 14, 15

Unit 4 Lessons 5, 6, 14, 17, 18

Unit 5 Lessons 1, 4, 9, 11

Unit 6 Lessons 4, 7, 10, 11

Unit 7 Lessons 1, 2, 3, 5, 6, 9

Index

B

C

more or fewer, 289–290

unknown amount, 287

use comparison bars, 286–288

using data in a bar graph, 206

using data in a pictograph, 205

Computational algorithms, methods, and strategies. *See* **Addition; Subtraction**

Content Overview

Unit 1, 1–4, 11–14

Unit 2, 93–94

Unit 3, 165–166, 185–186, 199–200

Unit 4, 223–226

Unit 5, 271–272

Unit 6, 313–314, 333–334

Unit 7, 367–368

Count-bys

0s and 1s, 49

2s, 17

3s, 49

4s, 49

5s, 17

6s, 97

7s, 97

8s, 97

9s, 17

10s, 17

squares, 97

Customary Units of Measurement

capacity, 171–174

length, 167–170

weight, 177–178

D

Dash Record Sheet, 16

Dashes, 77–82, 125–130, 143–148

Data

analyze

from a bar graph, 206, 207–208, 210, 213

from a frequency table, 211, 212, 216

from a pictograph, 86, 158, 201, 205

from a table, 158, 306

from a tally chart, 212

compare

from a frequency table, 212

from a line plot, 211

from a pictograph, 86, 201, 205

from a table, 204, 211

from a tally chart, 211

display

using a bar graph, 206–208

using a line plot, 211–212

using a pictograph, 86, 158

using a table, 204, 211

using a tally chart, 212

organize

using a bar graph, 204, 209–210

using a frequency table, 211, 216

using a line plot, 212, 214

using a pictograph, 86, 158, 202

using a tally chart, 212, 216

Decompose Figures

two-dimensional figures, 51–52, 56–57, 339–340, 345–348

Distributive Property, 51–52, 56–57, 63, 339–340

Dividend, 23

zero as, 66

Division, 23–26

0s, 65–71

1s, 65–71

2s, 27–32

3s, 45–48

4s, 49–55

Expression, 276

evaluate by using order of operations, 135–136

F

Factor, 6, 279–280, 283–284. *See also* **Multiplication, by**

0,1,2,3,4,5,6,7,8,9,10

Family Letter, 1–4, 11–14, 93–94, 165–166, 185–186, 199–200, 223–226, 271–272, 313–314, 333–334, 367–368

Fast array drawings, 44, 106, 112

Focus on Mathematical Practices, 85–86, 157–158, 215–216, 263–264, 305–306, 359–360, 389–390

Fraction circles, to model fractions as parts of a whole, 381–381A

Fraction rectangles, to model fractions as parts of a whole, 369A–369B

Fractions, 169, 212, 373, 387–388

compare, 379–380, 381–382

denominator, 371

equivalence chains, 383, 385–386

equivalent, 383A–386

express as whole numbers, 376–378

locate on a number line, 375–378

numerator, 371

on a number line, 374–378, 380, 385–386, 387–388

part of a whole, 369A–371, 381–381A

unit, 369–372, 379–380

Fraction bars, 371, 373, 379

Fraction strips

to model equivalent fractions, 383A–384

Frequency tables, 204, 209, 211, 212, 216

Functions

finding and writing the rule, 10

function table, 10

using a rule, 10

G

Geometry, 315

adjacent sides, 326

angle, 315, 316, 318

concave, 319

convex, 319

decagon, 320–321A

hexagon, 320–321A

octagon, 320–321A

opposite sides, 324

parallelogram, 321–322, 325–332

pentagon, 320–321A

polygon, 319

quadrilateral, 319A, 323–332, 333A

ray, 315

rectangle, 322, 323, 326, 329–332, 343–344, 369A–370

rhombus, 322, 327, 329–330, 332

right angle, 315

square, 322, 327, 329, 330, 332

tangram pieces, 353A–358

trapezoid, 324, 332

triangle, 370

acute, 316

classifying, 316–319A

isosceles, 317

obtuse, 316

right, 316

two-dimensional figures, 353A–358

decompose, 345–348

polygons, 319A–321A

Glossary, S13

Index (continued)

N

O

P

estimate differences, 234, 237

models, 247, 253

  drawings, 247

  equations, 276

  Math Mountains, 273–275

multidigit

  3-digit number subtracted from
    3-digit number, 259

relate addition and subtraction,
  255–256

ungrouping, 247–250, 252, 253, 258

vertical format, 255

word problems, 253, 257, 259–260, 275,
  277–284

Sum, 237, 245–246. 273 *See also* **Addition**

Symbols

  equal sign, 276

  is greater than, 285, 382

  is less than, 285, 382

  is not equal to, 276

  multiplication, 6

T

Tables

  analyze data from, 158, 306

  compare data from, 204, 211

  finding and writing patterns for data in,
    158

  frequency tables, 211, 216

  solve problems using, 306

  using data from, 306

Tally chart, 211, 216

Targets, 31

Technology

  Think Central, 89–92, 161–164, 219–220,
    267–270, 309–312, 363–364, 392

Three-in-a-Row **Game Grids,** 75, 152

Time

  addition of time intervals, 195

  before and after the hour, 187, 188,
    191–192

  A.M. and P.M., 188, 193, 194, 197–198

  analog clock, 187A–187B, 188,
    190–192, 197–198

  digital clock, 187, 188, 189, 190

  elapsed time, 193–194

    using a clock to find, 193–194,
      197–198

    using a line diagram to find, 195–198

  subtraction of time intervals, 196

  tell and write time

    to the hour, half-hour, quarter-hour,
      187, 188, 190

    nearest 5 minutes, 191

    nearest minute, 190, 192

    word problems, 194, 197–198

Trapezoids, 324, 332

Triangles, 316–321A, 370

  classifying, 316–319A

U

Ungrouping

  from the left, 253, 258

  from the right, 253, 258

  in subtraction, 247–253, 258

Unit Review and Test, 87–92, 159–164,
217–222, 265–270, 307–312, 361–366,
391–396

V

variables, 35–36, 283

© Houghton Mifflin Harcourt Publishing Company

Index (continued)

Multiplication Table and Scrambled Tables (Volume 1)

A

×	1	2	3	4	5	6	7	8	9	10
1	1	2	3	4	5	6	7	8	9	10
2	2	4	6	8	10	12	14	16	18	20
3	3	6	9	12	15	18	21	24	27	30
4	4	8	12	16	20	24	28	32	36	40
5	5	10	15	20	25	30	35	40	45	50
6	6	12	18	24	30	36	42	48	54	60
7	7	14	21	28	35	42	49	56	63	70
8	8	16	24	32	40	48	56	64	72	80
9	9	18	27	36	45	54	63	72	81	90
10	10	20	30	40	50	60	70	80	90	100

B

×	2	4	3	1	5	10	6	8	7	9
5	10	20	15	5	25	50	30	40	35	45
3	6	12	9	3	15	30	18	24	21	27
1	2	4	3	1	5	10	6	8	7	9
4	8	16	12	4	20	40	24	32	28	36
2	4	8	6	2	10	20	12	16	14	18
7	14	28	21	7	35	70	42	56	49	63
9	18	36	27	9	45	90	54	72	63	81
10	20	40	30	10	50	100	60	80	70	90
8	16	32	24	8	40	80	48	64	56	72
6	12	24	18	6	30	60	36	48	42	54

C

×	8	6	4	9	7	9	6	7	4	8
5	40	30	20	45	35	45	30	35	20	40
3	24	18	12	27	21	27	18	21	12	24
2	16	12	8	18	14	18	12	14	8	16
3	24	18	12	27	21	27	18	21	12	24
5	40	30	20	45	35	45	30	35	20	40
9	72	54	36	81	63	81	54	63	36	72
4	32	24	16	36	28	36	24	28	16	32
7	56	42	28	63	49	63	42	49	28	56
6	48	36	24	54	42	54	36	42	24	48
8	64	48	32	72	56	72	48	56	32	64

D

×	6	7	8	7	8	6	7	8	6	8
2	12	14	16	14	16	12	14	16	12	16
3	18	21	24	21	24	18	21	24	18	24
4	24	28	32	28	32	24	28	32	24	32
5	30	35	40	35	40	30	35	40	30	40
7	42	49	56	49	56	42	49	56	42	56
8	48	56	64	56	64	48	56	64	48	64
6	36	42	48	42	48	36	42	48	36	48
9	54	63	72	63	72	54	63	72	54	72
8	48	56	64	56	64	48	56	64	48	64
6	36	42	48	42	48	36	42	48	36	48